Your Life is a Series of Meetings…

Get Good at Life

By
George M. Prince
with
Kathleen Logan-Prince

ISBN: 1-4033-1092-0 (e-book)
ISBN: 1-4033-1093-9 (Paperback)

This book is printed on acid free paper.

1stBooks - rev. 08/27/02

Acknowledgments

We are greatly indebted to W. Timothy Weaver who participated in the early development of Mind-Free®. He not only contributed many ideas about content and process, he furnished live bodies in the form of graduate students with whom we could test our evolving program. The program would not exist in its present form without his accomplished and creative help.

When we were in the midst of our early experiments with Mind-Free® and needed money to rent equipment, the very first support came out of the pocket of Richard Harriman, who, since he became president of Synectics® Inc. in 1975, has given wholehearted support to every experiment, no matter how strange and non-logical, undertaken to learn more about creative thinking. Our special thanks for his unfailing assistance.

We also want to thank the Mind-Free Brain Trust. These stalwarts graduated from the Program and joined us in weekly meetings to further the cause of Mind-Free in every way possible:

J. Allyn Bradford
Beth Gilliam
T.K.Gilliam
Marie Kenerson

Jean Trescott Lambert
Julian Miller
Alan O'Hare
Marilyn Susan Yas

We also want to acknowledge the many contributions and editorial help given us by Jean Trescott Lambert and Julian A. Miller.

We want to thank Robert Weintraub, who, even though busy publishing his own book, made himself available to help with ours.

"A grasp of the concept of anxiety...will...prevent a great many commonplace stupidities..."

Harry Stack Sullivan

Contents

Part 3—The Self

Part 4—Anatomy of Relating

Part 5—Meaning and Learning

Part 6—Managing Fields

Part 7—Inner Field

Forward

Whether it is a meeting with yourself—the most common of the meetings in our lives—or a meeting with your significant other, or with a colleague or child, the quality of your meetings, your relationships, determines how satisfying your life is. Your meetings deserve your devoted attention and your most effective behavior.

Consciously managing the meetings of your life requires that you understand the forces that govern your own and others' behavior, and that is the focus of this book. Most of us take for granted that the action taken by any individual is a result of the circumstances plus the personality of the actor. If we take the literal meaning of circumstances—"the total complex of essential attributes and attendant adjuncts of an action: the sum of essential and environmental characteristics"—plus the literal meaning of personality—"the complex of characteristics that distinguishes a particular individual or characterizes him in his relationships with others"(Webster's) we see that the multiplicity of influences in a given situation can be mind boggling.

We will call the sum of these forces *fields of influence.* The idea of field is derived from the force field surrounding a magnate. This force field is *three dimensional.*

When neuroscientists observed the behavior of sub-atomic matter, what their tests 'revealed' at first, was a tiny, invisible field. Further, more exhaustive tests, showed that on one examination, the matter appeared as a particle. A second examination showed that the same matter was also a wave. Both could not be seen at the same time. Their unexpected conclusion: the sub-atomic matter was a particle surrounded by a wave. They explained the dual nature of a particle/wave as, particle=substance, wave=information. When the field of one particle/wave came together with the field of another, a new field—a relationship—was formed; a new field of influence with new characteristics.

Neurocientists have concluded that *everything* in our world is composed of sub-atomic particle/waves. When they clump together tightly, they become a solid, like a rock, or a person. A part of each rock or person is a wave of information, fields of influence, which communicate the nature of the rock or person. Each of us is a large bundle of sub-atomic particle/waves. Each particle/wave is connected and interacting with every other, and the combination forms a giant relationship field of influence. If something happens to my little finger, every particle/wave in my body is aware of it. Each of us creates, and is surrounded by our unique field of influence. The content of my field informs an apprehending mind of my state of being at the same time your field informs me of your state of being.

When my field comes into contact with your field, a new relationship or field is formed, as invisible and visible information is exchanged, and this new, combined field of influence has characteristics that are different from either of us alone. You have undoubtedly experienced this—a close friend gets married. That friend, now in relationship with her husband, is in a different state of being than the friend you knew before.

When a third person joins the married couple, a new relationship comes into being—a new field of influence. Every group generates a field that is unique to that collection of individuals. To add to the complication, whenever a group member undergoes a change, the field of the group changes to reflect that. For example, you are with a small group of friends. A cell phone buzzes and a member of the group speaks and listens for a moment. He hangs up and his expression signals a change in his field. He says that his brother has been in an accident and is seriously injured. The field of the group changes to reflect the distress of this member.

I am like a compass

Each of us, like a sensitive compass, is being pointed in one direction or another depending upon the combined fields of influence inside and surrounding us. Since our behavior is determined by these fields, it is important to be aware of their impact.

Everyday examples of interpersonal fields

- You are talking with a co-worker in your office and your boss comes in
- You are discussing an intimate matter with your spouse and one of your children comes in

- You come home from work and your partner is reading in the living room. Before a word is spoken, you know what mood she/he is in
- You go to your child's school to meet her teacher. You immediately sense what it would be like to have her as your teacher
- When you go into a hospital for treatment you get an instant message about whether they are friendly and caring, or not
- You call on a couple you know. You know immediately whether or not they are on good terms
- Walk into a church or a bookstore—each has its distinct field

The nature of internal field

A critical element in determining behavior is the information coming to us from our internal field. What is its make-up?

The Triune Brain

"Dr. Paul MacLean, an evolutionary neuroanatomist and senior research scientist at the National Institute Of Mental Health, has argued that the human brain is comprised of three distinct sub-brains, each the product of a separate age in evolutionary history. The trio intermingles and communicates, but some information is inevitably lost in translation because the sub-units differ in their functions, properties, and even in their chemistries." (Lewis et al, 2000, pg 21)

The three parts of the triune brain are, from most ancient to most recent, the Reptilian, the Limbic, and the Neocortical.

The Reptilian brain is the oldest and first developed. "This brain houses vital control centers—neurons that prompt breathing, swallowing, and heartbeat, and the visual tracking system…The startle center is here, too, because swift reaction to abrupt movement or noise is the principal reason we have brains at all.

"We will be disappointed if we expect the reptilian brain to play a major role in the structure of the emotional mind. Reptiles don't have an emotional life." (ibid)

The Limbic brain began its development with an astonishing mutation: instead of giving birth to infants in eggshells, the new mammals carried their young inside their bodies until the infant is ready to be born. After this gestation, human babies are not ready to operate on their own for *years*. Reptiles, after seeing their young out of the nest, show little concern about them. Humans, in contrast, have a very long period of dependent interaction before the young develop the behaviors that allow them to operate on their own. And the bonds of family persist through life.

The limbic brain evolved to deal with this new reality. It is the center of advanced emotionality. The original purpose was to monitor the external world and the internal environment and get everything ready to handle the situation. It is the home of feelings and emotions.

The neocortex

This most recent of the three brains manages speaking, writing, planning and reasoning, as well as the experience of our senses—awareness. Another of its capacities is that of abstraction and hypothetical thinking.

The mammals invent love

"The dangers of the outer world have a greater importance for (the infant), so that the value of (parents) which alone protect it against them and take the place of its former intrauterine life, is enormously enhanced. This biological factor then establishes the earliest situation of danger and *creates the need to be loved* (italics added) which will accompany the child through the rest of life." (Freud in *Inhibitions, Symptoms and Anxiety,* 1926)

Human infants must be born "prematurely" because of that extraordinary organ, the human brain. "The fetus must be born in an unreasonable state of unpreparedness for life…The human brain weighs roughly 350 gtams at birth, but by the end of the first year of life it will have grown to 825 grams! The adult brain weighs 1400 grams." (Gaylin, 1986)

"It is the gestation of a sensitive, perceptive, and aware "fetus" who, while helpless to protect himself, is all too capable of understanding the perilous nature of his position.

"This aware "fetus" with his huge brain, is learning lessons which will be indelibly marked upon him and will be sustained into adult life. Among those lessons, perhaps the most crucial is the link between helplessness, love, and survival.

"Another intriguing aspect of emotions is that they may be transmitted, one to another…feelings are contagious…emotions are powerful motivators of behavior…they are also an instrument of communication." (ibid)

"Love is not the icing on the cake, it *is* the cake"—Gaylin

In human mammals love, and the search for it in its many forms of expression, is a universal driving force in behavior. It is important that we understand some of the ways love and the search for it manifest in our daily lives.

Limbic resonance

The relationship between parents and infants in early mammals gave rise to an entirely new type of behavior that never existed among reptiles and aquatic life forms. It created a new *attachment* between people—a bond and involvement that was *emotional*. It was centered in the new limbic brain. As parent and infant interacted, the dependent infant is looking to parent for everything to sustain life. Studies of infants have shown that infants focus great energy on engaging parents, and most parents are available. In a healthy situation, the infant and parent take turns sending and receiving. Mom smiles. Infant observes, then smiles back. Infant gurgles, Mom observes and then gurgles back. In the course of hugs, kisses, talks and feeding, Mother and infant take part in *limbic resonance.*

This limbic connecting is the introduction to love. In a very real sense, the need for the reassurance of being loved, of having meaning for another becomes the underlying motivator for most, if not all, behavior. John Bowlby made exhaustive studies of infants and children who were institutionalized. They were fed and maintained, but had little intimate human contact. Their death rate was many times that of children with mothers. They grew up with serious emotional and physical deficits, and uniformly had trouble relating to others.

Meaning, love and behavior

Reptiles, who do not go through the long mammalian initiation of intimacy, being cared for, and developing the pivotal knowledge of loving and being loved, are indifferent to each other. Other than to reproduce, they ignore each other. In our formative interactions with mother and father, we humans develop a deep, implicit awareness of the critical importance to our well-being of other people. At a primitive level I come to believe that if I am not meaningful, I will cease to be.

Being and feeling meaningful becomes my primary need. I become an *informed specialist* at reading the fields of influence in and around me. I am looking for reassurance that I am meaningful. Any indications that I am not, I perceive as a threat to my be<u>ing</u> and call forth actions ranging from subtle non-cooperation to outright battle, to demonstrate that I am meaningful.

Since our need for meaningfulness is such a profound influence on our behavior, we will be examining the various roles played by our ever present search for meaning. The purpose is to discover the anatomy of our internal fields of influence and invent ways to modify our behavior—our thoughts and actions to increase our effectiveness in the meetings that make up our lives.

A Brief History of *Your Life Is a Series of Meetings* and Mind-Free®

Your Life Is a Series of Meetings is the book describing the Mind-Free® process. Mind-Free® is a result of combining the Synectics® Inc. body of knowledge about creativity (George was co-founder) and Kathleen's body of knowledge about relationships gained in 20 years as a marital psychotherapist.

Synectics® is used as the name of a company and also to represent a system of thinking and interacting designed to elicit more of an individual's potential for creativity. The system differs from many others in that the process and theories were developed by studying videotapes of people in groups working on real problems. Since the founding of Synectics® in 1960 they have worked with and observed many thousands of people and it is evident that few of us use more than a fraction of our potential for creative thinking. By systematic and informed *management* of themselves and the "field" around them it is possible to increase substantially the amount of creative potential a person can actualize.

Synectics® experience in training people to use their system has been disappointing in that very few participants are able to adapt the proven productive behaviors to their lives outside invention sessions. If they were able to "live" the procedures it would bring out more of their latent potential for accomplishment and satisfaction.

Kathleen's training and experience with couples in difficulty suggested that some of her procedures are more effective than Synectics in producing long-term change in behavior. Mind-Free® is designed to help participants internalize proven self-management practices. 14 years of testing and development have convinced Kathleen and George that such a change can be made by careful and protected experiments with one's internal practices and with interactions with others.

Creativity the Tip of the Iceberg

Pooling their experiences led Kathleen and George to a surprising conclusion: while we identify creativity as a very special kind of thinking that produces newness, that thinking process is the same as that which every one of us uses every waking hour of every day. It is the same process we use for understanding and learning. As new-born infants each of us is surrounded by what must seem like total confusion and chaos. With help from our parents and teachers we gradually develop the remarkable capacity to make sense out of the confusion and chaos and establish relationships with others.

This miraculous thinking-to-make-meaning process is the very heart of being a human <u>be</u>ing. Some of us, because of the way we are "socialized" from infancy through adolescence, become more skillful than others in thinking, yet we *all* use it *all* the time. It is analogous to a physical skill like running. Almost everyone can run. Some develop their running skills to become champions. The big difference with thinking is that the brain we are all given has such an enormous latent capability that virtually everyone has the "mental muscle" to become a champion thinker.

The governing factors in whether I use my mental muscle effectively are the mental models I fashion in my early years. By definition, I do this development with immature judgment and my decisions, while appropriate for that time, are seldom the best for my long-term good.

An example of a mental model is how I deal with competition. Some people consider themselves highly competitive and they behave competitively in all their relationships, others limit their competitive behaviors to games. These are different mental models, with different consequences.

Taking Control of Mental Models

Most of my thinking practices, developed long ago, deserve revisiting.

Many, such as assuming the wisdom and authority of all grown-ups, can be counter-productive in the present. Mind-Free® is designed to use the insights gained in Synectics® research and in psychotherapy to gain greater use of the almost limitless thinking resources that are a given. Participation aids me in becoming aware of my various mental models and I can modify them to better serve my adult purposes.

Mind-Free® and the Real World

Since joining Synectics®, Inc. several years ago I have had many opportunities to use the Mind-Free® principles. There is no doubt that it is possible to generate productive fields even in difficult situations.

The Mind-Free® Program can make your mental models visible to you. Only you can figure out what to modify and by how much. You need to do the perceiving, connecting, and creation of meaning. I hope it gives you as much satisfaction as it has given me.

T.K. Gilliam

"Different settings and people evoke some qualities from us and leave others dormant. In each of these relationships, we are different, new in some way."—Margaret Wheatley

Introduction

When I was in fourth grade the teacher asked the class "Who is a good reader to read this part of the book?"

My hand shot up and she called on me. "I am", I said.

"George," she said "That is a selfish and conceited thing to do. You should let others recommend you—or you should recommend someone else."

The whole atmosphere of the classroom felt different. Everyone seemed to be looking down on me with contempt. I was so hurt that I had trouble holding in the tears. I can still remember the pain of that moment. My relationship with that teacher was forever changed. For the rest of that year, I was a drop-out in her class and it was one of life's lessons that altered my behavior forever. I have been reluctant to recommend myself in any situation. In that exchange in fourth grade I was experiencing a radical addition to my interpersonal "field"—the collection of information in my mind and body that governs my behavior. When my field encounters the field of another, a relationship is created. The quality of my relationships determines the quality of my life.

In years of Synectics® study of thousands of small groups it became evident that the words, tones and non-verbal signals of group members had a critical influence on success.

In recent years scientific inquiry has supported the idea that we are sensitive to far more than these overt signals. Such "invisible" things as mood, optimism, anxiety and other emotional states can affect the field and our behavior. "Each person in any…relationship is involved as a portion of an interpersonal field, rather than as [a] separate entity, in processes which affect and are affected by the field." (Sullivan, 1953)

We now believe the field is made up of information which is generated by *everything* in the field and is carried by sound and electromagnetic waves, some of which are visible like the colors in a rainbow, and some of which are invisible like radio waves. As this external field of information envelops me, it interacts with my internal field and determines my behavior, which, in turn, influences the general field.

> "…nearly half a century ago [it was] discovered that nerve cells in the human brain are sufficiently sensitive to register the absorption of a single photon…"—Danah Zohar

My internal field is formed of the stored interpretations of the fields that were around me as I grew from tiny cells in my mother's womb through infancy, childhood and adolescence to maturity. We believe that one's internal field has four components that determine how effective we will be: genes plus 1. Empathy, 2. Self-Awareness, and 3. Integrity. The interactions between these create my relationship with myself. My interactions with the fields generated by other persons and things create my relationships with them.

We have all been conscious of the importance in our lives of the relationships we form, and aware also of the way actions of others can deeply affect us. The recent findings of quantum physics, brain research and the study of the consequences of early mistreatment and trauma have put solid scientific support under the theory of fields being the ground out of which our behaviors grow.

Each of us is extremely sensitive to the fields around us. I can remember when I was five, I could tell if my father was in a good or bad mood the moment he came in the door and it had a big influence on whether I went to greet him, or went somewhere else to avoid possible trouble.

Few of us have been fully aware of the enormous influence of field on how each of us fulfills her or his early promise. We now believe the field is *all important,* far more important than we had previously thought. And the internal field, the external field, and the interactions between the two determines the success of all of our transactions.

Success, in this sense, is a spectrum: after an interaction, the two (or more) people involved are whole heartedly recruited to whatever the exchange was about, or at the other end of the spectrum, they are completely at odds.

In between are the half hearted, those partially "on strike" emotionally and those who don't get it.

We have come to appreciate the potency of fields partly from the unusual way we developed the Synectics® creative process, partly from the observation of hundreds of couples and families in emotional trouble, and partly through becoming aware of the relevant findings of brain research, trauma, and quantum physics.

From the 1960's we were in the business of helping companies invent new products and processes and solve problems. Our clients brought small teams of five to ten people to our laboratory in Cambridge, Massachusetts.

We facilitated "sessions" in which they produced the ideas and plans to carry out their assignment. We tape recorded those session, first with audio tape and then with videotape as that became available. We studied the tapes to learn which activities aided in the production of ideas and which hindered. In the next twenty years we observed several thousand people working in groups to solve problems. We learned to appreciate the critical impact of actions that advance and those that hinder idea-getting. And these same actions determine whether people will collaborate or compete. We continually modified our procedures to avoid the negative inputs and increase the positives. We were not aware of the term at the time, but we were managing the "field".

It was only after Kathleen, with her experiences in marriage and family therapy, and I began to work together in 1987 to develop Mind-Free® that we began to realize that there seemed to be consistent, underlying "laws" that might apply to *all* behavior. It subsumes the laws of nature and laws of nurture which determine human behavior.

> "We are now in a position to integrate the perspectives of three large fields: psychology, biology, and physics…[resulting in] a picture that is quite unexpected.—Harold J. Morowitz

Emotional Field Theory

Our Emotional Field Theory holds that: behavior is governed by our internal field—the collection of information in our minds and bodies—and its perception of the information coming to us from the world. This information comes to us through all our senses in the form of words, vocals (tones, hesitations, etc.) and non-verbals, thoughts, feelings, signs and signals such as facial expressions and gestures. It is transmitted by sound waves, electromagnetic waves and gravity. All behavior and relationships grow out of these fields of information.

As we came to realize the power of these fields to determine how we live our lives, we decided to focus on them to make them into something we can consciously use in every area of our lives to bring out the best in us and in those with whom we interact.

Part 1—Field and Relationship

> "In quantum physics, this interdependency between the *being* of a thing and its overall environment is called [field], and the implications of it are vast, both for our whole conception of reality and for our understanding of ourselves as partners in that reality."
>
> —Danah Zohar

My field monitors

As a part of knowing myself I need to understand how fields influence me. It is an important part of managing myself and also of managing my relationships with others.

The organ that first senses fields is my amygdala. It is a walnut sized part of my brain and acts as my emotional "switchboard". Signals from all my senses first pass through my amygdala so it can do a preliminary scan for significance—is this signaling a threat, or is it friendly?

The amygdala is part of my primitive nose-brain, a critical operator designed to ensure survival. It is my emotional memory and it looks for two different kinds of information: is this situation dangerous to me; a threat to being and feeling meaningful, or does it offer the possibility of nurturance and support.

Any threat to my meaningfulness is an emotional threat. I scan for three things: 1.evidence of caring, 2. will this person be responsive to me, and 3, do I have power to influence this person.

When it is a mating possibility it tends not to be urgent and I pass the information to other brain functions and to my neocortex for more rational examination and planning before taking any action. When the information contains *any* threat, whether physical or emotional, it triggers an immediate alarm reaction *before* seeking rational analysis. I feel a stab of anxiety, get a shot of adrenaline and am ready to fight, flee or freeze.

Anxiety almost always plays a critical role in my operations and it deserves special attention. It is often confused with feelings of fear and worry, and a good self manager needs to know the difference as each has a quite different function. Fear has a specific cause that can be focused upon and perhaps removed or taken care of. For example, fear of the dark or of a tiger. A light can take care of the dark and a weapon can take care of a tiger.

Worry, in the same sense, has a focus and something can be done about it, such as mindful examination, preparation and rehearsal Anxiety is different in that it is a dread or awful feeling that has no focus or target that can in some way be managed. To understand the power of anxiety it is necessary to know its origin and its underlying significance.

"…it is anxiety which is responsible for a great part of the inadequate, inefficient, unduly rigid, or otherwise unfortunate performance of people…"—Harry Stack Sullivan

Anxiety first emerges as an event for an infant in about the eighth month. It happens when the mothering one goes away longer than the infant can tolerate. He interprets this long absence of assurance as abandonment and has an intense reaction. Beneath that horror and dread is the instinctual conviction that abandoned, he will cease to exist, will die. He is not capable of this kind of thinking, yet that significance is imprinted on anxiety forever after and is what gives anxiety its remarkable power.

The Conditioning of Anxiety

The amygdala, as my emotional memory, is designed to keep track of events and actions that are threatening so that it can forewarn me when something life-threatening happens again. The more events in childhood and adolescence that trigger anxiety—such events as abuse, neglect and rejection—the more sensitive becomes my amygdala. On the other hand, the more seemingly anxious events that I am able to work through to learn that there is no real danger, the more balanced, appropriate and mature I become.

A key factor in my development is the amount of support and reassurance I get as I explore my expanding world and do things that involve uncertainty and risk. For example, when I am learning to progress from crawling to walking, I get constant appreciation and encouragement for each sign of progress. In contrast, as I learn to make connections in thinking—I point to a table and call it a chair—I get corrected. I am wrong, and being wrong is to be anxious. This different way of dealing with thinking vs. physical learning is significant.

T. Berry Brazelton, the child expert, tells us that infants and children spend a large amount of their energy attempting to establish mutual contact with the mothering one. If the caretaker shows indifference or mistreats the infant or child, it has a permanent effect on development. Any abuse or neglect registers on the amygdala and the child becomes more easily moved to anxiety—a far more serious handicap than we have appreciated.

Foresight Function

Anxiety is such a disturbing feeling that we learn to think ahead to see if some future event will trigger anxiety. Thus a child may look ahead to going to school, realize he is going to be anxious and try to avoid going.

More important than avoiding situations like school is the effect of foresight function on thinking, learning and creating. The steps of the thinking/learning/creating process are, approximately:

1. Perceiving—becoming aware of/observing a problem or puzzling situation (a learning opportunity)

2. More or less confusion

3. Trial connecting the unfamiliar with things I know to make sense of it, or get an idea to solve it

4. Deciding on a connection to form an idea to solve the problem, learn and understand

5. Testing to see if the new idea matches reality and makes sense

6. Repeat steps 2 through 5 until it seems right

Connecting to create meaning/understanding

Grandson, six year old Max, is with me on a boat. He is pumping water, invisible beneath the floor-boards, out of the bilge. It is his first time. The pump sucks air. I say "What does that mean?"

Max says "It means I have pumped out all the water."

"How do you know that?" I ask.

"From sucking a soda with a straw."

Going through these steps presents many opportunities to make "mistakes" or feel mistaken and uncertain. If, in my past experience I have been rigorously corrected and disapproved of when I made mistakes, all of these thinking processes may trigger anxiety. If my internal field or the field around me is unfriendly or punishing, my foresight function will urge me to avoid the risk of proceeding—in other words, to stop thinking.

Connecting to create a new idea

Sally needed a better place to study for exams. Her roommates distracted her and she did not want to go to the library. She needed a new way to think about it so she went on an "excursion". The image of a mushroom popped up in her mind. She pretended she was inside a mushroom. It was cool and damp as though in a cave. The walls were nubbly and moist. There was a faint pulse as though the mushroom was breathing—it was a little like a heartbeat…

Sally thought, "Heartbeat…it would be comforting, as though I am in a womb. It would block out other distracting noise. That is what I will do. I will record my heartbeat and then play it back into earphones. Wherever I am will be a place to study."

When my foresight function sees any threat in the direction I am proceeding, my anxiety increases. As my anxiety rises, I become less and less willing to pursue that line of action. My most basic strategy is to act to reduce anxiety. When a perception confuses me, my foresight senses threat and I tend to *stop thinking* in that direction. When my foresight function gets thoroughly trained, I may not even *perceive* something that *might* lead to confusion. I conceal it from myself. I am being governed by my policy for controlling anxiety, which in turn is determined by field. We can get an insight into the effect of a poorly designed field on children's thinking from the research reported below.

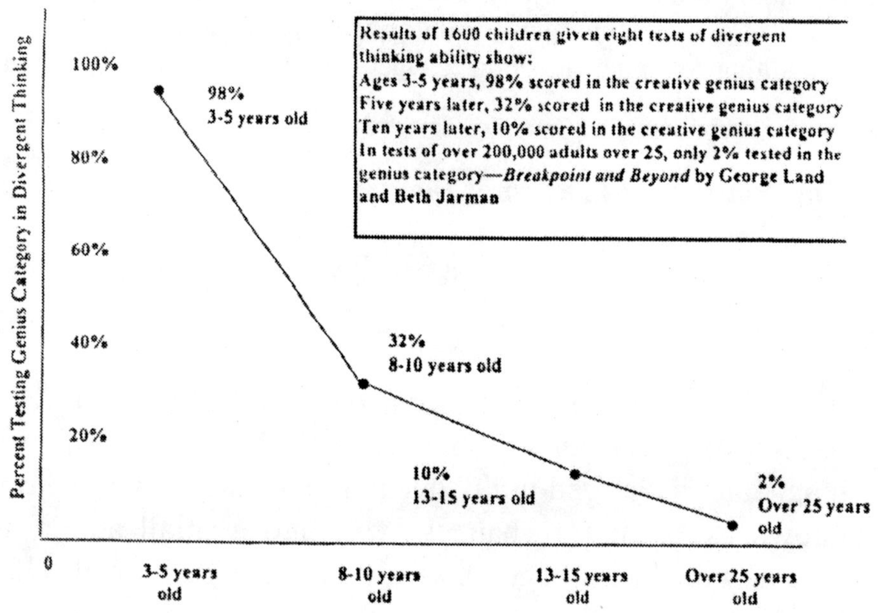

Since fields are such a critical influence in our lives, the rest of this book focuses on the anatomy of fields and what we can do to manage them for effectiveness.

"…the child's capabilities and sense of well-being deepen in proportion to the individual's ability to bring his or her [self] into a condition of rapt attention…"-Jack Zimmerman and Virginia Coyle

The Anatomy of Internal Field:

Empathy

In *The Once and Future King,* the story about King Arthur of the Round Table by E.B. White, Merlin, the magician, is charged with educating the future king, who is known as Wart. He changes Wart into a small animal to give him the knowledge of what it is like to be hunted. Then he changes him into a bird so that he can experience the fears and joys-the meanings of that way of being. This is the ultimate identification-actually becoming the creature. It equips Wart to experience empathy later, that is, to know intimately the thoughts, feelings, and meanings of being another without losing himself and *his* thoughts, feelings, and meanings.

Empathy is one of the three critical elements of field that supports collaboration with others. The other two elements, as we have mentioned, are self awareness and integrity.

Merlin wanted to prevent Wart from suffering the "king" disease-the tendency of persons in power to become isolated from and immune to the human needs and desires of others. As Lord Acton said, "Power corrupts. Absolute power corrupts absolutely."

Empathy is the antidote to the blindness that goes with the need to exert power-over and control. It is a receptivity that enables me to synchronize with the field of another and produce true synergy. Empathy, self-awareness and integrity are the pivotal elements in great partnerships, great marriages, great friendships, great companies, and in raising great children.

Whenever a person in power-a parent, a teacher, a boss-lacks empathy he or she sets up a field that will bring out the least in the those subject to the Power. We are all so finely tuned to lack of respect that we know instantly when a person has no empathy with us and our ideas.

Empathy is an exploring, learning, accepting capacity-the means of arriving at a deep understanding of a person and even of a thing. For example, Carl Marden, one of the founders of Synectics@, was a gifted machinist and inventor. When he was struggling to make a new device work, I often heard him say things like "This valve doesn't want to close against that pressure ". He was empathizing with that valve to understand how to help it do what it needed to do for the device to work properly.

An example of a whole group using empathy to create a field of understanding for each other, occurs in the New Guinea tribe called the Fore. (Smithsonian Institute Magazine, May, 1977, Pg.107). The anthropologists who studied them marveled at their openness, harmony, learning ability, lack of sibling rivalry, and general well-being. They had achieved a high level of mutual regard and equality.

One of the traits most valued among them was the ability to guess how another was feeling and, for example, bring a drink of water before the thirsty one realized that was exactly what she wanted They have no equivalent of our notion of punishment and I wondered if, when there is true empathy there is no inclination to punish.

> "To grasp the meaning of a thing, an event, or a situation is to see it in its *relations* to other things."-John Dewey

Webster defines empathy as "The imaginative projection of a subjective state into an object (or person) so that it appears to be infused with (my sensibilities) or the capacity for participating in, or a vicarious experiencing of another's feelings, volitions or ideas and sometimes another's movements.

This capacity to accurately create in myself the feelings, perceptions, desires and thoughts-the meanings-of another is one of the most important skills I can develop. It transforms the connectivity of my field for another and makes mutuality possible. To the degree I fail to develop my capacity for empathy, I am doomed to a life of isolation and incomprehension. I cannot create an engaging field without it.

Empathy and Identification

There is a critical difference between empathy and identification. In empathy, I retain my own identity, thoughts and feelings-my integrity. I recreate yours as I *imagine* them to be, but I do not lose touch with my differentiated self. When I *identify* with you, I imagine that I *am* you. I fuse with you and lose touch with my separate feelings and thoughts.

In empathy I accept the meaning you are conveying even though it differs from my own. I am able to think 'as if' I were you. As I listen to you, I temporarily put my own meaning on "hold" so that it does not prevent me from really connecting with and comprehending yours. In the developmental years of my childhood, it is appropriate for me to identify with parents and others from whom I learn. It is the central task of my youth and young adulthood to increase my capacity to be autonomous: self-governed and self-validating; to differentiate and become my own integrated person-to gradually shift from identification and dependence to empathy and independence.

Necessary Conditions

Empathy requires unconditional, wholehearted listening, that is, listening without the defensive barrier of my assumptions and prejudices. Three conditions make this possible. First, I need to be healthily differentiated, confident enough in my own basic beliefs and principles that I will not be threatened and become defensive by understanding those of another.

"*Creative fidelity* means to bear with their plateaus, regressions, imperfectness in such a way that these are transformed into new possibilities. Creative fidelity is to be for and with them, come hell or high water."-Ross Snyder

Second, if I am imperfectly differentiated, as most of us are, I need assurance that it is safe for me to relax my defenses and temporarily put aside my own best interests. No one will attempt to persuade or coerce me away from my point of view. Neither of these conditions is realistically completely possible so a third necessary condition is that I have enough trust in my own integrity and sense of self (awareness) that I am willing to risk the danger of giving up a position and being changed.

Empathy and Perception/Connecting

This phenomenon occurs when I have reached a point of minimal defense in relationship to another. I am able to give myself without reserve to the activity of making myself available to the total field of another without losing touch with myself. I know when I am approaching this level of attention because my anxiety gradient will urge me to cover up: make judgments, take control, feel bored, impatient, angry or otherwise defend my self from being taken over. When I summon up my courage to be with another in this wholehearted way, a remarkable transformation in field can occur. We together bring into being a field that glorifies and honors each other's real selves. We can experience a jolt of exhilarating positive energy as we release ourselves from the need to defend. The revelation of the richness of our undefended selves can be a truly blissful experience.

Realistically there are many people who are so heavily defended that when I reveal my availability they are impelled to deal with it as weakness. In such a case, my anxiety gradient urges me to raise my own defenses and strike back. If I have the courage to self-soothe, I can resist getting hooked, not respond in kind, and shift the interaction to the level of openness that is appropriate for such an anxiety-governed person.

In my experience, if I am able to contain my own defensiveness and be as available as such a person can tolerate, I may be rewarded with a growing relaxation of his defenses against me.

The Practice of Wholehearted Listening

I develop my capacity to listen wholeheartedly by inventing a step by step process to help me be more available to perceive and connect. Here, by way of example, is my process:

> Milton Erikson's principle of mutuality: a relationship in which participants depend on each other for the development of their respective strengths.

1. Tom is not in any way an enemy-for this time he has no power-over me. We are not deciding anything.

2. I focus my total attention on Tom. I go with the images and feelings Tom is activating in my head and heart. I use his statements as metaphors if necessary to make connections.

3. I will welcome the anxiety I feel. It is part of my aliveness. I will not let it enforce aloneness.

4. When a fear/defense rears its head, I mentally nod and say, "I feel your signals. We will review this later".

5. I *loan myself and my powers* to Tom. I am wide open to the waves of his field-the visible and the invisible. I put my imagination at his disposal. I may need to ask him to say more about some aspect.

6. I interact from wherever I find myself. This is still exploration time. We take turns exploring until we agree to decide something

7. When decision time comes, I introduce my preference by saying "This is what I am wishing for…"

Empathy and Synergy

My study of creativity in invention groups has led me to discover another dimension of empathy: when we have a common vision, and I listen to you wholeheartedly as described above, my acceptance and honoring of your thinking opens my resources to connect with and build upon the wishful meaning behind your thinking. We become more than the rational sum of one plus one. When a group achieves this quality of interaction, entirely new levels of originality can occur.

Empathic Wholehearted Listening to Self

One of the extraordinary benefits of learning to listen to others wholeheartedly is that it can become the path to listening to myself in the same way. Surprising as it may seem, unless specially trained, I am not an empathic,

> "...intimacy is the process of being in touch with or knowing *oneself* in the presence of a partner."-David Schnarch

wholehearted listener to myself. My inner field, as we will see in the section on Self-Punishment and Synergy, is not supportive in the total sense needed for synergy.

Empathy and Genius

When all the individuals in a group are skillful at empathic, wholehearted listening *and at managing the field that fosters it,* it becomes possible for them to multiply the capacity for connection-making almost exponentially. When thoroughly developed, such a group may well be able to replicate the thinking of a genius.

"In his 1988 book, *Scientific Genius* [Dean Keith] Simonton suggests that geniuses are geniuses because they form more novel combinations than the merely talented" (Newsweek, June 28, 1993).

"...iconoclasm disposes geniuses to *entertain* permutations of images and memories that more mundane thinkers toss out as too loopy. Similarly, creative geniuses are willing to take intellectual risks by merging disparate ideas." (ibid., italics mine)

Empathy and Self-Disclosure

As discussed before, early humiliations have taught me that it is dangerous to self-disclose and I have a well-established policy to present only my competitive image. Empathy on the part of another is a strong inducement to unfreeze. When all members of a group repeatedly evidence their empathy for one another, self-disclosure flourishes and I am able to experience those exhilarating moments of connecting with unforeseen, richly meaningful elements of myself and unexpected treasures in others.

Practical Intimacy™

Practical intimacy is not that which is sometimes achieved by loving couples, where the deepest secrets of the heart may be explored, but it is a state of mind and emotion in which I have the courage to be unrehearsed and undefended. This is a field that invites me to interact with whatever is emerging, unencumbered by old convictions, open to new connections.

> "Does the relationship leave [the parties to it] with feelings of increased strength and value, or of weakness and self-rejection? All human relationships can be judged by this one criterion."- Milton Erikson

Narcissism and Empathy

I have been puzzled about why some people do not seem willing to experience empathy. M. Scott Peck suggests a reason: "…we are all born narcissists…if we are supported through the natural humiliations of childhood by our parents and by grace…we gradually grow out of it.

"…narcissists do not think clearly about other people-if they think of them at all" (1993, Pg. 109).

My journey from being thoughtless of others to identification to empathy is uncertain. I do not learn it like math or spelling. The Stone Center at Wellesley has studied this process. The Center is dedicated to the study of women's developmental path to discover how it might be different from that of men. One of the central differences they see is the shift in a boy' s identification that happens at about age three. Then a boy begins to focus on father and maleness, while girls continue to develop interrelating skills with mother.

Dr. Stephen Bergman, at a Stone Center Colloquium in 1990, said, "Male psychology becomes fixated on achieving a separate and individuated self, what Joe Pleck calls 'male sex-role identity'. Self is based on separation from others and self-other-differentiation, *self-versus-other* which may then become *self-over-other."*

Dr. Bergman goes on to say that this shift is not "separating from the mother" or "disconnecting from the mother", it is a *disconnecting from the very process of growth in relationship,* a learning about *turning away from the whole relational mode.*"

The male model with its emphasis on rugged individualism, strength, dominance, and competition does not put much emphasis on attending to the thoughts and feelings of others. It almost seems like deliberate training in narcissism and therefore training away from empathy and toward power-over. Women are more fortunate in that the development of their relationship skills, of which empathy is chief, is uninterrupted throughout childhood.

"It is well known that the era of the rugged individual has been replaced by the era of the team player. But this is only the beginning. The quantum world has demolished the concept of the *unconnected* individual."—Margaret J. Wheatley

The Anatomy of Internal Field

Self-Awareness Vs. Hidden Self

Awareness of my self—my thoughts, feelings and wishes—is one of the three critical components that make up my internal field: the collection of information in my mind and body that governs my behavior and generates my relationships with the people and things in my life.

From the time I am born, my self feels at risk. I have an urgent need for tenderness and attention and when my parents fail to totally fulfill this demand, as nearly all busy parents do, I learn anxiety, uncertainty and become extremely sensitive to anything that even faintly seems to threaten my meaningfulness. It becomes necessary for me to develop some self soothing mechanisms…to make do until I can recruit my caretaker again.

Differentiation and Togetherness

My developing self has two instinctually rooted life forces: one which propels me toward being an emotionally separate, autonomous person who can think and act for myself; the other that propels me toward togetherness, a person who is connected with others, can get along with them, and belongs.

It is easy to see how I get confused between these two forces that can seem in opposition to each other. From infancy to adulthood I learn, through frustration and encouragement, more and more about how to walk the fine line between autonomy and dependence on others.

If I am mistreated, controlled too much, or ignored too much, my amygdala becomes inaccurate in its evaluation of the emotional significance of some events. I too easily rebel against control, even my own efforts at controlling myself. I am too quickly thrown off balance by what I perceive as slights.

Most civilized people believe that abuse of children, both physical and emotional, is destructive. What is not so widely realized is that *any* exercise of disrespectful power-over has consequences to my internal field—my relationship with and perception of myself. Every event that arouses anxiety interferes, to some degree, with my thinking process. Severe anxiety disrupts it entirely.

Unfortunately, I, like most of us, suffered enough over-control and neglect so that I have uncertainty about my self-worth. My amygdala is over-sensitive to signals that I am not meaningful and important—that I am being either "pushed around" or ignored. I am easily gripped by anxiety and the self I am aware of seems too often out of my control.

Prejudice Against Myself

There is a popular saying, "look out for number one". It strikes a chord in me because I am aware of my tendency to examine almost everything in terms of its effect on me. It is easy to believe that I really do look out for myself and protect my interests. It seems that I am prejudiced in my own favor, and superficially this is true. But beneath the surface, within my hidden self, in many respects hidden even from me, I treat myself in much the same way that I was abused when a child. My field of relating with myself is one of arbitrary superior/subordinate. My voice of self-appraisal is unrelentingly critical and discounting. The truth is, every discount I endured as a child, whether it was an actual physical beating, or a small humiliation, I perceived, at a deep level, as evidence that I might be meaningless and suffer "not being"—annihilation. The energy I mustered to survive, to "fight or flee" this threat, having no physical channel for discharge, accumulated in me as mounting proof of my helplessness and inadequacy.

> "The rules of the game cannot be fully comprehended, however, unless we develop an understanding of the hazards of early childhood, that time when the ideology of child-rearing is passed on to the next generation."—Alice Miller

As a child I am supplied with endless experiences of my inferiority compared to my main models—my parents and other grown-ups. This, together with the disparagement of discounting and the lack of respect and appreciation shown virtually all children, combine to create an inner field that is unfriendly to my own development.

Immunity to Favorable Experience

Although many of my experiences demonstrate competence, and often are appreciated by others, my negative internal field tends to intercept and keep my balance critical of myself. For example, when I was six my younger brother and I threw snowballs at a passing boy who was older and larger. He pursued us. I got to the front door before my brother, and shut him out to save myself. My father told me what kind of a person I was for doing that. For many years, whenever I was credited with accomplishing something, the voice in my head would remind me, "If they knew you are the kind of person who shut your brother out, they would not think this is so great."

Impression Management

Small wonder that early in life I begin systematically to conceal the "true" me from the outside world. I attempt to manage my relationships with others to appear effective and avoid discounts. False self is a term used to describe the carefully edited, cleaned up self I present when I wish to impress others or defend against the anxious feelings aroused by discounts—threats to my meaningfulness. I wear some version of this self when out in public and even in private with people I know. My cultural conditioning, as well as my personal experience, prejudices me against allowing others to see my weakness or know about my failures.

I have had the experience of revealing something about myself, and getting ridiculed or rejected for it. I remember being ashamed, embarrassed, and looking foolish. It felt

> "Virtually no aspect of our lives...is untouched by the violence that we do unthinkingly to children."—Philip Greven

terrible. I believed it diminished me in the eyes of people who were important to me.

Because of these unpleasant experiences, I am afraid that when I disclose anything that might make me look less than perfect, it makes me vulnerable to appearing inferior and being rejected. It can be used against me. I have learned that in most (if not all) situations it is best to be guarded, to hide my real feelings, admit to no unsatisfied needs or desires.

I create an internal field that guarantees that I will be disappointed in my real self—the self that necessarily experiments, makes mistakes in the process of learning and living.

I practice impression management rather than presenting myself as I really am—flawed and often uncertain, with a full share of weaknesses, together with some strengths and competencies. I fashion an ideal image of myself to appear strong, assured and comfortably confident, short of arrogance, but definitely *superior*.

I become centered on defense and safety. I am attracted to prestige and power because they promise less vulnerability. I engage in a genetically reinforced competition for the highest possible place in the pecking order.

If superiority is clearly not possible, I must manage to appear competent and respectable. My anxiety is triggered by anything in the field that seems to threaten my assumed identity. I am alert for opportunities to present information that puts me in a favorable light.

Developing and maintaining my false self becomes a high priority. In my adolescent years I spent most of my disposable time concerned with this project. If I never grow beyond this stage, the care and feeding of false self becomes a life-long, anxiety laden dedication. I have little appetite for the risky and often painful business of making connections, experimenting and growing. In fact, unless I am fortunate, my true self remains virtually hidden from me. It exists as a burden to be kept out of sight.

(There is considerable evidence that women are less centered on defense than men)

Being Other Directed

As a result of maintaining this false self, I get out of touch with my true or real self—the self with my own unique blend of weaknesses and strengths, fear and courage, blindness and insightful perceptiveness. In focusing on making my competitive self impressive to others, I become *other-directed*—dependent for validation on the opinion of others and unappreciative and discounting of my own worth.

> "While the etiology of depression undoubtedly is complex, punishment in childhood always has been one of the most powerful generators of depression in adulthood."—Philip Greven

This way of being in the world, of perceiving the world, moves me away from healthy differentiation and autonomy. I replace the dictatorship of my parents with the dictatorship of friends, fellow workers, bosses and leaders, with a cultural "dictatorship of the shoulds". *I create within myself a field that brings out the least in me.* I relate to myself largely with criticism, disapproval and punishment. I am even taught that it is bad form to show appreciation of my own accomplishments.

It is in the development of my real self that I connect, learn and grow more effective—that very growing demonstrates to me my own validity. To realize my full potential for thinking and acting I need to be able to connect with *all* of my assets. It may seem strange to label weakness and fear as assets, yet how can I feel empathy and fully understand the troubles of someone else unless I can make connections to my own feelings and experiences of joy and woe? And how can I modify and improve on my weaknesses if I deny them? A defensive field resists new information.

The essence of outstanding thinking and of creativity is to be perceptive and receptive—to connect with—people, new information and my giant reference storehouse of experience; to stay open in present time. When I am committed to defense, to self-protection, I do not risk the anxious confusion of processing new data. I stick with my old assumptions even in new circumstances. I tend to react in old and tested ways that *feel* safer. This becomes such an accustomed strategy that most of the time I am not even aware of doing it. Much of my everyday behavior is of this defensive type.

The problem is, protecting myself from confusion and anxiety also protects me from the very process of learning. When I focus only on presenting an acceptable-to-others self, I tend to lose touch with the full spectrum of what it is to be me. The ultimate aliveness is connecting with the *real* in myself and in others.

Safety and Risk

David Schnarch (1991 pg. 90), one of the giants in marital therapy, believes that the greatest obstacle to individual happiness and satisfaction is the unwillingness to share with another one's innermost thoughts and feelings, which, of course, include weaknesses as well as strengths.

> "The truth will set you free, but first it will make you damned mad—unknown

Nothing can make my world entirely safe. The field of a friendly group helps, but openness finally depends upon me and my willingness to push on the edges of my envelope to enlarge my zone of tolerance for anxiety—in short, to trust being myself. "Eventually [this zone of disclosure] becomes the arena in which individuals confront the issues of *integrity* and *cowardice*...In actuality the work of intimate relationships is self-maintenance in the face of fears of betrayal and abandonment. The most important "trusting relationship" is the relationship one has with oneself." (Ibid. pg. 130—131)

In my meetings with friends, when I repeatedly screw up my courage and disclose my thoughts and feelings, I am able to make new and exciting connections to elements of myself that had been dormant. This happens when I am hearing myself talk, and, miraculously, it also happens as I learn to risk wholehearted listening to what others say about *themselves.*

When I am willing and able to interact undefensively as my whole self, I am freed from much of the burden of impression management. This is the real me and it is exhilarating. Self disclosure is not just a process of personal biography. It is a way of tapping into my present-time self, the "just-in-time" me, the person who is here without rehearsal or ready-made response, aware of both my fear and my courage, with the energy to create and recreate myself out of the raw material of this moment.

This is what <u>be</u>-ing is about, and as Joseph Campbell has said, "Bliss is the rapture of <u>be</u>ing."

To achieve this, I need an internal field that supports me fiercely, not one that is quick to criticize and punish.

The ultimate purpose of the Mind-Free experience is to reshape my relationship with myself so that I can truly become my own best friend.

> "...people grow best where they continuously experience an ingenious blend of support and challenge."—Robert Kegan

Vulnerability

An Experience with Anxiety and Self-Disclosure

Recently I joined an experimental class in Dialogue at the University of Massachusetts. There were twenty-eight of us seated in a large circle: graduate students, the professor, and me. The Facilitator (as the professor called himself) asked us to pass a "talking stick". Below is what I wrote in my journal:

"As soon as [the professor] brought out that stick I recalled it from somewhere. My first thought was "he will start this way'" and that means I am seventh. He did. Ninety percent of my energy is churned into a struggle with anxiety. I listen with 10% and surprisingly, I can do OK which shows me how little of myself I give to everyday listening.

"I am supposed to let myself go with everyone who speaks and when it gets to me I say whatever comes to my mind. No rehearsal. No planning. Vomit me up, undigested. Anxiety gains the upper hand. I listen with 5%. 95% dedicated to the war within: anxiety urgently demanding a plan and some faking to make it more bearable, my coping self insisting that we go with the "rules" and play it as it happens.

"This continues until Gene passes me the stick. He avoided what was in him. I told about my anxiety and how it was blocking thought. Slipped into idea of impression management. This was, I realized, slipping into a previous plan. As I did that, the edge went out of my offering. To remain wholehearted I needed to hang with my anxiety and dig into it no matter how weak and embarrassed I felt.

"When I can hang in there and disclose what I am discovering in that painful whirl of anxiety, something thrilling is going to happen to me. And when others do the same so I can hang in there with both them *and* me, something even more thrilling is going to happen.

"The essential ingredient to make Dialogue work seems to me to be courage to self-disclose. I believe most of us know when we are being guarded and we recognize guardedness in others. It see ms a lot like the "Emperor's

> "What is even more destructive than such overt violence (and false excitement) [on TV] is that the senses, intellect, and emotions of the child gradually become deadened and the child loses the capacity for free movement of awareness, attention, and thought."—Bohm and Peat

Clothes. What would happen if each of us was required to precede his participation with a statement of how much he or she is self-disclosing. For example, David's talk about the ritual stick would be zero self-disclosure so he would have to say something like "I am willing to risk no self-disclosure". I would have had to say "I am willing to risk

30% self-disclosure". The purpose is to make sure I am *aware* that I am avoiding psychological risk and we are not colluding in fake dialogue. Or perhaps we require ourselves to rate ourselves after we have spoken."

It is uncanny how clearly I know when my field and that of others is aimed at defense and impression management.

A Procedure to increase my awareness

To get a reading on how self-protective I am, I began to rate myself, whenever I remembered, on the degree of self-disclosure I achieved after each exchange with another.

Integrity

Webster tells us that integrity is an uncompromising adherence to a code of moral, artistic or other values such as honesty…the avoidance of deception, expediency, artificiality or shallowness of any kind. It is the quality or state of being complete and undivided—material, spiritual wholeness.

Integrity governs my willingness to cope with, rather than avoid, situations that threaten me. It often requires courage and I do not always have it.

It can be particularly difficult in relationships that are important to me when the other person takes a position I disagree with. I not only need courage, I need emotional intelligence in the way I express my contrary position.

The formation my true self is movement to fashion, preserve and enhance integrity. The motion from being enmeshed with my parents and important others, toward differentiation independence and autonomy is the grounding phenomenon of mature personality

Kathleen introduced me to a whole new degree of integrity. She does not allow herself to say anything that is not the truth to the best of her knowledge. I would have thought this would lead to a lot of pain and rejection, and while she does not always feel compelled to volunteer her truth, when she does, her care in own her thoughts and feelings and expressing them in a self-focused way, has a remarkable effect. Dealing with a person I know is wholly honest and real is an exciting and rare privilege.

We will be dealing with ways of communicating honestly without damaging the relationship in the section titled: The Anatomy of Relating.

"A society may be termed human in the measure to which its members confirm one another."—Martin Buber

Self and Synergy

Synergy, according to Webster, is an ancient theological doctrine that holds that when a person renews him or herself after a failure or defeat, divine grace cooperates to make the renewal more effective than the person could achieve on his own. A second definition says that informed cooperation between two parties produces an outcome greater than one plus one, in other words synergy can be a multiplying force—the opposite of antagonism and better than operating independently.

For many years I have been thrilled by evidence of synergy—the flashes of brilliant connecting that appear in invention sessions that are going well. Usually the group is working on a problem that no one has been able to solve individually. It is synergy in action and it demonstrates that given the right circumstances (Field) almost anyone can "outdo" him or herself in short spurts. This suggests that I have gifts that I keep hidden or muted except in extraordinary circumstances. A physical analogy is the burst of strength that is suddenly available in an emergency, which demonstrates that the capacity is always there. People like Einstein, Newton, William Blake and Byron are different only in that they have devised ways of continually accessing their gifts while I conceal mine from myself except on those rare occasions when "the right circumstances" occur. This in turn suggests that when operating individually my inner field withholds or blocks myself from perceiving connection-making opportunities; that I have a cautious, anxious, *defended* relationship with myself; that I do not feel "safe" enough to permit myself the continuous high level perceptiveness and connection-making leaps necessary to do "genius" thinking.

Me, Myself and I

When I was eight, I was absorbed with airplanes. As I maneuvered tiny toy planes with my hand, I gave a running explanation of what was going on. I played all the parts and was storyteller and audience. Discussing things internally with myself was such an accustomed activity that I was hardly aware of it. My inner dialogue was without self-criticism—pure pleasure.

> "The hallmark of maturity is comfort and peace (rather than mere tolerance) in being alone. *This advance in one's relationship with one's self empowers the transition from dependence on other...*"—David Schnarch

It was an activity of imagination and I was so accepting that it was encouraging.

More recently, I was driving to work at about five one morning and thinking about the group with which I was working. I suddenly realized that I had driven through a red light, "You stupid *bastard!*" I said to myself. A few minutes later, as I walked upstairs to my office, I thought about the vehemence of that punishing statement. In the group I was working with, a statement like that would certainly toxify the field and trigger revenge. I wondered if I might be feeling like getting revenge on myself and how that might work. I had a fantasy conversation with myself. "You call me a stupid bastard? Wait 'til you need an idea…I am going to be out to lunch." The thought that I might deliberately sabotage myself in "revenge" for a self-discount started a new and surprising line of speculation: is it possible that my *relationship with myself creates the field that determines my effectiveness?*

An Examination of Internal Influences

I was so interested in the idea that I might sometimes be working against myself that I began to identify the characteristics of the two parts of my "split" personality. The fact of two voices now suggested that I might not be monolithic, but rather, a *relationship—a field*—fascinated me. Perhaps this was the core governor that controlled my use of my gifts. To differentiate the two voices, I named the tough voice of righteous safety my Safekeeping Self. The tentative, idea-getting subordinate voice I call my Experimental or Adventurous Self.

> "Addiction to perfection, as Marian Woodman reminds us, amounts to having no garden. The anxiety to be perfect withers the vegetation."—Robert Bly

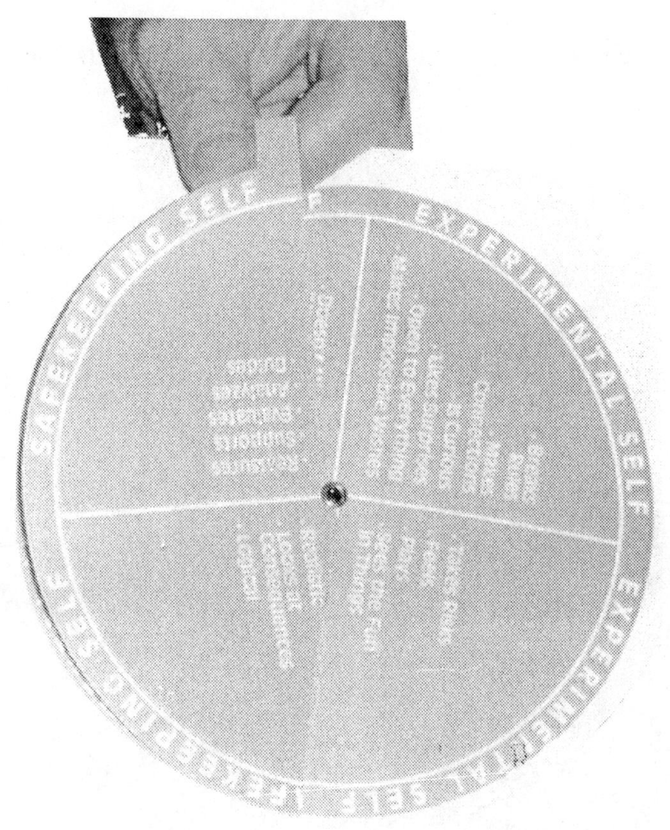

This is a picture of a Self-Wheel—a device that attempts to capture the way our divided selves get in their own way. Each of the two selves is represented by a wheel. Safekeeping is blue and as the boss self, can shut down Experimental. In the next pages we show how Safekeeping, depending on level of anxiety, can, with increasing anxiety, shut down all of Experimental self.

Ideally, Safekeeping oscillates from engaging all of Experimental to bringing into play all of its own valuable attributes (half of its circle). It keeps the punishing and cautious elements hidden until evaluation time, and keeps the punishing quadrant closed always.

Wide open and available for connections

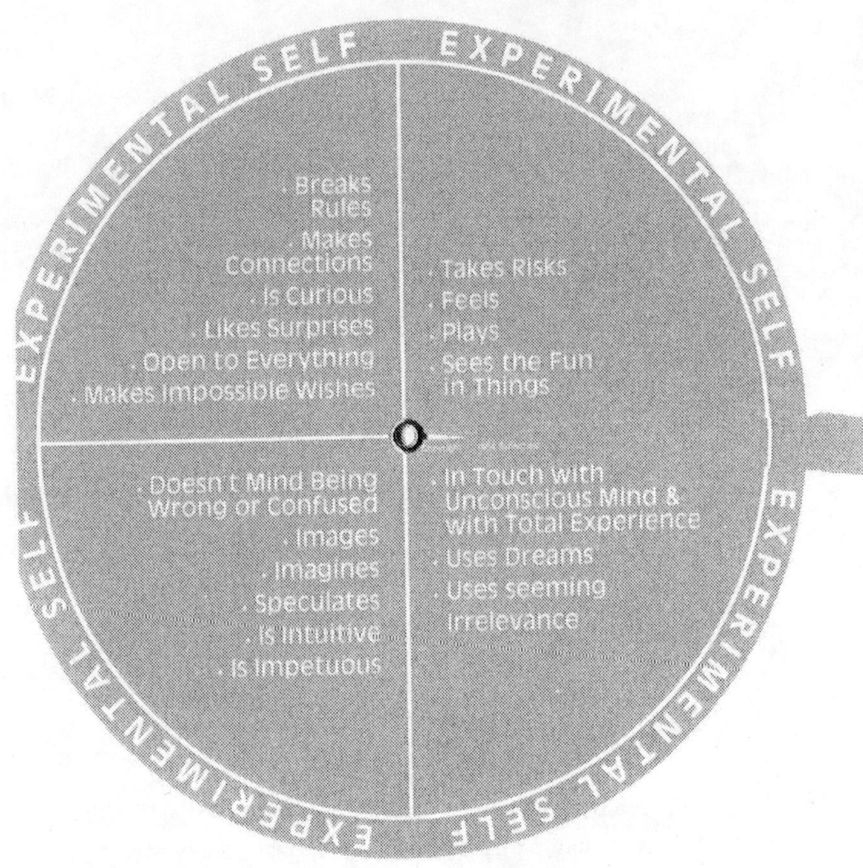

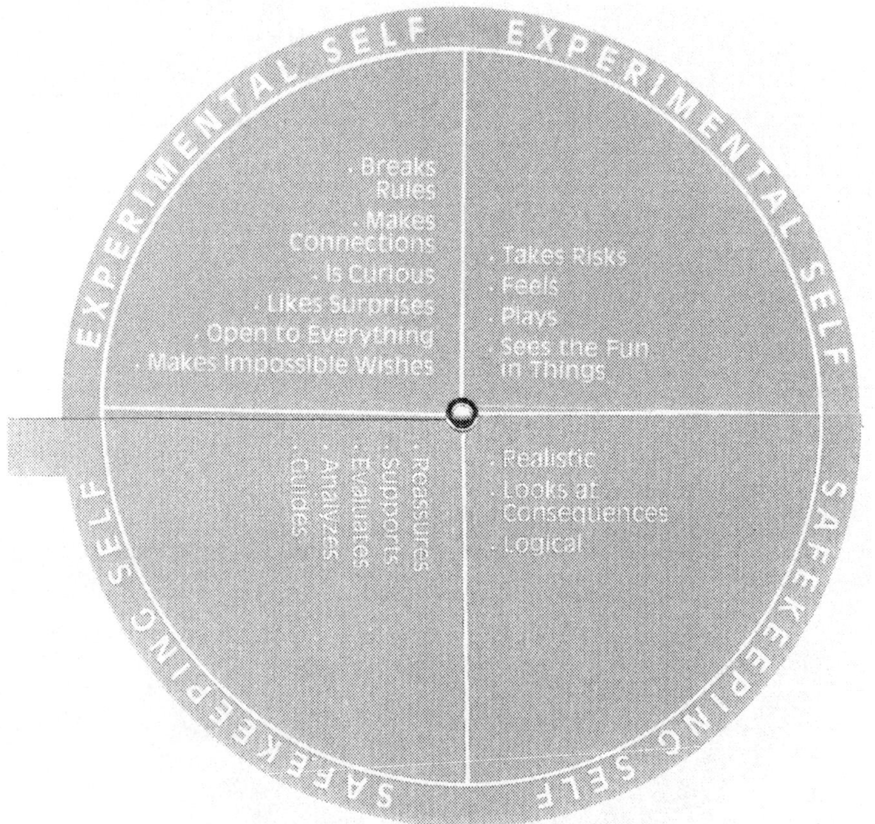

Evaluation of the connection

Anxiety is taking over

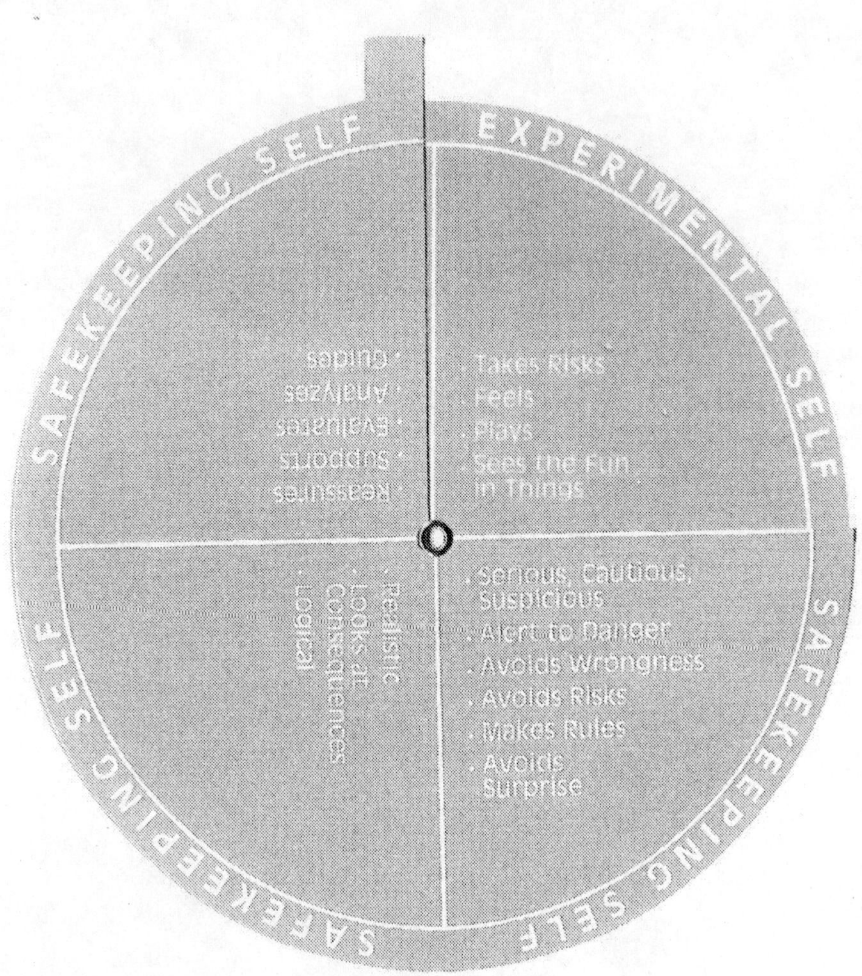

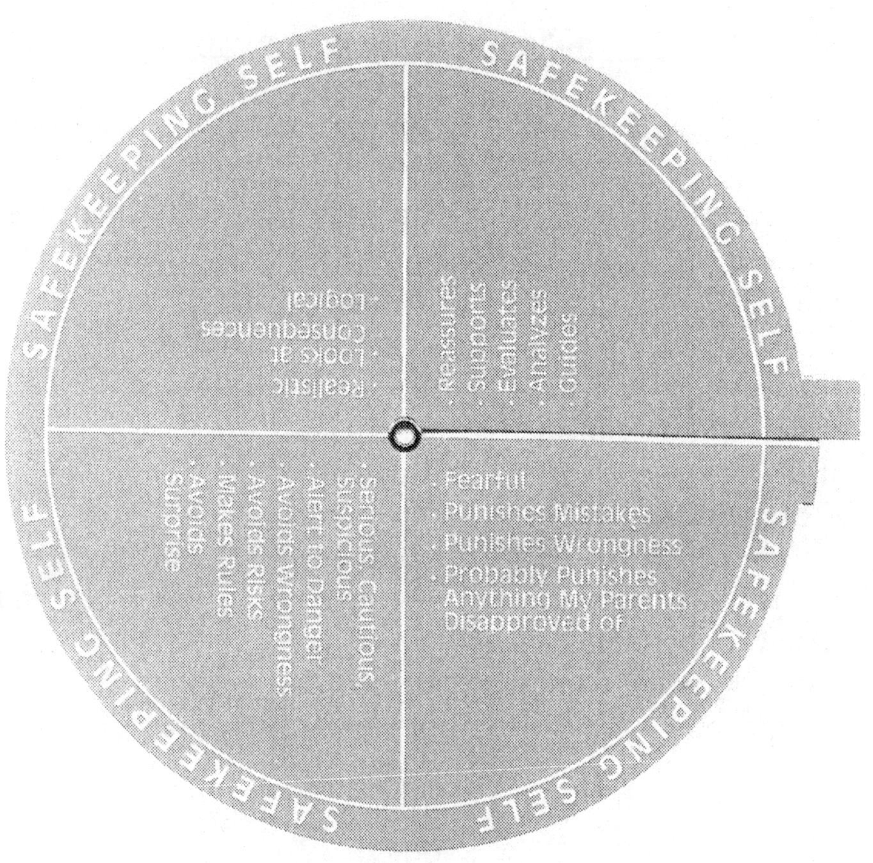

Unavailable

Psychological Division of My Self

Safekeeping Self	Experimental/Adventurous Self
•Evaluates	•In touch with total experience
•Analyzes	•Uses fantasy, dreams and wishes
•Guides	•Accepts irrelevance
•Makes rules	•Approximate thinker
•Realistic	•Impetuous
•Looks at consequences	•Intuitive
•Logical	•Speculative
•Takes things literally	•Curious
•Suspicious	•Accepts confusion, error and uncertainty
•Serious	•Open to *anything*
•Alert for possible danger	•Welcomes surprises
•Avoids risks, wrongness, surprises	•Risks
•Fearful	•Relishes ambiguity
PUNISHES ANY DEVIATION FROM THE ABOVE	•Plays
	•Makes connections
	•Breaks rules

This division of characteristics seems to be the result of the conditioning of my upbringing—my *interpretation* of all the fields of my life—parents, siblings, peers, teachers—and the resultant organization of my inner field—my thinking, feeling, acting self.

Reinforcement From Biology

Not surprisingly, there seems to be some support of the Safekeeping and Experimental division in the physical structure of my brain. The activities assigned to the left and right hemispheres of my brain reinforce my belief that I have internal influences that may not be cooperative. The chart below is intended to be suggestive rather than scientifically accurate. The qualities ascribed to right and

> "*Anything* we do generates action which can then be made meaningful. It is Okay not to know where you are going as long as you are going somewhere. Sooner or later you will find out where that somewhere is."—Weik

left hemisphere are roughly based on the early work of Roger W. Sperry, the great Caltech brain scientist.

Physiological Division of Myself

LEFT
Boss Hemisphere

Controls Right Side
Translations
Logical
Analytic
Semantic
Precise
Reading
Writing
Counting
ORDER
Precision
Right / Wrong
Yes / No
Black / White
Exact Connotation
Temporal Ordering
Sequence

RIGHT
Subordinate

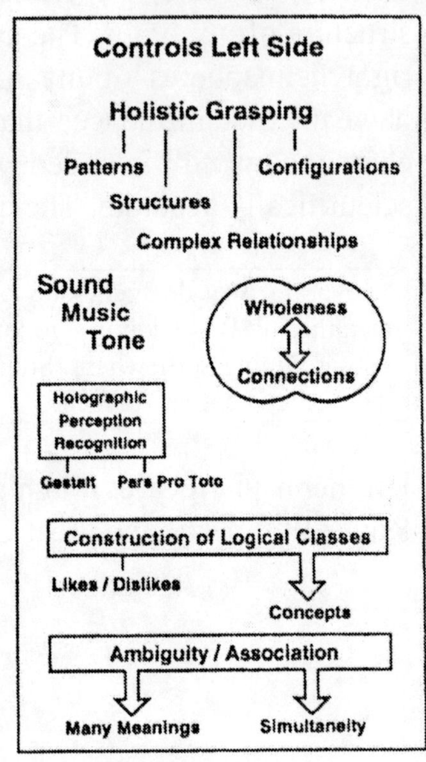

"To err is human, to forgive, divine."

A Self Divided Against Itself?

As I identified the actions typical of my Safekeeping/Experimental Selves, some elements are clearly adversarial. For example, my Experimental, Adventurous Self enjoys surprises, my Safekeeping Self does not; Experimental Self does not mind being confused and uncertain because that opens me to making new connections; Safekeeping abhors confusion and uncertainty because they may presage mistakes and danger. To better understand the relationship between these two selves I fashioned a wheel to suggest how they might relate (see figure of Self-Wheel). While both selves have important and desirable characteristics, *unless I make some conscious effort to manage the way they relate*, I slip into a boss-subordinate mode. I create in myself a field with all the draw-backs of an unfriendly partnership. My stop-light experience tells me that Safekeeping is boss—and a disagreeable one.

I am overwhelmingly critical of my ways of being—dissatisfied with my performance in many areas and quick to find fault. I am intolerant of mistakes and unforgiving. I hold grudges against my self. A great many of my transmissions to myself are *grossly* punishing. As in my stop-light experience, I do not hesitate to call myself harsh names—"stupid!" "idiot!" "incompetent" and worse are not unusual.

My standards for myself seem to require perfection and while I seldom live up to them, I do not revise my expectations to be more realistic and possible. *Any* shortcoming is punished. It is my practice to *expect* excellence (which increases my anxiety) and when I deliver only a competent performance, I almost *never* express appreciation.

If I were describing this as a relationship between two partners attempting to work together, I would consider this a poor, even destructive, alliance. When I see, accept and understand the adversarial *possibilities* of this internal field it is easy to see why I might be alienated from myself, uncooperative with myself, and blocked from effective use of many my resources. My "natural" internal field inclines me toward disagreement, disorder, agitation and waste of energy.

> "...bad is entropy—disorder, confusion, waste of energy, the inability to achieve goals; good is negative entropy...harmony, predictability, purposeful activity that leads to satisfying one's desires."—Mihaly Csikszentmihalyi

The Stone Center and Relationship

Since becoming familiar with the Stone Center at Wellesley College and their remarkable work on human development, I have used their illumination of relationship to help me understand how to improve the interactions between myself and others. Now I am applying that same illumination to the reactions, interactions, and actions-against that I engage in with the two voices inside me.

My Field

Margaret Wheatley explores the world of quantum physics for clues as to how the human universe works. The quantum world "...is a world where *relationship* is the key determiner of what is observed and of how particles manifest themselves." (1994, pg. 10) A Relationship is brought into being by the intersection of the fields between two people. What gives the relationship its energy, positive or negative is the quality of those fields. "Those who relate through coercion, or disregard for the other person, create negative energy. Those who see others in their fullness create positive energy…love…is the most potent source of power we have available."(Ibid. pg. 39). When I apply this theory to my relationship with myself, the inescapable conclusion is that I continually generate a negative, destructive field within myself. If, as Robert Kegan says, "…People grow best where they continuously experience an ingenious blend of support and challenge.." (1994, pg. 42), my internal field is stunting my growth. This is not only harmful to me, it is likely to project a negative field to others with whom I interact.

How Does This Destructive Relationship Form?

Robert Kegan (1982) tells me that my most fundamental activity is organizing meaning—understanding. This has been confirmed in my experience and it has become clear that I have a basic drive to *be and feel meaningful.* when something happens that threatens my being or feeling meaningful—a discount, a failure, a defeat, a weakness—it triggers anxiety that interferes with my thinking.

There is a critical sensing step that initiates meaning-making. It is perceiving/connecting. Nature, in her infinite wisdom, rewards me for perceiving/connecting because it is

> "It is essential to realize that "human nature" is the result of accidental adaptations to environmental conditions long since gone."—Mihaly Csikszentmihalyi

both the key to survival and the means of increasing my resourcefulness (to become ever better at surviving).

Whenever I make a connection on the way to creating a meaning, I get a small shot of the hormone endorphin—a tiny spurt of good feeling. From infancy through my early development, I am joyfully motivated to make connections. The actuality is much more complex, but Nature's plan is for me to be a *learner:* one who connects to make meaning and then organizes the implications so that I grow in capability, autonomy and complexity. A negative field within me works against nature's plan.

I Am Programmed To Get Attention

As we have learned, the attention of my parents was crucial. When I fail to get their attention it arouses my anxiety. I experience the fear that I am abandoned and will not survive. My determination to *be* and my terror of *not being* are, and always will be, driving forces in my life. I learn to scan *every* perception/connection; every transmission. The threat of *not being, of being meaningless*, activates all my defensive/aggressive systems. This is a genetic imperative for survival. I get a jolt of energy—adrenaline to prepare me for fight or flight. The objective is to secure control of my physical well-being.

This is an effective design for dealing with physical danger, but it is ill-suited and probably counter-productive for processing emotional and psychological threat. Yet, emotional threat, like physical threat, translates to, "I am in danger of not being" and I get that same jolt of adrenaline. I am ready for fight or flight, but those powerful impulses are simply irrelevant to my situation. The blind energy for attack or retreat creates confusion, disorder, and destructive actions. I believe that much of my rebellion, misbehavior, tantrums, and upheavals of childhood were rooted in my *misperceptions* of threat to my meaningfulness. The resultant shots of adrenaline propelled me *out of control* into senseless defensive actions.

The Paradox of Control

In childhood, control is a fundamental issue for me, and it remains one as an adult. Much of my inappropriate behavior, because it is provoked by an unrealistic assessment of the situation and fueled by anxiety, is, in one way or another, an attempt to express, demonstrate or protect my meaningfulness by controlling myself and others. As a child, I need and want to be cared for. At the

> "Nothing ever stays the same. Either let entropy get the upper hand, or try to beat the system."—Mihaly Csikszentmihalyi

same time, I need and want to develop my independence and autonomy. I develop a sensitivity to control and attempt to differentiate the kind of guiding and teaching actions that help me grow, from those that seem arbitrarily to "push me around" and defeat my need to be autonomous. Distinguishing between the two is often not possible and the competitive culture tends to confuse the issue even more: winning is being in control, losing is being controlled and often *feels* like a threat to my meaningfulness. In life, which in reality is not a game, this confusion may propel me into defensive reactions that make no sense. Power and control appear to assure winning, yet they often arouse such defensiveness as to make the short term victory very costly in the long term. While this is usually true in relationships with others, could it be true of my relationship with myself?

What are the implications of this for my internal field—my relationship with myself?

Attack and Self-Punish, or Self-Soothe and Self-Coach

Given my strict standards for myself I often make mistakes or fall short and whenever I experience that as a threat to my well-being, I get that spurt of adrenaline energy. David Schnarch (1994) in a seminar asserted that how I deal with that energy that often feels like anxiety, has a profound effect on my development of differentiation, autonomy and integrity. That energy will not go away and I must somehow *manage* it. To do so I have at least four options: attack and self-punish for the failure; repress and absorb the negative energy—a course that may lead to depression, or "kicking the dog"; deliberately use a self-soothing ritual to dissipate the energy; connect with the reality of the failure and learn from it.

Attack and Punishment as a Self-Management Strategy

My self-punisher originates out of early confusion. Following the model of my parents correcting me, I adopt self-punishment to correct errant behavior. It is to protect me from abandonment. Given my limited experience and the enormity of the fear, it is not surprising that I make my self-punisher "heavy duty". Further, it gets reinforced by every correction, disapproval, and fault-finding of important others. At the time my punisher is developing, I have almost

> "Alienation from one's real self...not only arrests personal growth; it tends to make a farce out of one's relationship with people."—Sidney M. Jourard

no capacity for discriminating between mild, forgivable impropriety and barbarism on my part. Any action or inaction of mine that falls short of perfection, or goes counter to my parents' *wishes* merits heavy to devastating punishment.

Perhaps the reason that a punishing action far outweighs an appreciation in it's impact on my self regard, is that it carries with it the unconscious threat of abandonment.

Punishment and Connecting

I organize meaning by exploring and experimenting to make connections—pulling a lamp cord to see what happens; forming patterns that make sense out of anomaly and confusion. An *essential* component of connection-making is error, as in trial-and-error, trial-and-success. But error triggers punishment and since my built-in punisher is not good at discriminating useful-error that leads to connection and understanding, and action-error that sends a lamp crashing to the floor, my early policy becomes: punish *every* error, punish *every* mistake and thus attempt to avoid abandonment and the terror of feeling meaningless. The attack and punish self-management strategy is a powerful deterrent to whole-hearted connecting to learn and to form ideas.

No wonder when someone asks me "How is a tree like a tractor?" It brings my "scanner-for-threat" to full alert and I prepare to punish. I will need to screw up my courage to risk a connection that is likely to be a mistake.

No wonder when I feel a rush of joy as I make a brilliant, un-obvious connection, my punisher, my ever-present killjoy says, "Watch it! There is bound to be a mistake here." This is a powerful part of the field in me that puts a damper on my healthy appetite for connecting to understand, to learn, to experience the rapture of being.

I have observed thousands of intelligent people in invention sessions and it is entirely predictable that when one person offers an idea that might help reach the goal, another person will point out a flaw in the idea. I am aware that when I am presented with an idea, I instantly look for the flaws. I have an insistent urge to tell the originator about the flaw I see. These negative impulses of mine are expressions of Mahr's Law, "Don't get any on you". I attempt to distance myself from a possible mistake. They also distance me from participating in synergy and being.

"If punishment make not the will supple, it hardens the offender."—John Locke

Punishment—the Acceptable Blight

When I thought of self-punishment as a way of managing myself, I began to examine it more closely. I asked several hundred people about their experiences with self-punishment. I learned that the phenomenon is virtually universal. The usual response was, "It's normal, isn't it?"

Together we did balanced evaluations of the possible benefits and possible damage done by self-punishment. Here are some of the results:

Possible Benefits of Self-Punishment

It preempts punishment by others. If I promptly punish myself, it will make it unnecessary for others to punish me.

It protects me from feeling meaningless. When I preempt, I make it unnecessary for someone else to send the message "You are meaningless"; my self-punishment may tell me I am stupid or wrong, but not that I am meaningless.

It will help me change my behavior. Nearly everyone believes that punishment will help avoid the mistake next time. The more intense the punishment, the more likely the mistaken behavior will be extinguished.

It focuses my attention on my shortcomings. The punishment assures that I will not simply ignore a flaw in myself. To avoid future punishment I will be motivated to correct the flaw.

It gives me feedback on how I am doing. This has the connotation of helping me evaluate my hour-by-hour performance. With this feedback, I can determine how well I am doing compared to how well I might or should do.

It is payment for the mistake. I believe the punishment is just retribution that makes up for the mistake, or at least demonstrates that I do not approve of what I have done.

It suggests that I am a better person than my action demonstrates. If I show that I disapprove of what I have done, I demonstrate to the observer that I am not ignorant of the proper behavior. This action is not typical of me.

> "...positive statements you make to yourself have little if any effect. What *is* crucial is what you think when you fail, using the power of 'non-negative thinking'."—Martin Seligman

It is a motivator. I have a deep down belief that without punishment I would stop being responsible.

It is the basis for self-discipline. Punishment, or fear of it, is what makes my self-discipline work.

It keeps things in balance. This is rather mystical, and it was mentioned often enough so it needs to be included. I believe that I must have a balance between good feelings and bad. If things get too good, I am inviting disaster. By giving myself a steady stream of small punishments, I protect myself against a large punishment.

It is apparent that when I examine self-punishment, I find it an important presence in my life. It seems to do a lot of things that need doing. But self-punishment has a darker side.

Possible Damage from Self-Punishment

It lowers my self-esteem. As I examined the extent of my self-punishment, I become aware that the steady stream of criticism within strikes a blow at my own self-regard.

It makes me other-directed. The standards that guide me in my self-punishment are based on my *childhood* understanding of what my parents and others expected of me. Instead of dealing with me and what is real now, my self-punisher reacts to outdated information.

It reduces my joie de vivre—my joy in being. In a simple weighing of "ounces of bad feelings and ounces of good feelings", self-punishment weighs in more heavily.

It slows my learning. Skinner, Lozanov, and my own experience suggest that I am not very available for connecting when someone is standing behind me ready to punish me for the slightest mistake.

It slows my understanding of something new. I do not leap to conclusions for fear of making mistakes. In most thinking situations (as opposed to acting) the fast, efficient way to understand *is* to jump to a tentative conclusion (in the scientific method it is called a hypothesis) and then

> "By improving your awareness of how you talk, and learning the skills to communicate fully and clearly you can literally make connections happen."—Miller, Wakman, et al

modify it as more data comes in. The slow way is to wait until all the information is in (if it ever comes) and then arrive at a conclusion or understanding.

It creates fear of newness. I will avoid situations where I cannot predict outcomes because they are more likely to breed mistakes and punishment.

I lose confidence in myself. It produces feelings of incompetence and low expectations of myself, which can be self-fulfilling prophecies.

It positions me as one-down and vulnerable. It tends to make me feel more helpless than I really am.

It undermines initiative. To avoid the risk of a mistake in thinking for myself, I 'wait for instructions', or worse, pretend the situation is routine when it is not so I can say "I acted as I am supposed to."

It produces imbalance. I focus on avoiding mistakes and punishment so my attention tends to be on the negatives in my enterprise and I may not relish the accomplishments.

It creates poor self-discipline. Contrary to the accepted belief, self-discipline depends largely on self-regard. With high self-regard I have high expectations of myself and I tend to live up to them. Self-punishment undermines this and leads to poorer self-discipline.

It causes a lack of wholeheartedness and commitment. Fear of mistakes and punishment encourages caution and suspicion. I hold back until I am certain to be right. I do not jump in and help make something go before anyone can be sure. I am a waiter-for-the-bandwagon.

It makes me avoid ambiguity, confusion, and uncertainty. In these situations I am in danger of being mistaken so I avoid them. Ambiguity, confusion, and uncertainty are the precursors to new connections.

It encourages denial. To avoid punishment I may not admit a mistake. I look for a scapegoat to blame and I do not learn from the mistake.

> "As long as pain, even at a very low level, continues, the computer (which is one's mind) tends to program a negative pall."—John C. Lilly

It discourages learning from experience. When an experience is unpleasant and involves self-punishment, I focus on the punishment and do not dwell on the mistake itself as a learning opportunity.

It can make me sick. There is considerable evidence that negativity in the mind-body connection can lead to depression and sickness.

It creates an anti-growth field within me. Which means that I carry with me everywhere and all the time a powerful self-limiting force.

The Paradox of Punishment

There is abundant evidence that abuse, physical or emotional, destroys the capacity to empathize and leads toward narcissism and sociopathic behavior. Nine out of ten inmates in our prisons were abused as children. There is a determined resistance in me to accepting and making meaning out of punishment from others because the message is, “You and your needs are meaningless”, and to accept that leads me to hopelessness and despair—perhaps toward suicide.

But punishing *is* rewarding to the punisher. Often my “misbehavior” is experienced by my parent as a willful disobedience and swift punishment not only teaches me a lesson, it is, in a sense, revenge for my discount, my flouting of a rule. Parents who punish would do well to tell me, “I am doing this for my own good, not yours.” However, punishment *seems* to get results, and since it handles the punisher’s anger and feelings of being discounted, it is firmly embedded in our culture. It is difficult to imagine bringing up children or operating a company without depending on the reward/punishment combination. But in the interest of dealing with reality I need to acknowledge that with punishment, the punishment itself *becomes the noteworthy event*, not learning. In other words, I connect to the punishment to make meaning, not necessarily to the offending action. Only by recognizing that, can I begin to think about inventing an alternative, more effective way of managing myself for change and growth.

The Net Effect On My Internal Field

As a result of the ever-present faultfinder, my internal field is the antithesis of the supportive holding environment that would facilitate growth and development. This leads to tendencies that inhibit learning:

> "The goal of supporting...the evolution of consciousness [is] a more ambitious undertaking than skills training." But "...a single investment could pay multiple dividends."—Robert Kegan

Some Tendencies Observed in

Self-Punishing Learners	Self-Affirming Learners
•Suspicious—skeptical	•Open—immediately ready to 'try it on for size', experiment
•Want precise, step-by-step instruction	•Reserve judgment until they have experienced the proposal
•Do not jump to conclusions	•Jump to conclusions (form tentative hypotheses)
•Do not make connections to understand until they are *certain*	•Tolerant of mistakes
•Immediately frustrated by confusion	•Make many connections—some 'off the point'
•Continually evaluate	•Tolerate confusion—use it
•Guarded vs. available	•Accept all and discard that which they cannot make useful
•Have an all or nothing posture	•Oscillate from approximate guessing to logical precision
•Put responsibility for their learning on a teacher	•Take responsibility for their own learning
•Avoid any risk of mistake	

Adopting a Creative Self-Management Strategy

Since self-punishment may provide some important benefits, it made sense to see if I could get the good without the bad. Initially I attempted to extinguish self-punishment by making policy. I *resolved* to stop all punishment of myself. This had a reverse effect. I not only continued to punish, I felt disappointed in myself when I failed to keep my resolution!

Next, I singled out each punishment and resolved not to repeat it. This also was ineffective. I next focused on each punishment, as it happened, and asked myself "How can I keep the benefit I am supposed to get from this punishment, but eliminate the pain?" When I first began to analyze the happening that initiated punishment and invent a way to be successful the next time, I discovered that I was using self-punishment to *avoid* close examination of the error. The punishment was the event, not the error. This proved to be the turning point in my campaign to reduce self-punishment.

> "Real learning gets to the heart of what it means to be human."—Peter Senge

Focus on the Error, Not the Punishment

I developed a procedure that eventually was effective for me. Whenever I experience a bad feeling I trace it. If it comes from myself, I look beneath the punishment for the cause. For example, I found that when I was typing and hit a wrong key it was my practice to wince and grimace and get a bad feeling. I analyzed what was causing me to hit wrong keys. It happened when I was pushing myself to type faster. I decided to attempt to type just a little slower than I was able to, and if I hit a wrong key, that was just a normal part of my typing and did not rate any punishment. I stopped wincing, grimacing and having a bad feeling when I hit a wrong key. A month later I suddenly realized that I was typing nearly twice as fast as I ever had, and while I still hit an occasional wrong key, there was no punishment, just awareness.

In my experience, every individual case of self-punishment had to be dealt with in this problem-solving way. At first, it required quite a lot of attention as I found that I was punishing myself in small and large ways many times a day. In retrospect it was a lot like untangling a ball of string. There were many tiny tangles. As I untangled them, the ball loosened. At first there seemed to be little effect on my life—a few less punishments, yet still a field of strictness and disapproval.

On my way to eliminating self-punishment I experimented with ways to take the sting out of that tough authoritarian voice in my head. One particularly effective experiment was to give that hypercritical authority in my head, the voice of Donald Duck. It was a giant step toward success!

About two months after I began my systematic analysis and problem solving, I was returning a rental car to Hertz at an airport. This was usually a high tension operation, punishment at the ready, with me on full alert so I would not miss the various turns. In this case I was late so I expected an increase in tension. Instead, I felt as though I had a friendly coach encouraging me: "Relax, you can easily see those signs—no sweat." And I *did* easily see the signs, return the car and catch my plane. As I checked in, I realized that this was a new, calm experience. My internal field had changed.

Good Me vs. Bad Me

Harry Stack Sullivan traces the generalized tendency to be self-critical to early experience. "The child's sense of self evolves gradually during the first year of life, primarily as a

> "...problems of conduct are the deepest and most common of all the problems of life...the deepest plane of the mental attitude of everyone is fixed by the way in which problems of behavior are treated."—John Dewey

consequence of the ministrations of the person who takes care of the child. If this caretaker is loving, comforting and meets the infantile needs, the infant has a generalized feeling of 'good me'. On the other hand, if the caretaker is anxious, tense, and rejecting [in my terms, punishing], this too is communicated to the infant who experiences a generalized feeling of 'bad me'." (1957, Pg.162)

I believe that in the two months when I had been painstakingly analyzing and problem solving each of my self-punishments, I had reached a critical mass and my internal caretaker shifted from "anxious, tense, and rejecting" toward "loving, comforting and meeting [my adult] needs". Complete change will require much more time, but I was on my way.

Reframing My Relationship With Myself to Develop Synergy

The first step toward a more effective internal relationship is to define what it needs to be like. Rewarding relationships between two people have specific characteristics:

- Mutual—the two parties are equal in the sense that they respect each other. Neither attempts to dominate.
- Listening—each listens to the other to connect and build.
- Empathic—each makes the effort to understand and honor the thoughts and feelings of the other.
- Dialogue—they communicate, not in argument and discussion, but in dialogue…to increase intimacy and deepen the relationship.
- Available—each party is free to move and to be moved by the relationship.
- Motivated—each wishes to expand connections, to collaborate to create new meanings and new insights.
- Managed—each *consciously* avoids actions that disconnect and distance or control.
- Interactive—each resists impulses to be reactive.

> "…the role of anxiety in interpersonal relations is so profoundly important that its differentiation from all other tensions is vital."—Harry Stack Sullivan

As a grown-up, I will need to take my development into my own hands. Kegan (1982) suggests that I experience several "holding environments": family, school, extended family, job and others. He describes the characteristics that encourage me to differentiate—to move toward becoming a whole and effective individual. First, the field holds heartily, supportively, but does not hold onto. Second, it assists in the emergence of competence with coaching, but does not push harshly. Third, it remains in place so I can touch base during uncertain beginnings.

My various holding environments allow me to experiment—trial and error/trial and success—and learn as I go. They give me a safe zone in which to change. Some holding environments are not optimal—e.g. an extremely competitive family where winning is the focus. However, when I convert my management style from self-punisher and merciless critic to a loving coach, I create an ever-present holding environment that nurtures my continuing movement toward differentiation and accessibility.

This Internal Field Greatly Influence My External Actions

It is predictable that this internal dynamic, this field, greatly influences my interactions with other people. Unless I am careful to control for it, I send punishing transmissions not only to myself, but also to others and often get punished in return.

In Summary

The most important action I can take in developing effective behavior in myself is to generate a continuously positive internal field.

Scientific Support for the Power of Inner Positive Field

Excerpts from:

Language, Thought, and Disease **By W. C. Ellerbroek, M. D.**

Co-Evolution Quarterly, Spring 1978

THE THEORY

Postulates

1. In order to avoid dissecting the human being, we will not use such words as physical, mental,organic, or psychological.

2. We will attempt to see the person in his/her field situation, including his family and friends and his/her cumulative behavior and experiences.

3. We will be aware that she interacts with the whole world.

4. We will keep in mind that our observations are subjective data.

5. We will note all the variables of which we know; we will also be aware that there are plenty of variables that we do not know.

6. We will remember that the field includes the observer.

7. We will not fall into the trap of "The fallacy of misplaced precision".

8. In this theory we will call each observation a behavior e.g. illness will be called a behavior.

Hypotheses

1. A person can contact the reality inside and outside of himself only through his perceptions. There is no way he can entirely verify these observations.

2. We cannot be sure these observations are right. Ambiguity can never be reduced to zero.

3. These perceptions produce a fantasy picture in the brain of what is going on. Fantasy is a better word than image because it has a connotation of error and spuriousness that is desirable.

4. We will avoid the delusion of perception=truth. A person looks at something and thinks he sees it. Actually he only *thinks* he sees it.

5. The person has his own ideas of the way he believes things are now; he also has ideas (constructs, fantasies) of how past, present, and future should be, or should have been.

6. When the reality he perceives does not match his idea, he wants it to change and match his idea of how it should be. When it does not do this, he becomes frustrated, irritated, angry, unhappy, depressed, or some other unpleasant emotion.

7. *Every* unpleasant emotion is linked with a thought or statement that is contrary to the observer's wanted reality.

8. These unpleasant emotional reactions are *always* harmful to the person; they cause unnecessary alterations from normal in various organs and systems. These then require correction. If there are many of these alterations and corrections, the corrective system may fail and Disease behavior results.

9. Conversely, love, happiness, pleasure, and good feelings occur when the person notes that the reality he observes is matching his idea of what it should be.

10. Language, with its errors and distortions, leads to additional difficulties in perceiving reality accurately.

11. It is very easy to make statements that are contrary to reality. These repeatedly stimulate the harmful responses of the body and brain.

12. It may be that by learning to be more accurate in our observations of reality we can eliminate or reduce harmful behavior.

++++++++

It is easy to test the above hypotheses: Pretend for a moment that today your partner drove into one of the garage doors causing extensive damage. If you repeatedly say, in appropriate tones. “He/She shouldn’t have done that!”, you will become aware of increasing tension and anger. Conversely, if you then say, “Considering everything I know about my mate, and bearing in mind that there are many factors of which I am unaware, *since the event has already occurred,* it is obvious that today is the day that my partner *should* have driven into the garage doors!” You will note a prompt decrease in gastric acidity, serum free fatty acids, and cholesterol.

The first statement is contrary to reality; The second is in accord with reality. Nothing about this says that you should be pleased about the accident. You are encouraged to do whatever necessary to prevent it happening again. The main consideration is to *avoid behaviors that are harmful to self.*

The Experiment with Patients Suffering from Acne

Summary

There were thirty-six subjects involved in this experiment. There were six therapeutic failures. These patients declined to change their life styles (of self-punishment). Thirty of the patients were judged 80% improved after eight weeks. At sixteen weeks, seventeen patients were cured (had clear skin); the rest were improved from 80% to 90%.

This rate of cure and improvement is quite remarkable compared to patients getting orthodox treatment

The therapeutic program

- Each patient was given a complete physical. During this time, and in following interviews, attention was drawn to harmful language habits, depressed postures, faces, voice tones, and sighing.

- Skin creams and lotions were advised against; their use reinforces the mistaken idea that acne is a skin disorder, thus decreasing the attention paid to the behavioral aspects of the program.

- Diet was de-emphasized.

- Posture and facial expression were emphasized.

- Patients were told that acne is related to feeling picked-on. Lesions will not develop without the picked-on feeling.

Examples of directions given

1. At each interview a statement like the following was included: "Since acne is related to feeling picked-on, it is important to stop picking on

yourself. Instead of punishing yourself for the way you look in the mirror, learn to say "That big pimple should be exactly where it is". or "My face *should* look this way."

2. The patients were advised to watch for itching as an indicator of irrational thinking e.g. observing that something is not the way you think it should be and getting bad feelings from that. "Every time you itch, it is a clue to you that immediately before the itch (or bad feeling) you have had an irrational or erroneous thought. You can use the itch (or bad feeling) as a valuable tool in spotting unhappy thoughts.

3. An attempt was made to teach the patient to avoid the feedback implications from negative words by not using them. Instead of saying "I am feeling miserable" use something like "I certainly do not feel as chipper as I'd like to".

4. Patients were told that unless forced, no human being can perform *any* act without wanting to. They were asked not to use the following words when referring to themselves: should, must, have to, ought to, got to, and will power. Each of these words imply that they are somehow being *forced* to do something when actually they themselves *choose* to do whatever it is they are doing. They were advised to use the phrases "I want to…" or "I choose to…", instead of "I've got to…".

In Summary

Dr. Ellerboek is saying that it can be demonstrated that when I create an inner field that is supportive, nurturing and non-punishing, I will avoid destructive reactions. It pays dividends in well-being and effectiveness when I relate to myself like a loving coach.

Part 2—Tools of the Field

> "Whenever...creativity is impeded, the ultimate result is not simply the absence of creativity, but an actual positive presence of destructiveness."—Bohm and Peat

Creativity, Thinking and Life Skills

This program is designed to help me identify the actions—the field generators—my own and those of others—that discourage connecting and reduce my thinking effectiveness. Awareness is the first step in modifying my behavior. If aware, I can *manage* my words, vocals and non-verbal actions to create fields that invite cooperation and generate synergy.

Michaelangelo and museums the world over have misled us about creativity. I ask a person, "Are you creative?" and most will answer "No, not really." And if I pursue it and ask why they believe they are not creative, they answer "I can't draw a straight line." or "I can't really put words together like Wordsworth."

These responses suggest that many people believe that in order to qualify as creative and do original thinking they need to produce art or literature. There is little recognition that the thinking operations called creative are the *same* as those I use in my everyday operations, from deciding what clothes to put on, to imagining how it might be to kiss my girl, to figuring out a work assignment, to getting cooperation from my companions at work.

Misconceptions about thinking, learning and creativity are not harmless. Not knowing about the thinking process is a constant disadvantage to my growth as an effective person. Because my internal field is firmly oriented toward self-protection, programmed in ancient times to react to *any threat* however trivial, I am often defensive, and resist information that contains any hint of emotional threat. Such every-day transmissions as criticism, impatience, dominance, indifference, or coldness can trigger anxiety and interfere with my thinking.

When I am unaware of field forces, I may unwittingly generate fields that inhibit creative thinking and learning, for example I may disapprove of guessing, when actually a guess is a hypothesis, an important thinking tool which we will examine below.

Webster's tells me that "create" means "to bring into existence; make out of nothing and for the first time". We interpret that to mean that if I develop an idea, in order to qualify as "creative" it must be the very first time anyone thought it. It also means that I must start with "nothing". This definition does not fit the process I have studied for thirty odd years. It would be more accurate to say "Create: to imagine or bring into existence or awareness, by means of connections, an idea or understanding." According to John Dewey, the great educator, all thinking is making connections to detect relationships to get an idea. "…an idea," he says, "terminates in an understanding so that an event acquires meaning…an idea is a mental picture of something not actually present and thinking is a succession of such pictures."(1933, Pg. 5)

> "What is even of greater danger...is that [denial of creativity] eventually brings about violence of various kinds. For creativity is a prime need of a human being and its denial brings about a pervasive state of dissatisfaction and boredom [and search for excitement]."—Bohm and Peat

So *thinking itself is a creative act.* The product of this process can range from a memory to a combination never before made. Thinking *always* involves the formation of mental images—imagination—though I may stop being aware of them.

The difference between a memory and a new combination is the degree of risk required of the thinker.

When I make the connections to figure something out for the first time *for me,* I risk being mistaken, and from infancy, those who teach me, begin to condition me to avoid mistakes. I begin to feel increasing anxiety whenever I start to make a "risky" connection. Creating something that conveys new meaning for everyone is the same process. In the case of Michaelangelo it is used with extraordinary skill.

My first need is to understand what my thinking/creative process really is and why the continual appreciation of it in myself and others is so essential. The creative process is driven by my most fundamental need as a human being: my need to *be and feel meaningful.* Robert Kegan says, "...what an organism does is organize; and what a human organism organizes is meaning...we literally make [create] sense." (1982, Pg. 11)

When I fail to make the connections to understand something, I feel less meaningful—it is a self-discount.

Kegan goes on to say "Thus it is not that a person makes meaning, as much as that *the activity of being a person is the activity of meaning-making*."

(Ibid. Pg. 11) Thus, creativity/thinking—creating meaning—is essential to being a person. The more skillful I am at perceiving/connecting and making meaning, the *better I am at being a person.*

> "[Misleading assumptions are] deeply and pervasively conditioned, for example, the general tradition that takes the absolute necessity of rewards and punishments for granted."—Bohm and Peat

At the heart of all thinking/creativity is the activity of making connections, of manipulating images—imagining. When I realize that, I can confidently say that *any behavior that discourages connecting will work against my growth and development.*

Guessing

Unless it is in a game, guessing is frowned upon as irresponsible.

Questions are thought to be an excellent strategy when we are uncertain and confused. In my study of invention groups, I found the opposite to be true. Guessing stimulated thinking and connecting, while questions brought the thinking down.

While there *are* situations when questioning *is* appropriate, in the vast majority of cases, questioning is an avoidance strategy or a power-over and control behavior. A more positive field generator and better connection-making practice is to guess and ask if I am close. A guess is trial connecting to form a tentative hypothesis.

Guessing behavior, while good for both relationship and connection-making proficiency, exposes me to anxiety. It *feels* like an unacceptable way of being. To name a few risks: being irrelevant and irresponsible, being mistaken and foolish, inviting rejection, and many other damaging implications of inferiority. I learn that when I am in a classroom or *any* competitive climate, questioning is the safer strategy.

> "[Inhibiting assumptions and beliefs] are a kind of pollution and we need to stop this pollution or introduce some factor that will clean it up."—Bohm and Peat

Yet, guessing—making speculative connections in a trial-and-error, trial-and-success procedure—exercises the thinking process I need to use to continually improve my skill at being a person.

As I get clear about the minute particulars of the thinking/creative process I become aware that the same cultural fields that inhibit guessing-to-make-meaning, also inhibit connecting to learn, and discourage remembering, imagining, feeling empathy, planning, critical thinking, and all the other thinking and feeling activities that by definition risk being mistaken.

There is a further destructiveness in actions that discourage connection-making. Because thinking/creativity is a fundamental activity of a human organism, when someone or something thwarts me (does things to discourage my connection-making) I experience it as *punishment*—a denial of my need to be autonomous, of my life force. It stirs in me powerful self-preservation impulses that are connected to my fight, freeze or flight instincts.

Field awareness can help me become clearly informed about my own thinking/creating behaviors—the thinking practices and policies I have invented for myself. Because I have done much of this inventing when young and inexperienced, my mental models are based on a much more limited "me". Mind-Free provides opportunities to see myself in action. It does this first by taking me through "Think Tanks"—a thinking/creative procedure designed to increase connection-making.

> "An example of this pollution is misinformation—creativity is necessary only in specialized situations and fields."—Bohm and Peat

Second, and perhaps more important, Mind-Free focuses my attention on concepts like Self-Punishment, Implication Thinking, Self-censoring, Discount/Revenge, Learning and Knowing. I learned in my study of creativity that early misconceptions often support beliefs, assumptions—behaviors—that work against connection-making. I explore them by examining experiences from my life that might illuminate these self-imposed restrictions.

(Note: The concepts in this book can be valuable to you if you are reading and thinking by yourself, but you will get the most out of this book if you read it with a partner or with two or three partners—a study group.)

A third way Mind-Free helps me become clear about my thinking practices is the attention I give to the transmissions between me and my world. *Every* situation in which I find myself brings into being a field. Whether I am confronting a flat tire or having a meeting with my boss, *the combination of my thoughts and feelings and the signals originating from the other party create a field that powerfully influences the outcome of the encounter.* Every such relationship in my life has the potential to be a positive or negative influence on my ability to connect. I need to become aware of my own behaviors when reacting to words, tones, and non-verbal actions and of my transmissions—their impact on the field. The purpose is to free myself from practices that hinder or prohibit connection-making so that I can become better and better at being all the person I have the potential to be.

Self-Discover or Lose Self

Being and feeling meaningful means that I am constantly engaged in making connections between my situation and my behavior aimed at accomplishing something, whether it is getting the cooperation of a colleague or inventing a way to get a job. I am most effective, when I understand the situation as it really is at that moment. This is possible only if I am open to all the information in the field, and often my own defensiveness works against this.

When alive and growing, I am in a continual state of change. My *knowing* gets out of date. Strategies that were appropriate for the "me" of last month are slightly obsolete for the current me who has been connecting and learning, awake and asleep, for over 700 hours (a standard college course is only 40 hours!), let alone the me of a year ago…or five years ago.

> "To pay serious attention to this need for sustained creativity is extremely relevant for bringing about a creative change in culture and in society."—Bohm and Peat

The reality is that if I am to be *current*—be all I can be—I need to have the courage and energy to continually recreate myself anew to be my most appropriate, up-to-date self to interact with the present situation. We think of this as just-in-time "me" or momentary me—me without rehearsal or ready-made response.

This is what <u>be</u>ing is about, yet my anxiety works against me. It seeks relief in defensiveness. It does not want openness to risky new connections with their mistakes. It wants the safe old prejudices. This is such an accustomed strategy I am not even aware of doing it. Much of my everyday behavior is of this defensive, closed-minded type.

To complicate matters, my old genetic instructions also urge me into a limbic-brained competition for the highest possible place in the pecking order. In order to get anywhere in that outmoded, pre-Neanderthal competition, I must maintain the appearance of superiority if possible. The maintenance of this demanding posture requires a considerable amount of energy and focused consciousness and this leaves very little of myself available to make connections for re-understanding or new understanding.

I call this posture self-sacrificing or self-hiding. I abandon my developing true (neo-cortex moderated) self and present a false front to stay in the competition. In a real sense, I self-destruct. This leads to diminished being and decreasing quality of life. I become more and more committed to developing relationships between my pseudo-self and the pseudo-self of others—pseudo-relationships. This is the path of entropy.

In the protected field of a Mind-Free exchange, I can risk disclosing "how it *really* is with me". The discipline of positive field requires that I do no discounting of others and so I must invent ways of disclosing that reveal my thoughts and feelings without blaming others.

Metaphorical (Wholehearted) Listening

Metaphorical listening focuses on implications rather than the literal. A speaker says, "I am a pro-life person and abortion is simply not permissible." If I am pro-choice and listening literally, I not only disagree, I react to this adversarial field we have created by summoning up angry and opposing feelings and arguments. If I am listening metaphorically, I perceive the speaker as enmeshed with an idea that has implications I can agree with: the great value

> We continually make decisions and do things that tend to impair as well as promote the functioning of others. All of us participate in groups that function in ways that make it more difficult for certain group members to function."—Kerr and Bowen, 1988

of life, and the tragedy of abortion as a solution. When I am able to listen in this way, there is the possibility that together we can work toward a way of thinking that we can both embrace. Even if he is unwilling to listen to *me* metaphorically, I can deal with him without cutting myself off from my resources with non-thinking prejudice.

This phenomenon occurs when I have developed an inner field of low defensiveness. I am able to give myself without reserve, to the activity of listening and making connections. The difference between this and ordinary good listening is in the objectives.

Ordinary listening, as suggested above, devotes energy to defense. I am alert for statements I disagree with so I can prepare my rebuttal. I spot any word or inference that discounts me, my beliefs, or that threatens my place in the pecking order. For example, if the speaker reveals that he has a Rolls Royce, I will need to search my possessions for status symbols and do my best to match him—and figure out a way to drag this in without being too obvious. I do not wish to *appear* threatened.

Connecting to discover something new

Archimedes needed to calculate the volume of the king's crown to determine how pure the gold was. It was too irregular to measure. As he lowered himself into his daily tub, the water overflowed. He connected "My body is an irregular shape, like the crown. As I lower it into the water, it displaces its own volume. I can measure the volume of the King's crown this way. EUREKA!"

Ordinary listening has complex assignments including constant evaluation of the statements and continuing judgment of the speaker as a person and his position in the pecking order. Even with friendly intentions, this is *competitive* listening. Few of us know any other kind.

Metaphorical listening has none of this defensive purpose. The speaker and I have arrived at the mutual acceptance of each other as real people, complete with weaknesses as well as strengths. We have no need to

"Learning is most effective when it is in the form of feedback from one's own activities."—Win Wenger

establish or defend our positions in the pecking order. That has been made irrelevant by our acceptance of each other as we *are*. Each of us has more in some areas and less in others. There is no need to conclude superiority or inferiority. My objective is to comprehend your reality—to connect with your meaning as completely as I can. I use it to know you more deeply and be rewarded by being in touch with your true self. I use it to experience empathy—feel, as best I can, what it is like being in your shoes. And I also use it to make connections with whatever of my experience I am able—to know myself more deeply.

What I find is that the first-person, undiluted impact of your experience, which I am not resisting (quite different from opinion, advice, or hearsay), often enables me to connect with long lost memories and repressed "secrets" that have significance and may be supporting limitations. I use your experiences to continue to "learn" myself.

Since I also grasp your *meaning* I am free to make new connections and build on the implications of the event you are revealing. We can, together, imagine and create new meanings altogether different from those we start with.

Through awareness of these interactions and the fields generated, I am able to identify the behaviors that tend to reduce my thinking/creative effectiveness. Once identified I am encouraged to invent ways to immunize myself to these toxic, anti-<u>be</u>ing influences.

"We reflect in order that we may get hold of the full and adequate significance of what happens. Nevertheless, *something* must be already understood, the mind must be in possession of some meaning that it has mastered, or else thinking is impossible."—John Dewey

Implication Thinking

A word is like a microchip. There is the word itself and the approximate dictionary meaning. I say approximate because when I look up a word I "know", I am usually surprised at some meanings of which I was unaware.

There is the word itself as a label on the microchip, and within the microchip there are the fifty or so connotations, implications, associations, and connections. This cloud of background "meanings" is unique to each of us. Yours will be different from mine, and in this variety and richness lies one of the strengths as well as one of the difficulties of a collaborating group.

The Johnson O'Connor Research Institute has discovered a positive correlation between vocabulary size and success. They say that a common denominator among the outstanding people in any field is the large vocabulary possessed by each person. I believe the way this works is: the more extensive my microchip for a word, the more I can connect with the world and what is in it, and the greater my chances of making connections to make meaning out of confusion. My effectiveness depends upon the comprehensiveness of my microchip, my willingness to use more than the literal, and how well my connection represents reality. When I am attempting to resolve an uncertainty, each of the implications, connotations, and associations I possess is like an antenna seeking a connection to help me make meaning out of the confusion.

The difference between a poor thinker and an outstanding thinker is the number of options each can create, and how well she sorts through them to select the one that makes the most sense. As a skillful meaning maker I am continually open for tests of my connections to reality.

> "The acquisition of ability to understand…is immensely furthered by language and by elaboration of a series of meanings."—John Dewey

Example:

GERM-1.) (a)a small mass of living substance capable of developing into an animal or plant or into an organ or part…(b)the embryo with scutellum of a cereal grain that is usually separated from the starchy endosperm during the milling 2.) something from which development takes place or that serves as an origin 3.) microorganism.—Webster.

My Microchip

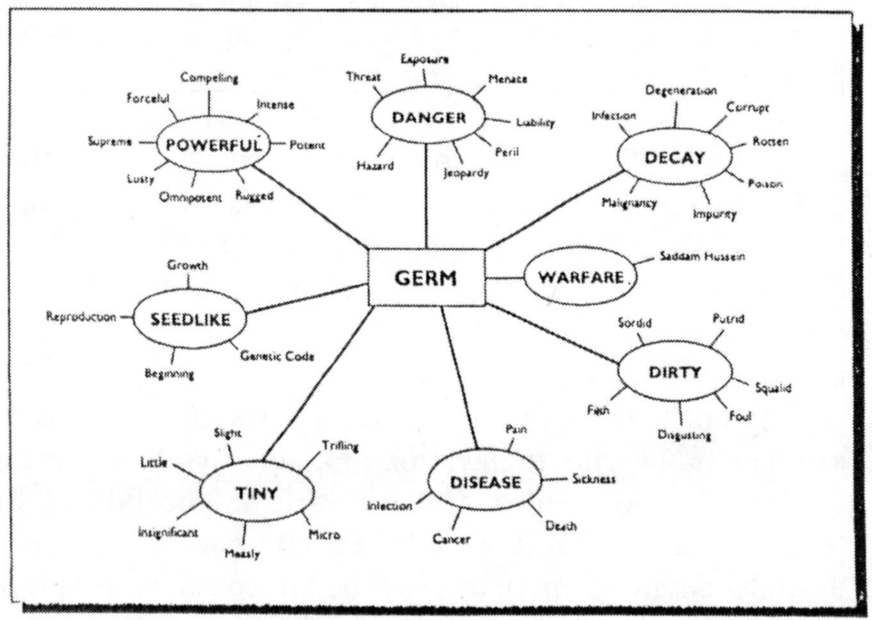

My interest in implication thinking is focused on two areas, both having to do with connecting. The first is learning (creating meaning or inventing). If I am to access my resources I need to be willing to *use* my microchips.

Let us revisit Sally and her problem of a place to study. In actuality, Sally was working with a group. Her group suggested a) the library, b) the park, and c) in a mushroom.

She instantly understood a and b, and had the strong impulse to reject c as irrelevant and *wrong*. But she was developing her skill in using her resources so she tolerated her anxiety about being mistaken and continued to think about mushroom. It represented the most promising path to newness.

> "…the moment a meaning is gained, it is a working tool of further apprehensions, an instrument of understanding other things."—John Dewey

The poor thinker gets this idea of taping her heartbeat and evaluates it on whatever merits she is *able* and *willing* to see: "I think that is an interesting idea" or "I think that is a poor idea" and makes an either or decision. This is a defensive and limiting behavior.

The outstanding thinker probably does the same instant evaluation but with no intention of a decision. She searches for further implications. One valuable implication of the heartbeat idea is that it opens an entirely new search area—a study environment that may be independent of place. Another interesting implication is that of countering one distraction with another that is less toxic. This is a field that keeps me open to learning and growth.

So the first area of interest is to learn to use the richness of my microchips to search out implications that help me think about my problem differently.

The second area of interest is connecting with other people. All relationships depend upon how well the people in them connect. The more extensive my microchip, the more possibilities for some overlap. Intimate relationships are maintained by each party being available for many implications and then exploring them for friendly connections rather than possibilities that arouse bad feelings. The choice is between interacting and reacting, between connecting and disconnecting.

If my associate says she has the germ of an idea and I possess only the bad implications of germ—sickness, danger, poison, infection, etc. my posture toward her idea is quite different from that I have if I hear implications for seed-like, powerful and compelling.

The difficulty with each of us having unique microchips is that the same word may have quite different connotations for each of us. Therefore, I may have trouble connecting with you. There is much opportunity for misunderstanding. Also, if my field is defensive, I stick with literal meanings, I may not connect at all. The answer is to develop a positive, supportive internal field that allows me to assume value and guess and test.

When I stick with my literal meaning of words, I am cutting myself off from many possibilities of connecting. The force in my field is mistake anxiety—I do not want to risk making a wrong connection and making a mistake or looking foolish. As I get older and more experienced, my field tends to become more defensive and I may get even more governed by mistake anxiety. The consequences are serious inhibitions: misplaced caution, premature rejection, resisted involvement, low level of learning (meaning

> "Interaction is a two-way exchange of energy, with an amplification of the energy of the two forces."—J. C. Pearce

making)…high second-hand connections, inadvertence, feelings of aloneness, and boredom.

At a social gathering, after a session to invent a new product, I overheard the conversation between two research directors from different companies. Joe, I will call one of them, said, "In developing new products we get our directions from the people in the field…"

Mike broke in, "That is bull—t. We originate new products in our lab and when they are ready, we bring the field people into the picture."

These two had disconnected, and staked out positions to defend. They were reacting rather than interacting. The chances of learning were not great.

Consider the possibility of learning and growing if Mike had been field aware, waited for Joe to complete his thought and then said "That is an interesting approach…mine is somewhat different, but what is your thinking?

Implication thinking is a way of interacting with and learning from the world and what is in it. It is a way of maintaining an inner field that fosters connection between human beings and ideas and creates connections and learning.

Wisdom Is Implication Thinking About Information

A third area of interest about implication thinking is its importance in the generation of wisdom. Wisdom is the judicious selection of a meaning or consequence from all the possible options. Implication thinking is the way I develop those options. When I think of wisdom this way, it clarifies the reason behind the saying that "a group is always wiser than any single individual."

> "As intelligent beings, we presume the existence of meaning, and its absence is an anomaly."—John Dewey

Connection-making

There is a path from ignorance and confusion to understanding and meaning. It begins with my initial perception and connection and *no matter how approximate* that connection, it is valid for me. The path is probably unique for each person because each of us has a unique accumulation of implications and other connection-making material.

Consider a sculptor. He/she often begins with something called an armature. It is a wire frame or core that has little or no resemblance to the final sculpture, but it is the frame on which the sculpture is built.

In thinking, that initial perception/connection is like an armature on which I can, if I am willing to be approximate, build the eventual precise meaning of the concept. As a skillful learner, I create an armature immediately. It is more efficient to build on or modify a concrete *something* than to hold back until I have a complete understanding and then accept it. The hold-back posture creates a field that is a far more serious handicap to me than it might seem. When that is my field, I delay accepting an observation until I can make sense of it. If I cannot make immediate connections, I move along my anxiety gradient toward increased discomfort. So I tend to stop the learning process. This seems paradoxical. How can I evaluate an observation without *making* an observation. Of course, I cannot. My well-developed foresight function allows me to make a lightening fast evaluation *out of my awareness.* When there is a high probability of not understanding, anxiety goes up, I stop trying to connect, and attend to my anxiety by changing it to impatience, boredom or even anger. I make no effort to perceive and guess a connection to form a beginning armature.

My defensive field is keeping me focused on safety rather than connecting and learning. This is anxiety-governed thinking and it tends to cut me off from my resources. I avoid thinking about difficult subjects. Prejudice is a mental model I often substitute.

I remember many times when a teacher or some other authority was explaining something and I became confused. My practice was to drop out, feel bored and focus on something else. I was obeying the directions from my anxiety gradient. This strategy to reduce anxiety is not uncommon and it is at the heart of a vicious cycle that makes for very poor thinking and learning.

> "All routine and all externally dictated activity fail to develop ability to understand…"
>
> —John Dewey

It suggests that remedial programs might do well to concentrate on creating internal fields that give the learner feelings of security.

Axi and the skateboards

Axi, who is 7, has been blind from birth. He and his Daddy, and I are walking down a hill. Three kids on skateboards come thundering by. Daddy says "Axi, those are skateboards."

Axi says, "Is that like a gun?" That was Axi's armature.

"Yes", says Daddy, "it makes a loud noise like a gun. When you feel a skateboard it feels like a board with wheels on it—it's about the size of a tennis racket. A kid stands on it."

Whenever Axi asks "Is it like______________?", Daddy *always* answers "Yes".

When I questioned this, Daddy explained, "It is a lot better for Axi to have a few temporary misconceptions than it is to have him lose his speculative confidence."

Speculative confidence

Is the willingness—the courage—to make and accept that initial connection between the new, not-yet-understood, and something known—perhaps quite approximate—a beginning, an armature. This is one form of jumping to conclusions and it is mistakenly frowned upon.

Early training, with the best intentions, can create an internal field that reduces speculative confidence to near zero. As a result, I am reluctant to risk that initial perception/connection (don't be wrong! Don't be approximate!) without guidance from a teacher or "one who knows". I lose faith in my own independent capacity to figure things out—to think things through. This is serious for it has a paradoxical consequence: a dependent revolt. I am dependent on others to help me make meaning, and I resent them for it and develop defensive reactive strategies to resist learning from them. This puts me in a double bind as a perceiver/connector.

When there is abuse or heavy punishment in the early years, the problem becomes more serious. Children tend to try to make sense of mistreatment as due to some shortcoming or mistake they have made. Initially they attempt to become perfect, without mistakes. As punishment persists, they numb out to defend themselves. It makes for a handicap in later learning and growth.

> "I believe that it is fairly safe to say that anybody and everybody devotes much of his lifetime, a great deal of his energy—talking loosely—and a good part of his effort in dealing with others, to avoiding more anxiety than he already has and, if possible, to getting rid of this anxiety."—Harry Stack Sullivan

My Sight Has More Courage

I am much more willing to jump to a trial conclusion about something confusing that I see. For example, see if you can find the Dalmatian in the illustration below.

"When we listen devoutly, the heart opens."—Jack Zimmerman and Virginia Coyle

I believe that my tolerance of the approximate in *seeing* is the primitive need to see danger very early. For early man, survival probably depended on quickly jumping to conclusions. While that has persisted in my visual practice, I have been trained out of my childhood willingness to jump to a conclusion and form an armature to begin understanding.

Jokes can teach us

Play changes my field. Risky connecting is approved. The connection-making to enjoy a joke is a demonstration. Here are some jokes that work because of an initial connection being modified by a new connection that surprises:

The Arkansas Medical Dictionary

Artery..the study of paintings
Barium ....what doctors do when patients die
Bowel..a letter like a,e,i,o, or u
Dilate ....to live a long time
Impotent.....................................distinguished, well known
Seizure ....Roman Emperor

> "For the things we have to learn before we can do them, we learn by doing them."
>
> —Aristotle

Guessing as a Trial Connection

Axi made a guess about skateboards by connecting the loud noise with another loud noise he knew about: a gunshot. John Dewey says, "Logical ideas are like keys that are shaped with reference to opening a lock." (1933, Pg.134) I believe the word 'guess' better captures the tentative spirit of this action. My guess is a beginning idea with a special purpose: to make a connection I can test and modify to reach understanding. That uncertain and anxiety-inducing step is the essential beginning of Perceiving/connecting to make meaning.

Questions Are a Poor Substitute for Guessing

Each of us is born a naturally gifted perceiver and connection-maker. As we experience disapproval for making approximate connections, we learn to avoid the anxiety of disapproval by asking questions. This is a giant step backward in developing my thinking ability. Speculative thinking, hypothesis formation, autonomy and differentiation, and much of the pleasure I get from exercising my competence are all diminished by a field that punishes guess-and-test whenever I encounter the unknown.

> "Active, persistent, and careful consideration of any belief or supposed form of knowledge in the light of the grounds that support it and the further conclusions to which it tends constitutes reflective thought."—John Dewey

Reflective Thinking

Reflective thinking is the essential thinking process needed to make meaning out of the confusions of "unorganized" information.

A great capacity for this kind of thinking is present in the infant and child as he or she makes sense of walking, talking, and the world around him. In physical actions the consequences are clear and connections can be made without a lot of outside help, other than support. The development of thinking skills requires much more deliberate cultivation and few of us parents realize it. We are lulled by our observations of the remarkable progress of our child.

As a result, most children learn thinking in a field that is so goal and "right answer" oriented, where mistakes and approximations are punished, that the *connecting process* is discouraged. Unless the child is fortunate enough to have a supportive field, some of the essential connection-making skills for outstanding thinking are effectively blocked. The person may be so well defended against the risks of learning that she is only partially available.

An ideal developmental program

The absolute necessity is a field of mutual appreciation.

The field of the womb might be thought of as perfect for mutual responding. The fetus makes demands, and the demands are met. There is complete safety-unless the mother imperils the fetus with toxic substances.

At birth the situation becomes more complicated and dangerous, but if the bonding process continues there are a great many exchanges of mutual pleasure and appreciation. It is called mirroring and is an almost miraculous positive field generator in the infant.

"In order for full thinking development to occur, the non-verbal physical and the oral forms of communication must pass back and forth between the infant/child/youth and other persons with each party speaking and listening—sharing, expanding, and reflecting on each others' experiences."(Belenky et al 1986, Pg. 26)

> "New thoughts generally arise with a play of the mind, and failure to appreciate this is actually one of the major blocks to creativity"—Bohm and Peat

These interactions are experiments—a continuing series of trial and error/trial and success learning experiences, that test ways of operating that will win approval for the child. *The critical focus needs to be on process, not correctness.* Thus, when my child identifies a horse as a big cat, I need to appreciate the *connecting*. That is the important thinking operation, not being instantly correct. Repeated disapproval of mistaken connections can permanently change the internal field of the child and cause him to abandon the trial and error way of learning. He relies, for safety, on authority. He becomes unwilling to risk mistaken connections and becomes uncertain at being a person who can construct meaning for himself.

Equally important, through being in a loving, attentive field, the individual develops an internal field and field generating skills to enable her and him to recruit friends and lovers—to be welcome in the social and intellectual life of her community. The complex ability to generate positive fields needs to be nurtured by example throughout infancy and childhood. Recent brain research has shown us that infants and children are far more sensitive to disrespect and inattention than we realized.

Without field awareness and the interaction skills of Emotional Intelligence, individuals are isolated. Without tools for representing his experiences, a person is also isolated from self. Internal storytelling is the way one makes sense of the events in life. One of the keys to successful dialogue is finding the courage to self-disclose so that one's true self can be made visible not only to others, but to one's self.

Another essential ingredient in developing skill in reflective thinking and learning is play. Play is an intellectual, emotional, and physical interaction with an imagined reality. It is an efficient way to experiment with a repertoire of ways of behaving. It involves the kind of inventing and testing that are needed throughout life to cope with uncertainty and the unexpected—to contend with the feelings of helplessness that can poison a learning opportunity.

Some destructive field generators

Dr. Thomas Gordon in *Parent Effectiveness Training* (1970) identifies the twelve typical responses he has observed in parents he has worked with. These establish the field that evokes the child's response and teach him how to behave with others (and self). It seems clear that we need better early relationships to infuse our lives with what

> "Parental civility, then, provides the springboard from which children can leap into a separate, independent adulthood."—M.Scott Peck

Joseph Campbell calls "the rapture of being". So the problem becomes: how can I remodel my field so that I automatically live *without* transmissions that are disrespectful and discounting, competitive, contentious, aggressive, or dominating—without any behavior that devalidates and leads to reactivity?

On page 108 are Dr. Gordon's "Terrible twelve" destructive ways of dealing with children. My own feeling when studying this list was "I have to invent a whole new way of communicating!"

As I buckled down to the task of understanding I realized that the quality all these typical twelve have in common is that they put the listener in a one-down position. Each creates a power-over field and I know it will be experienced as demeaning and will trigger fight, freeze or flight defensiveness.

> "In the creative orientation the most powerful question you can ask yourself is "What do I want?" "What result do I want to create?"—Robert Fritz

ORDERING, DIRECTING, COMMANDING

Telling the child to do something, giving him an order or a mmand:

"I don't care what other parents do, you have to do the yard work!"
"Don't talk to your mother like that!"
"Now you go back up there and play with Ginny and Joyce!"
"Stop complaining!"

2. WARNING, ADMONISHING, THREATENING

Telling the child what consequences will occur if he does something:

"If you do that, you'll be sorry!"
"One more statement like that and you'll leave the room!"
"You'd better not do that if you know what's good for you!"

3. EXHORTING, MORALIZING, PREACHING

Telling the child what he *should* or *ought* to do:

"You shouldn't act like that."
"You ought to do this. . . ."
"You must always respect your elders."

4. ADVISING, GIVING SOLUTIONS OR SUGGESTIONS

Telling the child how to solve a problem, giving him advice or suggestions; providing answers or solutions for him:

"Why don't you ask both Ginny and Joyce to play down here?"
"Just wait a couple of years before deciding on college."
"I suggest you talk to your teachers about that."
"Go make friends with some other girls."

5. LECTURING, TEACHING, GIVING LOGICAL ARGUMENTS

Trying to influence the child with facts, counterarguments, logic, information, or your own opinions:

"College can be the most wonderful experience you'll ever have."
"Children must learn how to get along with each other."
"Let's look at the facts about college graduates."
"If kids learn to take responsibility around the house, they'll grow up to be responsible adults."
"Look at it this way—your mother needs help around the house."
"When I was your age, I had twice as much to do as you."

6. JUDGING, CRITICIZING, DISAGREEING, BLAMING

Making a negative judgment or evaluation of the child:

"You're not thinking clearly."
"That's an immature point of view."
"You're very wrong about that."
"I couldn't disagree with you more."

7. PRAISING, AGREEING

Offering a positive evaluation or judgment, agreeing:

"Well, I think you're pretty."
"You have the ability to do well."
"I think you're right."
"I agree with you."

8. NAME-CALLING, RIDICULING, SHAMING

Making the child feel foolish, putting the child into a gory, shaming him:

"You're a spoiled brat."
"Look here, Mr. Smarty."
"You're acting like a wild animal."
"Okay, little baby."

9. INTERPRETING, ANALYZING, DIAGNOSING

Telling the child what his motives are or analyzing w. is doing or saying something; communicating that you him figured out or have him diagnosed:

"You're just jealous of Ginny."
"You're saying that to bug me."
"You really don't believe that at all."
"You feel that way because you're not doing well in schc

10. REASSURING, SYMPATHIZING, CONSOLING, SUPPORTING

Trying to make the child feel better, talking him out feelings, trying to make his feelings go away, denyin strength of his feelings:

"You'll feel different tomorrow."
"All kids go through this sometime."
Don't worry, things'll work out."
"You could be an excellent student, with your potential
"I used to think that too."

"I know, school can be pretty boring sometimes."
"You usually get along with other kids very well."

11. PROBING, QUESTIONING, INTERROGATING

Trying to find reasons, motives, causes; searching fo information to help you solve the problem:

"When did you start feeling this way?"
"Why do you suppose you hate school?"
"Do the kids ever tell you why they don't want to pla you?"
"How many other kids have you talked to about the wo have to do?"
"Who put that idea into your head?"
"What will you do if you don't go to college?"

12. WITHDRAWING, DISTRACTING, HUMORING, DIVERTING

Trying to get the child away from the problem; with ing from the problem yourself; distracting the child, ki him out of it, pushing the problem aside:

"Just forget about it."
"Let's not talk about it at the table."
"Come on—let's talk about something more pleasant."
"How's it going with your basketball?"
"Why don't you try burning the school building down?"
"We've been through all this before."

- GORDON, THOMAS; PARENT EFFECTIVEN TRAINING, PETER H. WYDEN, NEW Y 1970

"...fields—invisible forces that structure space or behavior."—Margaret Wheatley

Thinking Tools

When I am at my creative best, I use a number of thinking tools that help me perceive and make connections to get new ideas. As my old partner, Bill Gordon (1960), says, I use them to "make the familiar strange". This is not always easy. For example, in the Dalmatian puzzle, once I have seen the Dalmatian, it is difficult to look at the earlier picture and *not* see it.

Here are some thinking tools that multiply the number of options for perceiving and connecting to see things differently. All of these procedures are aimed at changing my internal field to make it more open to my almost limitless imagination.

Wishing

My everyday thinking is packed with perceiving and connection-making as I make sense of the thousands of symbols and signals in my field—such subtle signs as the noises my partner makes as she gets out of bed can tell me what mood she is in. And as I drive to work there are all the moves of other drivers to interpret.

When I am faced with a problem or a decision, I tend to search my connection-making material for items that worked before. In the interest of efficiency, I censor any connections that seem irrelevant. When I need *new* connections to solve the problem in a different way, my censor has trouble loosening the specifications and admitting the unexpected. As soon as I label my search "wishing", my field changes and my censor relaxes. Anxiety is diminished. Wishes can't get me into trouble so there is no need to be strict with them.

Learning to wish without restraint takes practice. I have spent too many years believing it is childish and useless to wish for things I cannot have. As I relearn wishing I discover that it is a marvelous way to get in touch with many facets of myself that are usually barred from my consciousness by my careful and practical censor.

> "Panic of error is the death of progress."—Alfred North Whitehead

> "…the relaxation of the tension of anxiety…is the experience, not of satisfaction, but of interpersonal *security*"—Harry Stack Sullivan

What Wishing Can Do for Me

1. I remove the restrictions of reality.
2. I give my imagination free rein.
3. I can entertain mutually exclusive impulses without logical censorship and thus learn the wants and needs of my whole self—not just my civilized, impression management self.
4. I can ignore tradition, common sense, and convention to consider only what I *want.*

5. I can imagine an impossible outcome being successful and think backward toward reality, spotting the obstacles and wishing them away.
6. I can explore dream solutions and, as Carl Sandburg wrote, "Nothing unless first a dream."
7. Giving myself permission to wish puts to sleep my anxiety, judgment and negative caution and activates my courage to dare.
8. I remove any need to defend or justify.
9. I get in touch with facets of myself that I ordinarily repress.
10. I become progressively more daring and unlimited in dreaming for myself and others.
11. I experience the exhilaration of thinking without the constant restrictions, repression's, strictures, reservations, strings and confinements I impose on myself in the name of reality and practicality.
12. As I repeatedly experience this exhilaration without being arrested or ostracized, I become aware that it is liberating the best in me to *think anything* as long as I evaluate before *acting*.
13. It puts me in touch with resources for connecting that I usually repress.

Imaging

Imaging is seeing with my mind's eye. It is my display system—a way to keep track of my thoughts. When you tell me something, I image it to better understand it. It is a very efficient process. I can make changes instantly, look at things from different angles, enlarge or shrink the image, and in general get a better understanding.

> "...understanding...must always be through acts of experiencing directly or in imagination..."—John Dewey

As a child I was an automatic and skillful image maker. I could take a block and turn it into a truck or a fort. As I got older and imaged as a person told me something, I found that my instant images were often wrong—never mind that I modified them as data came in. Being wrong made for increased anxiety so I began to repress images until I had enough data to know I would not be wrong. Eventually I stopped being aware of imaging most of the time.

As I relearned the value of imaging, I reinstated it as a thinking tool. Imaging is a great aid to my imagination. That may seem a truism, and what I mean is that when I want to imagine, if I create a concrete image as a starting point it makes it easier to make things happen. My imaging is not as clear as it was when I was young. Often I do not see a picture. When that happens, I fake it. I pretend I have an image and use the pretend image as though it were the real thing, and this works perfectly well.

Approximate thinking

Precise or apposite thinking is an essential skill and when I am doing it I am eliminating possible alternative connections. The extreme opposite of precise, apposite thought is irrelevant thought. In between these two types of thinking is a vast territory I call approximate.

When I am considering a problem or decision, my field pressures me to consider a thought irrelevant if it does not precisely fit. This eliminates a great many possible connections. When I want new connections, to form into new ideas, I deliberately relax my field's insistence on precision and welcome *any* thought into my consciousness. I probe its implications to see if I can forge a connection and make a new idea.

> "To some physicists chaos is a science of process rather than state, of becoming rather than being."—James Gleick

Excursion Thinking (Safe Chaos)—Analogy, Metaphor, and Irrelevance

This is a thinking strategy to break mindsets and invite new kinds of connecting. Say I am dealing with a communication problem in a company. If I use an analogy, for example, communication is like blood circulating in the body, it helps me see the problem in a different way and making those connections may lead me to a new idea.

> "These are new principles that highlight the dynamics between chaos and creativity, between disruptions and growth."—Margaret Wheatley

In Think Tank there is an Excursion—a deliberate generation of analogy and metaphor and seeming irrelevance—to give me more connection-making material.

What Excursion Thinking Can Do for Me

In general, it transforms my internal field from defensive and exclusionary to accepting and inclusionary.

1. It changes the rules about what is relevant and increases my tolerance for out-of-the-ordinary thinking.
2. It makes approximate thinking acceptable and transforms billions of pieces of information formerly labeled irrelevant into "possibly useful".
3. It makes me comfortable with "silly" connections and thus opens me to many more possibilities.
4. It helps me not insist that a speaker be precise and accurate. I am more able to entertain proposals that have obvious (to me) flaws.
5. It gives me practice in stretching the limits of my ability to free-associate.
6. It exercises and strengthens my capacity for making unlikely connections.
7. It alters my internal field toward relaxed tolerance of the thinking of others..
8. It enlarges my appreciation of my own *limitless* storehouse of images.
9. It shifts my listening mode from competitive, spot-a-flaw, to "get the point" listening, as in listening to a joke.
10. It puts me in touch with my remarkable capacity to imagine.

"...thought confers upon physical events and objects a very different status and value from those which they possess to a being who does not reflect."—John Dewey

11. As I make repeated connections I am bombarded by endorphins and in addition to feelings of aliveness, I am alerted and available to make further connections and create new understandings.
12. It builds respect for my own resources and my ability to call on them.
13. It gives me practice in "chaining", that is, moving freely from one image to another without hampering myself by insisting on logical connections.
14. It gives me opportunities to experience and take pleasure in my miraculous thinking *agility.*
15. It hones my flexibility.
16. It breaks my mind-sets.

[There is] "no limit to the continual growth of meaning in human life."—John Dewey

Distinguishing Between Thinking and Acting

Perceiving the danger in a line of thought is important to survival. It is intended to protect me from doing something that might threaten my well-being or that of my friends. When I was a child I did not distinguish well between thinking and acting. I acted on impulse and this often got me into trouble. I identified impulse and the action as the same and I learned to censor the impulse as though it *was* the action. As my censor became more skillful, it would often stop a risky impulse or line of thought even before it became fully conscious. While this tended to take care of my anxiety gradient and keep me comfortable, it made speculative thinking difficult. I was treating thoughts as though they *were* actions. Trial and error thinking becomes very anxiety-filled when every error is punishable as an action.

As an adult I am able to use mature judgment to decide whether or not to move from thought or impulse to action. It is important in making my resources available, to encourage myself to think *anything,* confident that I will not take reckless action. By not censoring *any* thinking I open myself to all imaginable connection-making material in my storehouse.

Open-Minded Evaluation—The Itemized Response

This is a thinking procedure to manage my powerful (and healthy) impulse to spot flaws in any new idea. As noted above, perceiving danger or shortcomings in a developing idea is important in advancing it to practicality. However, unless handled with care, a negative reaction can toxify the field and interrupt learning all the implications of a beginning idea. It can also stop adventurous building.

> In the early sixties I identified a way of dealing with ideas that was helpful
> "We act, or fail to act, not because of "will" as is so commonly believed, but because of imagination."—Maxwell Maltz

I called this process The Spectrum Policy and it asked that I treat every idea as a point on the spectrum from totally acceptable to totally unacceptable (1970, Pg. 38). Over time the name changed to Itemized Response to emphasize the need for concreteness. Peter Elbow enriched the thinking behind Itemized Response with his concept of Methodological Belief and Methodological Doubt. He says, "...we can improve our understanding of [an idea or] careful thinking or reasoned inquiry...if we see it as involving two central ingredients: what I am calling methodological doubt and methodological belief. The fact that good thinking involves two mental processes that conflict with each other helps explain why the activity is complex and rare." (1986, Pg. 255)

He goes on to say, "...thinking is not trustworthy unless it also includes methodological belief. ***Believe*** **everything to find virtues or strengths we might otherwise miss."** (Ibid., Pg. 256)

"By methodological belief, then, I mean the disciplined procedures of not just listening but actually trying to believe any view or hypothesis that a participant seriously want to advance."

"...we must not ask, "What are your arguments for such a silly view as that?" but rather, "What do you see when you see [it] that way? Give me the vision in your head. You are having an experience I don't have: help me have it." (Ibid., Pg. 261)

"Methodological doubt represents the human struggle to free ourselves from parochial closed-mindedness, but it doesn't go far enough. Methodological belief comes to the rescue at this point by forcing us genuinely to enter into unfamiliar or threatening ideas instead of just arguing against them without experiencing them or feeling their force. It thus carries us *further* in our developmental journey away from mere credulity." (Ibid., Pg.267)

Ideally, when I spot a flaw in an emerging idea, I will attempt to invent a way to cure the flaw and offer it as a 'build'. If I can think of no way to overcome the flaw, I will make a note of it and offer it as a "How can we…" when the mature idea is evaluated later. If I see the flaw is fatal unless overcome, I follow a careful procedure: I imagine the proposed idea implemented, and it works. I think of a benefit it would provide, and talk about that. Only when I

> "A root feature of dialogue is that one must be ready to acknowledge any fact and any point of view as it actually is, whether one likes it or not."—Bohm and Peat

have demonstrated that my heart is on the side of making the idea work do I voice my concern as a wish or a "How to".

An example of Itemized Response in action: a member of a group working on credit card fraud says, "Let's use finger prints. Have the person validate his or her purchase with a finger print."

Member #2 knows that reading finger prints requires expertise and unless this is dealt with the idea will fail. “I like the certainty of a finger print. It would make fraud much more difficult. How can we make comparing finger prints easy for the check-out person?”

Compare the impact on the field vs. “Come on! Every check-out person would have to have a billion fingerprints on file and be a finger print expert.”

Open-minded evaluation or Itemized Response or Methodological Belief create a valuable mind-set not only to keep the field positive, but to make me more available.

Differentiating an Idea from a Direction

In our invention sessions we use the concept of idea in a special way. Idea denotes a new connection that forms a suggestion which is concrete enough so that the Client could, if he or she chose, run an experiment to test it. We differentiate *idea* from a *direction*—a new connection that forms a suggestion that indicates a line of thinking and is not yet concrete enough for an experiment.

For example, suppose we are working on the problem “How to reduce accidents caused by drinking and driving.” I make a new connection (for me) between an accident and the guilt that the drunk perpetrator must later feel. I say, “Lay a guilt trip on everyone who is thinking of drinking and driving.”

This may be a useful line of thought, and it is, in our terms, a direction, not an idea. The way to know the difference is to ask: "Can I test this suggestion?" And in this case we would not have anything concrete to test. A direction can be very useful in leading to more concrete ideas.

To convert this direction into an idea I push myself to think of a way of building testability into it. For example, "Have an 'exit booth' in every bar. Everyone must go through the booth and be exposed to several accident scenes. At the end ask "are you sober enough to drive safely?"

> "As one ages…the importance of the quality of daily human interaction becomes clear."—David Schnarch

The Client could, if she chose, actually test this suggestion so it qualifies as an idea. Direction thinking is extremely important since new directions lead to original lines of thought.

Paths to Effectiveness

In every beginning there is a field of energy that determines what will emerge. This field is a sum of all the influences present—the words, vocals and non-verbals, the background experiences of the players, the surroundings and anything else that is perceived. The field in a court of law elicits very different ways of relating than a playground.

Only when we understand fields and relationships will we be able to manage our lives to bring out the *most* effectiveness in ourselves and others. The difference between the behaviors of effective person and a ne'r do well, is knowledge and practice of *field management*. Often this knowledge is not consciously acquired but is arrived at implicitly, through trial and error and experience with parents and others who are loving or not.

When we compare a manager who is getting outstanding results with one who is getting mediocre results, there may be many different styles, yet the outstanding results will be coming from the manager who is skillful in helping his staff be and feel meaningful.

How does the effective person manage fields?

1. S/he helps people learn to protect themselves and each other from demeaning/dominating actions which trigger defensiveness and reduce availability.

- By being able to discriminate between actions that demean and those that support and nurture
- By learning and practicing "emotionally intelligent" communication
- By learning impulse control
- By understanding the anatomy of relationship
- By making interpersonal security a requirement

2. By systematically helping them improve their processes for making connections and making meaning.
    - By modifying their criteria for connectedness
    - By understanding the function of confusion and mistakes
    - By increasing perception and exposure to connection making material
    - By making play a practice

Emotionally intelligent communication

Emotional intelligence is the capacity to be aware of fields and respond to them to invite cooperation and friendliness—to bring about synergy. It requires us to manage our impulses and anxieties to avoid destructive or defensive actions. Emotional intelligence is the ability to manage our transmissions without demeaning or diminishing the other while maintaining our integrity. Emotional intelligence is knowing how to create relationship fields that advance interpersonal security, reduce defensive perversity and invite collaboration and synergy. In addition it is knowing how to handle destructive inputs.

"We are learning that sharing one's authentic experiencing with another person has important effects on both the discloser and the listener."—Sidney Jourard

Dialogue

One of our goals in the Mind-Free process is to develop skill in creating a field that enhances my interactions with others. If I can manage such a field, my dialogues with others will encourage collaboration in whatever task we are considering.

The correct definition of dialogue is taken from the Greek roots of the word: logos=word or meaning of the word; dia=through, not two. So dialogue is a stream of meaning flowing between us, out of which will emerge some new understanding. It is more about a way of listening than a way of talking.

Dialogue vs. Discussion

Discussion has a connotation of analysis where people present different points of view. Since the usual field in our culture tends to be competitive and adversarial, discussion often sets up win/lose positions where I am focused on maintaining my feelings of meaningfulness or status, and my associate is focused on maintaining *his/her* feelings of meaningfulness or status. In discussion, my focus is on me and my position, whatever that turns out to be. My associate's posture tends to be the same.

If I defend my opinions, I can't listen to really grasp your meaning. It will be a struggle of opinions and this is what usually happens—the one who is strongest or cleverest appears to win and it may not be right. This is a handicap when people work together because we all have different opinions, assumptions, and self-interests.

> "Opinions are the stakes one places on winning discussions."—T. K. Gilliam

Assumptions and Opinions

Assumptions and opinions are like computer programs in my mind. They take over against the best of intentions and keep me prisoner. I will attempt to keep myself out of this prison by disciplining myself to practice no persuasion and no defense.

I will feel free to present my assumptions and opinions in a special Mind-Free way: first an experience and then, if I wish, my conclusions. I will not attempt to champion my opinions. I will repress the urge to bring you to my way of thinking. This will permit me to share meaning with you. When I am freed of the need to espouse an opinion or resist that of another, the language and thought can become entirely collective. When I think with you in a coherent way it has tremendous power because I add rather than resist: I make connections with what you say and build on it rather than protect myself against it.

Relating at a Tacit Level

If I am thinking *with* you, not only at the level we recognize, but at the ***tacit*** level, and if I *comprehend you listening to me to grasp my meaning,* it has a powerful impact on the field between us. It transforms my relationship with you from self-protective to mutual. This makes a profound difference in the way I think and speak. I am free to become exploratory…open to wonder, along with you, about the implications of my meaning. Since my field conveys respect for you, you have no need to defend or attack. Our field nourishes cooperation and that can multiply our effectiveness.

I can learn a new way of being with myself and others. Stephen B. Levine(1991, pg. 263) in speaking of the impact of intimacy says "On the way to the solace of being understood, and on the way to the pleasure and privilege of hearing another person's inner self, powerful emotions can be generated in the listener(s) and the speaker." "…there is a feeling of attachment, a loss of the usual social indifference, a vision of the person as special. As a result of this conversation and, particularly if similar conversations occur…*the emotional power of these changes [in the way we experience ourselves and each other] can be enormous."* (Italics ours)

Tacit means unspoken and more…I know that meaning is conveyed by the field (words, tonals, and non-verbal gestures and expressions, mood, etc.). What I may not fully appreciate is that my meaning and yours are given an added dimension because of this tacit field between us that cannot be described. It is like the knowledge of how to ride a bike. A large part of the field between me and my bike is not describable.

Much knowledge and many meanings are basically tacit and what I can say explicitly is only a small part of it.

> "If genuine dialogue is to arise, everyone who takes part in it must…be willing to say what is really on his or her mind about the subject of the conversation…no one can know in advance what it is that he has to say."—Buber

To get the powerful leverage of really thinking together, I need to be in touch with you on a tacit level. If I can be with you at that level, I may be able to break out of my usual defense-oriented relationship and create new ways of using *your* thinking to learn more about myself.

New Levels of Self-Learning

My core self really wants to join and be appreciated (validation and connection). When I am able to get in touch with another's unspoken, tacit field, I get confident that there is no intention to discount me. I am free to trust myself and a different level of relating becomes available to me: I can listen to you with a feeling of safety that allows me to open myself to connections that are otherwise too frightening. I can go to new levels of self-learning.

> "We love those who can lead us to a place we will never reach without them."—Norman Mailer

However, if I am not able to suspend my defensiveness—if I am compelled by my internal field to take up my reaction strategies; I will remain out of touch with others as well as my own tacit self.

The Destructiveness of Defense

In 'normal' encounters I am using my defensive strategies—many of them designed long ago and now out of conscious awareness—my mix of strategies is *incoherent.* Anyone dealing with me has her own set of strategies that complicate our field. There are lots of minute reactions—acts against—that toxify the field and block a truly mutual exchange.

If I could magically know all your meanings and assumptions and you could know mine and we could appreciate them without reacting or acting against, then, my underlying, childlike, tacit self can get to a *coherent* understanding of you and can create my half of a relationship of mutuality and empowerment, and it would invite you to create your half.

Whenever I accomplish coherence with myself and another, I have a chance to reconsider my incoherent strategies and modify them to be more congruent with my needs for validation and connection—for meaningfulness. Ideally, I will use this new coherence to manage all my fields…beginning with my relationship with myself.

The Power of Coherence

In relating, I have to go through a period of 'not getting anywhere', of exploring your assumptions and disclosing mine. If I do this in the spirit of dialogue—that is, I do my best to understand your meaning and my own, and repress the urge to freeze a conclusion or judgment—I will be launched toward a coherent, mutual experience of fellowship.

When I am part of a field of this quality—where none of us needs to dedicate a quantum of energy to defense, the whole of my energy is available to propel me to a new level of coherence to say nothing of the bliss attendant to making new connections of this importance.

Changes can take place. I can invent new, more satisfying strategies and make meaning from a new perspective.

> "Each [person's] experience is a possible way for the world to be…if I can act and experience in some way, so can you. If you can, so can I."—Sidney Jourard

To be coherent with several people gives me a glimpse of salvation—deliverance from the condition of spiritual isolation and estrangement, to a reconciled relationship with my fellow men and women…deliverance from the world of defensive strategies into a world of openness and learning.

As I become more and more coherent, my tacit persona is allowed out for me to experience. I can feel and interact with you without my defensive assumptions and opinion armor. Through repeated experiences I learn to trust myself as I become more and more my real self out in the open.

As I practice this demanding (and rewarding) quality of be-ing I become more and more sensitive to meaning. I realize that it is not static. It is continually evolving and I will miss it if I waste myself on defending my assumptions and opinions.

The Catalyst of Equality

A necessary condition is equality. There is no place for hierarchy and authority which imply power-over or dominance, for they surely kill the possibility of letting down defenses and becoming intimate.

When I am dedicated to defending my opinions I am not serious about becoming all I can be. Or if I am avoiding something unpleasant in myself I am not serious. Society teaches us to be not serious, to espouse and defend trivial, prejudiced opinions the implications of which are self-defeating and perhaps fatal.

Love will go away if I cannot share meaning at a tacit level.

Ultimately love is everything."—M. Scott Peck

Reminder

In the moments before *any* meeting I need to remind myself that I intend to create a field that telegraphs my intention to respect and listen.

Much of the above comes from *David Bohm on Dialogue,* from the transcription of a meeting that took place Monday, November 6, 1989, in Ojai, California. David Bohm Seminars, P.O. Box 1452, Ojai, CA 93023

> "Changing *how* you talk is more effective than *what* you talk about."—Miller, Wakman, et al

Eye-Witness vs. Hearsay ("I" Statements)

In the days when horses were the equivalent of today's cars, horse trading was a male obsession. An owner would describe his horse in glowing terms and might shave a few years from the horse's age. The canny trader would look in the horse's mouth. The condition of the teeth told the truth about the horse's age. "I got it from the horse's mouth" came to be a phrase meaning 'this is the truth,'.

There is a special field about a first person report that invites me to *interact* with the information. I am in touch with the person who was there—the expert on that experience. It is immediate and real. When the person tells it like it was for him or her—using "I" statements—it is not a distant scene that is being interpreted for me. I am sharing the experience and interpreting it for myself. As I listen, the channels are clear for me to empathize…to experience with her the realness, to connect and make meaning for myself out of someone else's struggle

There is a quality of ownership in that kind f exchange. It says "This is *my* experience and it seems *to me* to be relevant to the issue we are exploring. It may or may not seem relevant to you." It creates a field of *respect* for my autonomy.

I, as listener, am completely free to engage or to remain aloof. I need not muster any defensiveness. I can trial connect—try it on for size—and see if your experience adds up to something meaningful for me or make no use of it.

This freedom provides me with the opportunity to learn in the way I like best: making what connections I want at my own speed. As a result, 'I' statements have a special attractiveness and power.

In contrast, when a person describes an experience by hearsay, or declaring, when referring to his own experience, "You had to be careful…" I listen twice removed. It is a report from someone who has distanced himself from the event, and perhaps, like me, was not there.

Part 3—The Self

..."Resolve to be thyself: and know that he who finds himself, loses his misery."—Matthew Arnold

The Self
Kathleen Logan-Prince

When I was thirteen, I became interested in boys. I was not dating yet, but was anticipating and fantasizing what it might be like. In my images, I did not know what to do, or how to carry on a conversation. On one occasion I asked my mother for help. She thought for a moment, then said, "When you're with a boy get him to talk about himself and you'll be fine. If he likes baseball, talk about that. Find out what he's interested in and talk about it, but the important thing is—*be yourself.*"

Her tone was reassuring, but as I walked away, I was gripped by a troubling question: "who *is* myself?" It seemed strange that I did not know. A little earlier, when I was ten, I knew just who I was and who I would be when I grew up. I was a good Catholic girl in a nice family with a brother and sister and a best friend. I liked school and did well. I was going to be a ballerina, a wife, and a mother in that order. Now, at thirteen, my world seemed to be so much more complex and I was confused and anxious as well as excited about what was to come.

My mother, like many parents, sent me mixed messages. She exhorted me to be authentic and true to myself and at the same time, encouraged me to develop certain traits, qualities, and behaviors that would help me live up to the expectations of others. Of course, learning what others want and expect from us is an important part of becoming a civilized human being. There is not a "true self" that unfolds in a vacuum, free from the influence of family and culture. But for me, building myself had special obstacles imposed by my mother's promotion of self-sacrifice and service as feminine virtues, and anything suggesting selfishness as clearly undesirable.

Concepts of the self have fascinated us for centuries and many thinkers from all walks of life have helped illuminate its meaning. Freud suggests that I am not necessarily one self; on the contrary, in developing my defenses against the slings and arrows I form many selves. This is not the pathology of multiple personality, it is the normal formation of defensive strategies to protect myself. The technical terms for some of these defenses are: repression, rationalization, regression, projection, and denial. For example, since I was angry and fearful of my father when he was drinking, I still tend to feel annoyed and anxious in the presence of a man who is drinking too much and am inclined to treat him rudely. Even if he is totally different

> "Some persons are likable in spite of their unswerving integrity."—Don Marquis

from Father, he elicits some of those old feelings that I experienced when I was thirteen.

The integration of my many selves into a coherent person who is able to cope realistically with the tasks of my life is a continuing series of challenges. How effectively I deal with each one determines what sort of a person I am making of myself. I find it more accurate to think of *making* myself rather than *finding* myself, and it is my lifelong assignment with continuing opportunities for trial and error/trial and success. Virtually everything that happens to me gives me a chance to move closer to being an increasingly developed self.

Eric Erikson, the psychoanalytic theorist, speaks of identity and the sense of identity rather than the self. His developmental scheme, which outlines healthy and unhealthy stages of growth, indicates that each stage is folded into the succeeding stage. No developmental battle is won once and for all; rather, my process of identity-making is lifelong and presents me with opportunities for creative invention as well as potential for disastrous regression throughout my life journey. This is why it is so critical for me to focus on my *process*, and the internal field that supports it—the attitude and the thinking and acting steps I go through—as I handle my life's crises. In each stage, I make decisions about the kind of person I am becoming.

Erikson's stages identify periods of time and specific issues which he calls psychosocial crises. For example, adolescence focuses on the issues of identity vs. identity confusion, and, at thirteen, I was certainly confused! Adolescence seemed like one long confusing crisis for me. I was detaching from my family (it seemed that they really did not understand LIFE as I was experiencing it) and it felt as though there was no dependable other instructor either. I was deep in a search for heroines and other role models who I could use as raw materials in the creation of my self.

Fortunately for me, the field my mother provided was loving, competent, and nurturing. Even though I was her third child, and in adolescence was busy breaking away, she had enough energy—and perhaps more important, she had a history with me—to be a good mother for me. Winnicott (1985) describes the "good enough mother" who provides for her child the basic ingredients for good mental health. In an earlier period, she had given me what I needed to develop a basic sense of trust, the beginnings of autonomy, initiative and industry. According to Winnicott, self is established by refraction through another. Being held and

> "Sex lies at the root of life and we can never learn to reverence life until we know how to understand sex."—Havelock Ellis

being seen are the basis for self-hood and identity. My mother was very good at mirroring and I always felt seen by her. Her special talent was seeing qualities and potential qualities I was not aware of. She was extremely supportive. I also developed a deep mutual bond with my father.

I was fortunate, too, in having a brother two years older who bonded with me. He loved and protected me and taught me things in such a way as to make the world seem a safe and interesting place. My second experience of intimacy (after my early closeness with Mother) was with him. I could tell him my secret thoughts and worries, and he would honor them and keep them secret. He was a constant presence in my life—a regular playmate in spite of his advanced age. When we disagreed and fought, he was careful not to hurt me or disparage me with discounts or superiority. The names he would sometimes call me like "Butterball" or "Blondi" did not hurt me. I was lucky. My sister, who was three and a half years older did not share our common interests and thus did not seem to compete in any obvious way.

The Adolescent Storm

Although I had negotiated the early developmental crises of childhood, adolescence was a storm of change: my body was blooming into womanhood and along with that came overwhelming awareness and anxiety about all manner of things I had never considered important: it became a matter of life and death to be friends with certain girls, to learn to flirt and attract certain boys; to wear exactly the right clothes, and the most effective make-up. My fair skin betrayed me—I developed acne.

I discovered that the sun and salt water of nearby Quincy Bay cleared my skin, and, the summer I turned fourteen, I *lived* at the beach. I became an expert swimmer and that brought growing feelings of competence.

One day as I walked to the beach in my summer uniform of shorts and tee shirt, a car-load of laborers from the Fore River shipyard honked their horn, shouted and whistled at me as they approached from behind me. I was embarrassed at the commotion, but there was a vague yet thrilling sense of power in attracting that attention. I was puzzled because they started honking while behind me and before they could see whether or not I had a pretty face. When I told my brother about this, he explained the male response to the

> "I think, therefor, I am."—Descartes
> "I see that I am seen, therefor I know that I am."—Winnicott

female body as a whole. I had thought a pretty face was the whole story. I was beginning to like my sexual self.

Shame

While the first psychosocial crisis of autonomy vs. shame and doubt occurs in early childhood, my most memorable instance of this crisis came that summer when I was fourteen. We were vacationing at a resort in Maine. While going into the dining room, my father stumbled on the threshold. As if I had been struck by lightening, I connected the stumble with the pre-dinner cocktail hour. During dinner he was angry, sarcastic and punishing and I felt stunned, embarrassed, and deeply saddened. I withdrew into myself. In that one epiphanic dinner hour, our field was changed forever. I was overwhelmed with the shame that this same nasty mood that had made him such a different person before, was really *drunkenness.* This person I was so attached to was a drunkard. The shame on him was a shame on me, and it made a lasting injury to the sense of my own worth.

The Long Step Toward Autonomy

The transition, when I was fourteen, from a Catholic parochial elementary school to a co-ed college preparatory school was a major revelation for me. The field of the school expressed a value system of the administration and students that was exciting and so different from parochial school that I felt confusedly reborn. My first day in gym class required changing into gym clothes. In the locker room, I was amazed to see that all the girls wore bras. I felt strikingly different; embarrassed to be the only one not wearing a bra. On the way home, I stopped at Sheridan's Department Store and bought a bra—my first. I also bought lipstick, blush, foundation makeup, and mascara—*all* firsts.

The next morning I appeared at breakfast dressed and made up in a way I considered appropriate for my new life. My mother was visibly shocked.

"Kathleen, that purple lipstick is horrid", she said.

My father was more careful. "I think you are prettier without all that paint," he said.

Reluctantly, I went upstairs and washed most of it off. I decided that my mother and father did not know what they were talking about. A made-up me was who I wanted to be.

"Nothing is beautiful from every point of view."—Horace

While self doubts lingered, I was launched on the perilous adolescent journey of making the grown-up me.

Self as a Developmental Achievement

True self and false self are notions that theorists and psychologists have studied in depth. Most agree that my true self is the self with all of my feelings, drives and instincts striving for expression. My true self is messy, egocentric, containing hate, envy, and destructiveness as well as honest talent for seeing reality. It is also the repository of yearning and of the desire to love and be loved. My open, unprotected self is extremely vulnerable to threat of abandonment and its civilized cousin, rejection. During adolescence, I was torn between the values of my parents and my Church and the free-wheeling, exploratory customs of my teen-age mentors. My true self felt almost constant threat from this non-facilitating field, and I often went into hiding, deep within the recesses of my being. To deal with the unsafe world, I replaced my true self with a false self which was designed to defend me from danger.

In one expression of this false, or public self I present me as a people pleaser looking for approval at any cost. This may lead to outward success, but, to do this effectively, I mute and stifle the demands of my true self for expression. I sacrifice vitality, genuineness, and feelings of aliveness. The central task of my life is defining and building a public or 'false' self that is consistent with my true self. It begins in my family of origin, but it certainly does not end there. At every age and stage of life, I am challenged to build a self—both public and true—that is competent to deal effectively with the many challenges of my reality. To the degree my public self is at odds with and alienates me from my true self, I will stunt my growth and be despairing.

The issue that recurs throughout my life is: how can I honor the dictates of my true self—my wholeheartedness, my rapture of being—and at the same time enter into the mutually rewarding relationships that make life worthwhile? My answer has been to conduct a continuing negotiating conference within; to stay in touch with the "murmurs of my heart" and yet stay empathically with the person or persons with whom I wish to relate.

It has been useful to me to use Margaret Wheatley's (1994) concept of field to describe this relationship. As described earlier, the positive or negative valence of this field has an important influence on the feelings we evoke in

"Equality breeds no wars."—Plutarch

each other. I build my part of this field by paying close attention to my transmissions: my words, tonals, and non-verbals. My objective is to trust myself enough to disclose how it truly *is* with me, without damage to our relationship, that is, without discount or blame to the other.

Mind-Free is a practice ground to help me master this most demanding task of my life. In years past it was considered acceptable to say of an exchange that hurt the feelings of another, "That is her problem, not mine." This attitude ignores the reality of mutual relationship which requires that both parties take care not to inject toxic transmissions into the field, not simply to be nice, but to avoid the inevitable discount/revenge cycle that poisons relationships.

Toward a Unified True Self and Public Self

Autonomy, differentiation, independence, selfhood are all concepts that psychotherapists embrace as primary values and goals, and so do the people who come for therapy. "I want to find myself." "I want to discover who I really am and what I want." "I want to be less concerned with other people's approval." "I want a close relationship, but I don't want to lose myself." These represent people's yearning to experience more of their true selves, to be less governed by a false self that has grown so distant from true self that it ignores their deep need to *be.*

When Rita came to me for therapy, she was in the throes of the intense pain of divorce. She experienced the loss of her husband as a piece of herself being ripped away. Although the field of her marriage had been troubled for years by irresolvable conflict, and a poor sexual adjustment, she had become deeply attached to her husband. His filing for divorce was a humiliating rejection, and it triggered her worst fears of abandonment. Her internal field felt shattered and fragmented and it influenced not only her, but her interactions with everyone in her life.

In the early months of our work together, Rita talked of herself as though there were different selves within her. There was the nine year old, dependent and vulnerable; the artist, talented and expressive; the dental hygienist, a professional caretaker; the adolescent, stubborn, angry, and vulnerable. She would announce, "The nine year old was out this week, and I could hardly function at work." or "I felt so horribly stupid…I was at a party and my angry, stubborn fifteen year old was out and I made a fool of myself."

> "Of my own spirit let me be in sole though feeble mastery."—Sara Teasdale

The core of our therapeutic work together was aimed at Rita establishing a more appreciative relationship with herself. She gradually was able to see that these different parts of her were valuable and deserved understanding and attention—respect. They were not other people, but all parts of the same Rita. In some sessions Rita got some parts to speak to other parts, and finally she integrated them into a whole with Rita in charge of herself. She is much happier and will speak of her true self which includes many aspects of her "old" self. She has found a new man to love and who loves her. In this relationship she continues to build toward a coherent true and public self that respects her needs as well as those of others.

The Language of Respect

In my work with troubled couples, as well as in my own development of myself, I am continually impressed by the critical necessity of shaping my transmissions to convey respect. This need is almost deliberately ignored in our competitive/defensive culture. I am tempted to make my public self as impressive as possible in order to *win.* When I yield to this temptation, I begin to distance my public self from my true self and it becomes my false self. For my true self—my heart of hearts—winning is in the rewards of mutual relationships where there is no competition, only collaboration and connection to achieve what no one alone can manage: maximum opportunity for <u>be</u>ing.

> "The way we want children to make meaning of events is without error, without confusion, without experiment.."—Robert Kegan

Making A Self
Kathleen Logan-Prince

When I entered therapy for problems in my relationship with my spouse, I was spouse-focused; a state of mind that is common among people who are beginners in the development of a differentiated self. In that state I see the behavior of the other person as the problem and I believe the solution is for that person to change. While I am speaking of a husband and wife issue, my bias toward blaming others, creates a field that has destructive consequences on *all* my relationships, and in particular, it contaminates my relationship with myself.

If I persist in looking outward for the causes of my troubles I cut myself off from learning new and better ways to cope with my anxiety gradient that pressures me to block my awareness, and interferes with my capacity to achieve my true heart's desire: to be and feel meaningful, by growing in personal mastery and competence and in ability to relate effectively to others. Each shift toward greater selfhood requires three important elements: first is awareness of the situation; what is going on both in the external field and in the field within me. Second is the courage to accept the reality of my own field: my internal experience of thoughts, feelings, desires as well as my behavior. It also means refusing to disown any aspect of myself. Third is accepting responsibility for my choices, my acts, and for the attainment of my goals. Whenever I deny responsibility I effectively render myself helpless.

Taking the focus off the other does not mean silence, distance, cutoff, or a policy of "anything goes". Rather, it means that as I become less of an expert on the other, I become more of an expert on myself. I shift my locus of control from outside myself to inside myself. As I work toward greater self-focus, I become better able to share my perspective; to state my values and beliefs clearly—to disclose myself.

Self As A Work-In-Progress

As an infant I am totally dependent on others. When one of my wants or needs is unfulfilled, I complain and my loving caretaker responds. It is no wonder that I am convinced that my well-being depends upon another. I am enmeshed with her. One of the critical factors in making my unique self is how well I progress in differentiating from

> "Much of what we say or don't say and the way we say it is governed by some kind of fear."—Miller, Wakman, Nunnally and Saline

my caretakers. To become whole, I need gradually to recognize and nurture the competencies necessary to get my needs met. I am naturally gifted with a drive to develop myself. Nature rewards me with good feelings whenever I make progress toward competence and meaning, whether it is becoming a sure-footed walker or getting skilled in understanding words. My progress from total dependence to differentiation and autonomy is a long and difficult assignment and remains a work-in-progress for my whole life. Further development is always possible. (see differentiation outline in Relationship, Unit 3).

Self-Focus The Key To Growth

Self-focus is the process I use to become consciously aware of *all* the dimensions of my "self in situation"—my total field. It is the process I use to identify and make cohesive meaning of my internal experience of thinking, feeling, wanting and sensing. It's the means by which I discover the wealth of information within me, thereby fostering my self awareness. It helps me distinguish the impact of external field from internal. With good self awareness I can consciously choose how I manage myself in the combined field and communicate to another with awareness of my contribution to the quality of the interaction.

It is *not* a procedure that comes naturally; I need to learn it and practice it to get the required skills. The alternative to self-focus is allow my impulses—my anxiety gradient—to govern my reactions to a situation. Spontaneity has some good connotations, such as free from pretension or calculation, natural and guileless. These are wonderful qualities that can put us in touch with the real, honest core of a person. Spontaneity also connotes acting without apparent thought or deliberation and can lead to indulgent reactions that are destructive to relationships.

Self-focus allows me to reveal to myself and/or another person how a situation really *is* for me without blame or guilt. It helps me sort through the confusions of mixed feelings, thoughts, wishes and intentions so that I am in a position to manage myself and the relationship with understanding and intelligence. The practice of it demonstrates the highest respect for both myself and the other parties and discloses me in a way that is just as real and honest as spontaneity, and is more reliably developmental.

> "Truly creative individuals are those who succeed against all pressures of instinct and worldly wisdom, in visualizing a way of life that will make the lot of others freer and happier."—Mihaly Csikszentmihalyi

Self-Focus Does Not Narrow Perspective

Self-focus does not mean self-absorption. It means, rather, awareness of myself in connection with my field in the broadest possible sense. This includes my immediate circle of influences—family, friends and acquaintances, my living spaces, my work, my faith, nature around me, as well as the larger world of politics, and the world. My mindfulness of what is going on around me, together with the responses it evokes in me, prepares me to take intelligent action on my own behalf. Psychoanalyst Jean Baker Miller (1986) is a wonderful example. She became aware that all the profiles of mental development were based on men and did not define the mentally healthy woman. She and her colleagues at The Stone Center at Wellesley College, developed a new theory of mental health that illuminated the unique differences between masculinity and femininity. No psychotherapist could claim to be well-informed who did not know their theories, and because they took action on their own behalf, they brought about profound changes in the understanding of male/female development.

I think another example of self-focus leading to constructive, broad change is the woman's movement. We acknowledged the effect on us of the field of discrimination, unfairness and injustice of the male-dominated culture and recognized that unless we clarified our own needs and wants and took action, no one else would do it for us. Intelligently self-focused women "...began busily writing women back into language and history, establishing countless programs and services central to women's lives, starting new scholarly journals and women's studies programs in universities, to name just a few actions. Women insisted on taking back control of their own bodies and decisions regarding them." (Harriet Lerner, 1993, Pg.)

Myself As Change Agent

Through self-focus I bring about change, not by trying to force change on someone else, but by developing explicit, clear-cut understanding of my own thoughts, feelings wants and actions, I can arrive at an "official policy" toward an issue. I can then communicate this, without threat, to other, concerned parties who are free to respond in whatever way they are able. If *they* self-focus we have a clear understanding of the significance of the issue for all parties and we can negotiate an appropriate course of action. If they persist in a course of action unfavorable to me, they are

> "Many people, including clinicians, don't recognize (and don't *want* to recognize) the level of suffering and deprivation that most relationships endure and perpetuate."—David Schnarch

aware of my policy and know I will act in accordance with it and they must take that into account.

As a psychotherapist, self-focus is critical in enabling me to help my clients. It is through my awareness of the impact on me of my client's disclosures and actions that I am able to tailor my responses and interventions to make them helpful. For example, it is not unusual for a client to describe an experience of loss or violent abuse and as I listen I experience a range of emotions such as compassion, anger, sadness and disgust. Rather than spontaneously reacting, I self-focus, bring into my awareness my response to my client's description. Then with my *client's* needs in mind, I devise an intervention to help him or her grow rather than venting to satisfy my own needs.

A characteristic of couples whose relationship is in trouble is that they have great difficulty self-focusing. Their focus is on the other and their transmissions are random and spontaneous. The result is predictable. And in my work with singles who are wishing they could find partners, I am impressed with how often those who have trouble maintaining relationships are *un*mindful of their transmissions; how often the field they create is not one that invites closeness. Often I am aware of a client's blindness, and when I self-focus and accept my feeling of disappointment or impatience, I can put them aside, and go ahead with an appropriate intervention.

For example, Frank had been divorced for two years and had been dating and searching for a significant other for over a year. He complained sadly that he could not seem to get beyond a second or third date with any of the numerous attractive women he found interesting. He was bewildered by the fact that women seemed to get a bad impression of him.

I asked him to reflect for a moment and then tell me ten things a man could do to deliberately turn women off. I asked that, as an experiment, he use "I" language. Reluctantly he began, "I deliberately turn women off by never giving them compliments. I deliberately turn women off by criticizing them…by looking over their shoulders when they consult their appointment books…by suggesting ways they could solve their problems better than the way they have chosen…by hogging conversations to talk about me, etc. When he finished, I asked if any of his statements were true about him. "They are all true," he said, chagrined.

> "An effort to increase one's level of differentiation does not require others to change and is not contingent on anyone's cooperation."—Michael E. Kerr

With that, I helped him consider whether his actions served a need, and he became aware, "I'm afraid of going from the frying pan into the fire." He had felt so burned by his first marriage, he was not yet ready to invest in a new relationship. Before he could move from that fear, he needed awareness of what was really going on in himself—to own responsibility for it and accept it. Then he could open himself to alternative ways of operating.

Validation—Belief In Meaningfulness

Practicing mindful transmissions requires awareness and habitual self-focus. Self-focus creates an inner field that recognizes that *I* am the ultimate authority on my experience, as you are on yours. As I am aware of how I value my own thoughts, feelings and wants, I can appreciate how you value yours. This acknowledgment honors the equal importance of our unique ways of experiencing our worlds and lays the foundation for respect and collaboration. Our relationship will be informed by this mutual empowerment and will be a source of validation for both.

Field and Behavior

The basic function of my mind is to create a field to govern my behavior to maintain and further my life. One area of governance is my work or profession where goals seem different than those in more personal circles. However, *every* interaction with another person is significant and reflects *me.* Chances are that the way I interact with casual acquaintances, close friends, and even my spouse is consistent and falls somewhere on the spectrum indicated below.

Field Generators

Random <——————————————————>Mindful

I think of random interactions as "doing what comes naturally". I speak and act without much processing, assuming that the impact on the other person will be favorable. That other person, almost without exception, has a top priority of first evaluating my transmissions (words, tonals and non-verbals) for possibility of discount, put-down, or implication of meaninglessness, and only after that, responding to the sense of what I am saying. And the

> "...intimacy is the process of being in touch with or knowing *oneself* in the presence of another."—David Schnarch

tenor of that response will be influenced by whether or not a discount is perceived. Understanding this, I know that random transmissions are hazardous to the health of relationships. My preferred practice will be mindful transmissions that validate and invite cooperation rather than random ones that risk kindling hostility. This seems to contradict the accepted view of the worth of spontaneity, but I do not see it that way. Mindfulness means being aware of consequences. When my spontaneous transmission will not be perceived as a discount, I send it. When it may hurt, discourage, or convey meaninglessness, I rethink and redesign my transmission so that it communicates my truth without discounting. My profession, where I must be mindful of every transmission with clients, has been good training for me. It helps me to be mindful in my other relationships.

Connections With My World

To maintain and further my life—to be and feel as meaningful as I am able, I need to be wakefully connected to both my inner and my surrounding fields. This means that part of my focus is on what is happening outside of me, part is on my instant, spontaneous response to it, and part on the wealth of experience that I have stored inside me. A simple example is an interaction I had with a gas station attendant. My request for gasoline was polite. His response was surly and rude. My spontaneous reaction was a little thrill of anger (my foresight saw rejection. My anxiety soared. Rather than flight I chose fight) and the impulse to say, "Forget it," and drive to another gas station. Self-focus, including past experience, put me in touch with what was going on. I felt discounted, hurt and annoyed. I thought, "He is rude and is probably having a bad day. He is not really aiming at me. I do not want to bother going to another station. I will see if I can model validation. I want to send an appreciation his way."

When he washed my windshield, I leaned out the window and thanked him. When he finished filling the tank and came to collect for it, he was pleasant.

Self-Focus For Self-Soothing And Balance

In the above example if he had not responded to my appreciation and continued to be unpleasant, my awareness of the realities(I *really* need not be anxious about being rejected by him)—the probability that he was having a bad

> "The assumption that emotions have an external explanation comes from *"indirect self-acceptance"*...in lieu of the more difficult and painful development of autonomous self-worth which develops from the courageous exploration of self-doubts.—David Schnarch

day and that his behavior did not reflect on me, and my experiences in similar situations gives me a broader perspective and allows me to think more calmly and, if necessary, self-soothe and self reassure.

This may strike some as self-indulgent but in fact, the ability to self-soothe is critically important for insulating me from reactivity to the many discounts, slings and arrows that are inevitable. Self-soothing enables me to cope with my anxiety gradient and deal appropriately with the situation rather than maneuver to reduce anxiety. It allows me to maintain my self-regard in painful circumstances. I can accept, rather than reject or deny, feedback and learn from it. It depends upon my skill in self-focus.

To the degree that I am in touch with all my experience, it is available to help me manage myself intelligently. For example, Sally (not her name) came to me when her distress about difficulties with her boss became intolerable. She was on the verge of being fired and was desperate to keep her job, having a lengthy record of job failures in her past. While taking her personal history she shared with me that her sister called her "ostrich". Sally had a habit of saying, "I don't want to talk about it," when any conflict arose between her and someone in her family. Sally's foresight function triggered her anxiety gradient at the slightest hint of censure and her avoiding strategies took over. Sally believed that this defense demonstrated strength and unwillingness to compromise. In actuality she was enslaved by her unwillingess to cope with her anxiety. One consequence was that she was unable to learn from experience. She persisted in behavior that was unacceptable to others. Her field projected disregard for others, and even though her relationships were unrewarding, she was not available to feedback. She entered therapy out of desperation, still not accepting responsibility.

Sally effectively cut off awareness of the consequences of her actions. Her focus was on the trouble "others" were causing her, and her defensive strategy of not being available withheld essential information from her self-focusing. She had never learned to comfort and soothe herself when a hurt or criticism triggered heightened anxiety. Self-soothing would have allowed her to cope with, rather than avoid, anxiety and to develop a strategy to incorporate the feedback, make it a part of her balanced self-focus and use her experience to grow in competence,

> "The initial impact of anxiety on a relationship is always one of increased reactivity".—Harriet Goldhor Lerner

self-regard and relating skills.

Blindness In My Self

Sally permitted her anxiety to govern her awareness. She blinded herself to important aspects of her environment. Her avoidance strategies prevented her from developing coping strategies. Whenever anxiety struck, she was trapped in self-defeating reactions.

I do not begin by repressing awareness of my external world. My repression begins with a toxic external field. It is a flight from inner experience—feelings of pain, fear, helplessness, and rage. As Sullivan suggests, I develop foresight. I learn the signs that give warning of trouble coming. My anxiety gradient serves to tell me if the danger is increasing. I even learn deliberate inattention, to numb myself, to protect me from those terrible feelings. This process becomes a kind of habit, a mental model, and I later resort to it to deal with bad-feeling memories of actions and thoughts. Unless I invent for myself some effective schemes for engaging my courage to cope with adversity, I will continually be tempted to slip into avoidance rather than healthy coping with my reality.

> "Family Systems Therapy assumes an instinctually rooted life force—*differentiation*, which propels the child to grow to be an emotionally separate person, with the ability to think, feel and act for himself. Family Systems Therapy also assumes an instinctually rooted life force—*togetherness*, that keeps family members connected and operating in reaction to one another."—Michael E. Kerr

Differentiation, Autonomy and Self-Focus

I think of the autonomous person as one who is self-directed and independent, one who goes his or her own way. While that covers an aspect of autonomy it neglects the interacting, relating elements of a truly autonomous, differentiated person. These are as important, and perhaps more so, in terms of a satisfying life, because many pleasures and accomplishments are the result of my relationships and the field I create.

The idea of independence is misleading when it stirs up images of me making my way in the world alone, by courageously solving my problems and persevering in heroic isolation. Real life seldom works that way. Even the most independent, autonomous persons, except perhaps hermits, rely heavily on the fields they create with other people. It makes sense to foster the skills that lead to rewarding fields. These skills that help me connect constructively with others are based directly on my skills in connecting with myself and creating my inner field; for this, the ability to self-focus is essential.

Power, Control And Cause

As I grow out of my infantile belief that I am the center and cause of the universe, my dependence on others in my childhood becomes overwhelmingly evident. I come to believe that power, control and cause are all outside of me. I learn, through experiment and feedback from my anxiety gradient, what works and what does not. I create a field to get the attention I need. I develop methods of *influencing* those outside of me to get what I want. The drawback is that I also tend to become other-directed. It is in these early years that I form most of my beliefs about power, control and responsibility. It is no wonder that I exaggerate the importance of power-to-control and tend to place responsibility outside myself. Those two beliefs—in the importance of having power-over and in the usefulness of placing blame on others, are adopted to protect me from the overwhelming anxiety aroused by the threat of being meaningless to my caretakers.

> "This motion, from being enmeshed toward differentiation—this evolutionary motion is the grounding phenomenon of personality."—Robert Kegan

I develop behaviors to get control and to avoid blame, but they cause me a great deal of frustration and misery because they tend to obscure me from myself, obstruct my connection-making/learning ability and alienate me from others. My craving for power-over others, creates a field in me that can pit me against every other human being in an often subtle, underground struggle that can pollute *every* relationship and make it impossible for me to deal as an equal. This destructive appetite is reinforced by the hierarchical organizations of our culture. Margaret Wheatley in *Leadership and the New Science*, develops the idea that each of us is *potential:* "In organizations, which is the more important influence on behavior—the system or the individual? The quantum world answered that question for me with an authoritative, "It depends." This is not an either/or question. There is no need to decide between the two. What is critical is the *relationship* created between the person and the setting. That relationship will always be different, will always evoke different potentialities."(1994, Pg. 34)

Autonomy And Gender

In traditional, male dominated organizations, the underlying "setting" is nearly always hierarchical and, in Wheatley's term, this sets up a "field" that is adversarial. As a man, when I am subordinate, I strive to *look* as-good-as, while I search for ways to become superior. When I am superior I must be vigilant to tastefully display my superiority and guard against losing it, either in fact or in appearance. I adopt a set of behaviors that discount those subordinate to me with almost every transmission (see chart). Every interaction is slightly poisoned by competitive feeling and the need to be on guard and manage the impression I create. My true self, my potential, is concealed—even from myself, and I am operating without the guidance of my full core wisdom, values and connection-making capacity.

Transmissions That Create Relationship "Fields"

Invention sessions often include three levels of management: a senior manager, his immediate subordinate, and the subordinate's subordinate. Observing the differences in the way these three levels dealt with each other clarifies one of the drawbacks of the traditional male hierarchy.

> "In order to hold things fixed the culture reacts in ways that are defensive and false."—David Bohm and F. David Peat

Words, Tonals and Non-Verbals Used

With Subordinate	With Superior
•brusk	•deferential
•authoritative	•subservient
•condescending	•respectful
•contradicts	•quick agreement
•corrects	•suggests
•impatient	•tentative
•interrupts	•listens intently
•questions	•patient
•talks to rather than with	•willingness to give
•judgmental	•good humored
•positive	•tactful
•relaxed	•tense
•expresses anger	•shows no anger
•sarcastic	•checks understanding
•blames	•accepts
•wins in discussions	•loses

Women Experience Hierarchies Differently

As a woman, I experience being subordinate differently, in part because it is my cultural heritage to be subordinate to men. Some social theorists believe that all of society, culture and thought is built on the Oedipal moment when a boy identifies with his aggressive father and I with my supportive mother. The message is that I should now focus my energies on the well-being, growth and development of men. The message is conveyed in a thousand ways and it deeply affects my sense of myself and the way I relate to others. The field is a pervasive force toward subordination and against the flowering of my true potential.

"The role prescriptions for men and women vary substantially, based upon the prevailing cultural mores of one's particular generation. For today's senior citizens the traditional role models still apply even though these models

> "Every woman's wish is to inspire the love of a man."—Moliere, and "A woman should be smart enough not to outsmart a man."—Arlene Dahl

are out of step with our post-industrial society. However, the "baby boomers" (i.e., those born between 1945 and 1960) are a transitional generation. Though raised with traditional bedrock American values the baby boomers have been forever transformed by the social upheaval of the 1960s and 1970s. The women's movement continues to enjoy its greatest numerical, spiritual, and political strength from among this generation. Interestingly, today's youth are not nearly so politically inclined. Only 16% of college age women consider themselves feminists"(Brown, 1991, P. 59)

"Even though the majority of women work, the sharing of family responsibilities to balance the work load is not occurring. While husbands and children participate slightly in housework, the vast majority of household labor is done by wives-between 74-92 percent of the major tasks. Employed women continue to do 4.8 hours a day of housework compared with 1.6 hours for their husbands."(Ibid P.58) These realities influence me in my struggle for equality with men. Self focused reflection has helped me develop my personal policy toward the men in my life. I am required consistently to use my courage to generate fields of equality.

Adolescence is a time when my capacities greatly increase. They divide in several ways; for example, sexual capacities, aggressiveness or assertiveness—the ability to act; cognitive capacities with the formal thought that expands my universe. However, many studies still indicate that in spite of much progress toward a more equal role, this is a time when I, as a woman, begin to contract rather than expand.

"Bundles of Potentiality"

Margaret Wheatley says, "...I read that elementary particles were "bundles of potentiality." I have begun to think of all of us this way, for surely we are as undefinable, unanalyzable, and bundled with potential as anything in the universe. None of us exists independent of our relationships with others. Different settings and people evoke some qualities from us and leave others dormant." (1994, Pg. 34)

The field generated by male domination has distorted the understanding and appreciation of my *whole* potential as a woman. Jean Baker Miller in *Women's Growth in Connection,* says,

> "…people create the environments which then impose on them."—Karl Weik

> "Another way to put this is to say that women's actual practice in the real world, and the complex processes that those practices entail, have not been drawn upon, nor elaborated on, as a basis of cultural knowledge, theory or public policy.
>
> "We have all been laboring under only one implicit model of the nature of human nature and of human development. Much richer models are possible. Glimpses of them have always been struggling to emerge through the artists and poets, and in some of the hopes and dreams of all of us. Now, perhaps, we can work at learning about them in this field."(1991, Pg. 26)

The Cultural Shift

In the last twenty years there is evidence of change. It is possible for me to show my competence and operate as an equal in many areas such as medicine, business and the arts—thank God for the woman's movement! In personal relationships am also accepted as a sexual creature by my significant other and can risk collaborating with my partner to bring my unique capacities into our equal relationship.

The Paradox Of Blame

One of the common problems that brings couples to therapy is the constant struggle of each to be in control and make the other party change and conform to the controller's model of how a person should be.

A paradoxical outcome of blaming others is that when I hold them responsible for my dissatisfaction and insist that he or she change, I assign myself the passive, helpless role. I am dependent upon the other to take action; I avoid rather than cope, which makes me more defensive and more dependent. This depressing, vicious cycle eats away at my respect for my true self. It is as though I cannot make it if I deal with you as an equal. The more I blame and attempt to control, the less meaningful my actual true self feels.

The reasons power-over/control and avoidance are so toxic to my own development is that both lead me toward "impression management" and away from a *functional* relationship with myself and reality. The most fundamental

> "When a person attempts to be more of a self in a relationship system, the absolutely predictable response from important others is, "You are wrong; change back; if you don't, these are the consequences!"—Michael E. Kerr

purpose of a functional relationship—a positive field—is to achieve and maintain a satisfying level of validation (being and feeling meaningful) by myself and others. Such a relationship depends upon being open to the feedback that comes from *every* experience. Mistakes, failures, and short-comings move me up the anxiety gradient and I am tempted to engage in avoidance strategies to repress my reception of negative feedback. This practice has an unexpected consequence. I resist *all* feedback. I not only fail to learn from negatives; I fail to learn from positive accomplishments and do not get the many benefits that come from acceptance and appreciation of myself. Having the courage to tolerate anxiety and accept all feedback is the basis for the most powerful forms of psychological learning. Avoiding psychological risk and personal responsibility for *both* failings *and* successes precludes learning (S. Epstein, 1973).

My tendency to escape from conflicts that arouse anxiety is an indication that I am "in avoidance". I develop strategies that often conceal this underlying purpose: escape from anxiety! For example, anger may be an escape from facing my fear of losing control. Cynicism may be a way of avoiding consideration of a new and anxious-making idea. Procrastination, mistrust and suspicion, adversarial and bullying actions may all be escape strategies to avoid the psychological risk of accepting personal limitations and responsibility. Blame and avoidance are blind alleys.

The Path To Wholeness

The path to true autonomy, self-validation and high self-esteem always lies through self-disclosure. This idea usually arouses instant anxiety and protest. But theoretically this is *the way* and would, perhaps, be practical for me if I give up impression management and competition and accept the fact that I have a full share of personal limitations as well as strengths.

Am I avoiding or am I coping. Am I taking personal responsibility or denying. When I *know* what is going on in me, I may then chose to self-disclose to another and move toward a relationship that is between my true self and another.

> "We must understand that reaching our potential is more important than reaching our goals"—Max DePree

This process is critical to getting in realistic touch with the extraordinary person I am becoming. The skills involved are straightforward but using them is difficult. Rising anxiety presses me to avoid personal responsibility and the vulnerable feeling of appearing weak and inferior. Jean Baker Miller tells me, "In its extreme form…vulnerability can be described as the threat of psychic annihilation, probably the most terrifying threat of all."(1987, Pg. 37) However, if I am to have any possibility of continuing growth in competence, ability to relate, and self-esteem—the areas that are important to self-validation—I need to master a procedure for courageously disclosing myself to myself.

Developing A System Of Self-Focus

To balance my fear of appearing vulnerable, I need to appreciate the usefulness of *knowing* what is going on within myself. This may seem a silly concern. Of course I know what is going on in me! In reality this is not necessarily so. In a great many situations in childhood I feel pressured to deny my thoughts, feeling, actions, and wishes because revealing them gets me into trouble. My habit of thought and feeling may become to mute or ignore—to slip out of awareness when something happens that arouses my anxiety. Sullivan, as we noted earlier, calls this "selective inattention".

Selective inattention, being the outcome of the foresight function, operates so quickly it is on the very edge of perception, and blocks awareness; thus it may be difficult to

> "...positive statements you make to yourself have little if any effect. What *is* crucial is what you think when you fail, using the power of "non-negative" thinking. Changing the destructive things you say to yourself when you experience setbacks that life deals all of us is the central skill of optimism."—Martin E. Seligman

re-establish close contact with some of my inner experience. I need to invent a systematic way to improve my perceptions of my inner experience. Avoidance precludes wholehearted <u>be</u>ing—I act without the benefit of all my resources for connecting to learn, to improvise and to invent.

What is Happening Inside *Matters*

Most people don't pay enough attention to their inner field: what they are thinking, feeling and wanting and how that affects those around them. Everybody has access to this gold mine but many do not tap it as a resource. Those who do, have mastered the art of self focus and responsible self-disclosure.

With the awareness wheel (Miller, Nunnally and Wackman) I can lift the veil of my inner self and get clear with my ideas, feelings, wishes and what my senses experience. This is necessary for effective communication. I can't possibly communicate clearly if I'm not aware of my motivating ideas, emotions and wishes.

Self awareness involves processing information abaout myself-about what's going on with me…the condition of my world at a given point in time. Much of my self is a product of:

1. l. What stimulates my senses
2. The interpretations I make of that sense data (what I think)
3. My feelings or emotions
4. My intentions (wants, wishes and desires)
5. My actions or behavior

All five dimensions of self ar always part of me even though I am not equally aware of each. No one has total self-awareness. It's a continuous process of seeking to identify each of those five dimesions.

Dimensions of Self

Sensations

Souces of all data about the world and a funnel through which all information comes to me. It consists of what I see, hear, smell, taste and touch.

Feelings

Slippery, elusive, wonderful or horrible—feelings are my spontantous, bodily responses to the interpretations I make and the expectations I have. (If I'm expecting to be elected president of my organization and a darkhorse defeats me I'm going to have some feelings of disappointment, sadness, anger, surprise, dismay and/or others.Feelings are inside my body but usually have outward signs.

Interpretations

What I think is the part of which I am most aware. Traditionally, men tend to value highly their capacity to be rational and logical. Interpretations include my impressions, beliefs, assumptions, ideas, opinions, evaluations, conclusions, reasons, expectations, stereotypes, what I think about myself, other people, things and events.

Intentions

What I want are my desires and wishes. My intentions are like "organizers". Probably the most important function of intentions is to help me consider alternative actions, things I want and don't want to do.

> "...people bring their best to work only if they can involve their whole selves. They must feel free to talk about the things they are passionate about, to explore opposing points of view."—Margaret Wheatley

Intentions can often be the hidden agenda in an encounter. Wants or wishes like, "I want to get even with you.","I want you to admire me' or "I want to look more competent than you in this situation," often do not get expressed directly.

My actions or behaviors usually provide clues to my intentions. I can believe my behavior. If I do something it's likely that I want to do it, or at least there is something I want for myself that the action seemed likely to get for me.

My feelings can illuminate my intentions. Positive feelings such as satisfaction usually mean that my major intentions match my behavior. Wants can be mixed too. For example, "I want to strike out at you because I'm angry but I don't want to put a barrior between us either." Being aware of mixed wants and feelings makes it easier to decide what to communicate.

Actions

What I do is comprised of the verbal and non-verbal expressions of what I sense, interpret, want or intend and feel; the output of information. My actions are a part of me and become the raw data that others take in through their senses. My actions are also a source of self information.

I like to believe, "I know what I'm doing." I assume I am aware of what I do or have done but frequently some of my actions are not part of my awareness while they are clear to an observer. For example, smokers will often reach for a cigarette as a way of punctuating, interrupting or delaying a conversation that's become tense.

I Need to Catalogue My Feelings

The first step is to reacquaint myself with the various nuances of *feeling* of which I am capable. An effective exercise is to take a list of all the kinds of feeling I have ever had or imagined (see charts) and then imagine myself in an emotion-rich situation and recover a sample of each of my feelings.

The most effective way to do this is with a partner and take an agreed upon length of time to articulate every feeling.

> "You connect by communicating and by facing the reality that mintaining relationships is a slow and painfully learned art."—Miller, Wakman et al

Typical Emotion-Rich Areas

School—grammar, high, college; teaching; parties; dances; job; sports; parent child interactions; marital interactions; encounters with bullies; a serious loss

Signals Of Avoidance

As I go into self-focus I may find myself avoiding it. There are signals that can, if I pay attention, alert me.

anxiety	blaming
impatience	boredom
anger	denial
procrastination	suspicion
mistrust	prejudice
dominance	antagonism
pessimism	inattention

> "The worst sin is inadvertence."—Joseph Campbell

Self Respect

Max, at seven, is a Cub Scout. His assignment for the next meeting is to learn how to fold the American flag in the proper way. He asks me for help and hands me the Cub Scout Manual in which there are illustrated directions. I get a good feeling from being asked to help, and I take a sheet of paper the shape of the flag and begin to show him how a flag should be folded.

This interaction would get high marks for nurturing from almost anyone in our culture: patient, helpful person teaching attentive child one of life's small skills. Both Max and I have been conditioned to slip into these comfortable roles, but what is the field?

It is superior/subordinate with me sending the message that he need not go through the anxiety of perceiving, confusion, trial-and-error connection making of learning something new. It is a toxic field that discourages thinking.

In this case, I catch myself. Instead of showing him, step by step how to fold a flag, I hand him the paper and point to the illustrations. "See if you can guess how to fold it to end up with a triangle like the picture. You can use the pictures to help if you want."

Max takes the paper, glances at the directions and begins to fold without much regard for the illustrations. It is not working. After a moment he turns to his father and says "Will you help me, Daddy?"

Daddy's impulse is to take over and help, but he understands what I am attempting and suggests that Max follow the directions in the book. Max believes he has already tried that and it does not work. He loses patience with both of us and with the problem. His foresight function triggers rising anxiety at the possibility of wrongness. He expresses this with impatience and the intention to quit the activity—a strategy of avoidance with far-reaching implications, but he overcomes this impulse and persists.

When I struggle to keep from doing Max's thinking by coaching, I help Max use his unique learning process, and avoid imposing my knowledge on him, I honor Max's self-hood. I free the field of the taint of domination and we can experience the bliss of connecting our true "self-hoods". As Max makes sense out of the puzzle of flag-folding, he experiences *his* joy and I experience mine in his growing competence.

> "...limitations are based on presumptions rather than actions."—Weik

Max's and my deepest, most compelling need is to be and feel meaningful. I make my judgments, as Max does, on how I am doing in that enterprise by observing how I *cope* vs. *avoid.* If Max had avoided taking responsibility for teaching himself how to fold a flag, it would not have spoiled his day, but it would have subtracted a small sum from his feelings-of-meaningfulness account.

Another important source of data about my meaningfulness is how others act toward me. If I had persisted in being more helpful than Max needed, it is a statement to him about my opinion of his abilities. Most of impression management distortions of my true self are designed to keep me safe from being "de-meaned". To avoid the normal mistake-anxiety of learning something new, Max attempted to get help he did not need. Max imagined that if he avoided the ineffectual *appearance* of guess and test learning he would seem more respectable. What Max does not yet appreciate is that the toughest judge of his action is Max himself. When he chooses to cope, tolerate the increased anxiety, and make the attempt, he wins more esteem for himself than if he avoids. This is true even if his coping attempt is unsuccessful.

It is asking too much to expect Max to know this, or to ask himself, "Will this action of mine help me to feel more meaningful or less meaningful?", but the earlier I learn to ask that question of myself, the more certain I can be that I will develop the habit of competence.

> "Through interaction, intelligence grows in its ability to interact. We are designed to grow and be strengthened by every event, no matter how mundane or awesome.—J.C. Pearce

Connectedness

The development of an inner field that supports and respects my self requires that I continually revisit earlier decisions that avoid emotional risk to reduce anxiety. The habit of self protection—defensiveness—tends to cut off my empathic connection to others. One of the notable consequences of child mistreatment is the failure to develop empathy.

The socialization process in my upbringing was haphazard. Through the close-coupled nature of child and parent, I learned thinking and behavior patterns out of my conscious awareness without much evaluation. An important motivator was and will always remain the complex dynamic of my foresight function, my anxiety gradient, and selective inattention. This expresses itself in my wish to please, be accepted, appreciated—validated—reassured that I am meaningful, and also in my reluctance to cope with issues that *feel* too dangerous to me.

To change myself I need to recognize that I am an integrated system—that song about the head-bone connected to the neck-bone, the neck-bone connected to the shoulder-bone applies to my thinking.

When I attempt to change one habit, it may have a consequence for many others, and every one will reinforce the status quo. That habit probably originated to protect me from an early threat. Changing is an anxious business just like learning.

Effective renegotiation requires that I deal with each insightful connection in a friendly-to-my-self, compassionate way. For example, if I want to change my early field of self-punishment to a field of support, a blanket policy change, "I am not going to punish myself anymore" does violence to many other decisions like those about self-discipline. I may believe that self-punishment is necessary to maintain discipline. Further, I firmly believed that my self-punishment policy was aimed at self improvement. When I actually focused on instances of self-punishment, I discovered that it had the effect of *avoiding* change. The punishment itself became the center of my attention, not change. Renegotiation means that I must isolate individual instances, analyze each, and decide about *it*. Then gradually and tolerantly deal with its implications.

> "[Love] is work or courage directed toward the nurture of our own or another's spiritual growth."—M. Scott Peck

To paraphrase Blake, if I am to do good to my self-hood I must do it in minute particulars. General declarations about my intentions are the refuge of self-deceivers.*

My world continually presents me with the necessary lessons. It is my assignment to make sense *for me* out of them. Joseph Campbell says that the real hero or heroine is he or she who sees her life as a warrior's journey in which the quest is to process every adventure to reveal new, added possibilities for herself and others.

It is important for me to keep in mind that my field is not fixed. A way of being that is wise at 30 may not be at 70. To achieve the most for myself I need to be continually modifying and bringing my field up to date to support the way I want to be in the future.

*What William Blake (1757-1827) actually said is:

> "He who would do good to another must
> do it in minute particulars;
> General good is the plea of the scoundrel,
> hypocrite, and flatterer:
> For art and science cannot exist but in
> minutely organized particulars."

Part 4—Anatomy of Relating

"There is no such thing as a genius, some of us are just less damaged than others."—Buckminster Fuller

Validation

The founders of Synectics® Inc. were a group of inventors working for the Arthur D. Little Company, a large consulting firm in Cambridge, Massachusetts. We had been repeatedly frustrated by seeing our inventions treated by clients with indifference or hostility. Even though we had been hired by executives of the company to create a new product for them, those who were assigned to put it into production, had little commitment to making it succeed. This rejection of ideas not originated in the company is known as the N. I. H. Factor—Not Invented Here.

Looking back, when I accepted the NIH Factor as a healthy fact of life, it changed my approach to practically everything. I began to believe that NIH is a profound truth about most human beings. Ideas presented to me from outside get far less of my understanding and commitment than those I form myself. That understanding has been a guiding principle in the development of the Mind-Free Program. It is designed and presented to give each participant room to make connections for her or himself. The use of "I" language is intended to make it clear that this is *my* experience and thinking. It may or may not be true for you. It is your responsibility to invent what is true for you.

We left ADL in 1960 to market our new understanding of how to implement creativity in the workplace. After our initial education in NIH, our approach was different from the usual consultant. It reflected our acceptance of the NIH Factor. Our position was that *for an idea to be most effective for a company, it needs to be implemented—put into practice—by the people who conceive it.* With this basic insight, the Synectics team focused on helping people enhance their creative thinking *process,* rather than offering solutions.

In our work with ADL we had used sound equipment to record our invention sessions. It was our practice to track back from an idea to learn how it had happened. This proved to be a fruitful way to learn the minute particulars of the creative process. Little by little we developed systems to produce the kind of field that encourages effective thinking and leads to new ideas. It was this body of knowledge we used in coaching our clients.

"…events, relationships, and transactions which give a sense of identity, worth, hope, and purpose are 'inspiriting'…those that make a person feel unimportant, worthless, hopeless, low in self-esteem, isolated, and frustrated…are 'dispiriting'."—Sidney M. Jourard

In time, we developed a procedure for videotaping the Synectics invention groups in action and it has been our practice to study these tapes much as a football coach studies game films. We examine each transmission (words, vocals, and non-verbal actions) to derive, if we can, its effect on the field and thus on behavior. During this process it became crystal clear that the way one person interacted with another was key to the positive or negative valence of the field. Seemingly small differences in the way team members treated each other could alter the field and determine whether a member participated wholeheartedly, dropped out, or became adversarial and competitive.

Wholeheartedness

Observations of thousands of sessions, together with the most current information about the psychology of learning and human development, have convinced me that there is a way to help a person mobilize him or herself to be more creative, more competent, and more effective—to get more of what he or she wants out of life. The term I use for this state of full presence in (and enjoyment of) a task or goal or person is wholeheartedness.

I become wholehearted when certain kinds of interactions happen between elements of myself (for example, between my strict self and my adventurous self), and between me and others. These interactions create a field that allows me to be wholeheartedly available or that dictates defensiveness. *The most fundamental characteristic of a positive field is that it quells anxiety and produces feelings of validation—feelings of being meaningful and safe—this frees up energy for connecting.*

Self-managing, "…the control of one's mental processes whenever it developed…was one of the most momentous events that happened on our planet." (Csikszentmihalyi, 1993, Pg. 76)

Since the field in and around me causes my behavior, learning how to create and maintain a validating field inside me and between me and others is the central purpose of the Mind-Free process. Developing a positive, supportive field frees defensive energy for constructive purposes and opens me to perceive and connect with more and more of my resources for outstanding thinking.

> "Intimacy is that type of situation involving two people which permits validation of all components of personal worth."—Harry Stack Sullivan

What is Validation?

Validation is a transmission that leads me to connect with my own best self—some aspect that is meaningful in a positive sense; it is support for who I am, as I am now. It is an action that helps me appreciate my positive worth. I may experience validation when I perceive and appreciate my own competence in coping rather than avoiding, and when I engage my courage and make a risky connection, and it may come to me from an accurate compliment; from the empathy, recognition, or appreciation of another, or from an expression of need for my presence and skills. It may come from containing my reactivity and accepting responsibility for a mistake; from my retreating gracefully from a wrong decision, or from keeping my balance when rejected.

When an action of mine validates, it creates a link between the two (or more) of us: it encourages me and the person who is validated to be inclusive rather than alienated, nourishing rather than withholding, collaborative rather than competitive, open rather than hidden. It generates a nourishing *intra*-as well as *inter*-personal field. Because I have such a long dependent childhood—a period in which I develop my strategies for surviving and getting what I need and want mainly through *watching and interpreting the behavior of others*—I am extremely sensitive to signals indicating approval or disapproval. This drive to observe, imitate, and learn is an expression of the great human yearnings that compel me toward validation: differentiation and integration, autonomy and belonging, competence and equality.

Competence and Equality

My drive to be competent (and be seen as competent) begins in my infancy. It is part of my healthy need to differentiate myself and become an autonomous, self-possessed person who is in control of my physical and social environment. As I grow older, my definition of competence is shaped by parents, peers, teachers, and others. I internalize standards. When I reach adulthood, I am constantly (and often unconsciously) measuring myself against those standards in everything I do. I give myself continual feedback about my competence.

One of the unfortunate aspects of our culture is that parents, peers, teachers and others are much more likely to criticize me than to appreciate me.

> "People who feel accepted by others also feel safe enough to explore problems more freely, take risks, play with possibilities, and benefit from mistakes rather than [endure] a climate in which mistakes must be hidden."—Alfie Kohn

I dutifully internalize *that* along with the standards. My evaluations of myself are skewed toward punishment.

My need to be included as an equal in relationships with others may be as fundamental as survival. In any case, this is a powerful drive in most of us and while we intuitively *know* this, a great many of our social structures violate this need. There is a firmly held assumption that because each of us has differently developed knowledge and skills we *must* be relationally unequal. I unhesitatingly accept the superior/ subordinate design of the vast majority of my relationships in spite of *knowing* that it greatly reduces the possibility of dealing with each other wholeheartedly. It will be one of my objectives in the Mind-Free experience to invent and practice ways of dealing with *everyone* as equal. I know more about some things than a child does, and the child knows more about other things than I do. When we create a field of mutual respect and empathy of equals, we make it a *given* that each of us is meaningful. We relieve each other of the need to defend and compete. We can enjoy mutual validation even when we have differences. Whenever I succeed in relating as equal, it will enrich the interaction. It will also make a crack in the overwhelming cultural conviction that relational inequality is a requirement of human nature.

Threats to Validation

My feelings of validation are under ceaseless challenge from infancy on. The slaps, dominating voice tones, anger, frustration, orders and critical comments that are directed at me in my cultural surround, skew my inner field toward reaction, self-punishment, and shame. Even though I get a fair share of appreciation and praise, one criticism seems to have enough negative weight to cancel out five positive transmissions. Over time, as these negative inputs continue, I lose my trust in myself and the outward manifestation of this inner mistrust is submission to the dictates of my anxiety. In the face of life's threats or uncertainties I obey my anxiety's pressure to defend myself with reactions such as cynicism, suspicion, alertness for flaws in others, closed-mindedness, bullying, adversarial attitudes, pessimism, prejudice, and hate.

While these attitudes are often seen as aggressive and hostile, I believe they are often behaviors—preemptive strikes—to defend against vulnerability.

> "Beatings, slaps in the face, verbal batterings are injuries. Blows that lacerate self-esteem, puncture our sense of grandeur, pollute enthusiasm, poison and desolate body image...these all make a defilement. They damage and do harm."—Robert Bly

Increasing amounts of data tell us that these behaviors poison the field and are unhealthy for both perpetrator and victim. They are destructive to relationships. We know for certain from thousands of observations that invalidating actions—actions that diminish my sense of competence and equality—reduce cooperation and accomplishment.

The hierarchical design of everyday life is also unfriendly to my hunger for validation. The rules and norms of our culture are focused on competition and dominance or power-over. Nearly every circumstance or enterprise is framed in some way as a contest in which one party will be a winner and another a loser.

These accepted rules of dominance and submission in the pecking order are upset by having women in the group. Women in business are in an anomolous position. Even though a woman has rank, men tend not to be comfortable with her unless she sends subordinate signals. We observe that many men persist in using dominant transmissions even when they are subordinate to a woman. It suggests that much sexual harassment is an attempt by a threatened male to underscore his traditional power-over position.

This competitive stance is not limited to relationships with women. Hundreds of videotape studies of traditional groups and committees, with or without a controlling chairperson, demonstrate that participants quickly create a somewhat adversarial climate of difference. It appears to be important for each person to establish an image of validity. Observe in your next meeting how each person usually weighs in early with a wise statement or information that conveys that he or she should be treated with respect.

> "Do we perform better when we are trying to beat others than when we are working with them or alone? *Almost never.* Superior performance not only does not *require* competition, it usually seems to require its absence. This conclusion, to say nothing of the near unanimity of the data, will be astonishing to most people."—Alfie Kohn

We see this as defensive. Any hint of incompetence or any sign of rejection, and I react with defensive strategies that effectively make me unavailable for *inter*action, for contributing, and for learning. Of course, this dynamic is not limited to business meetings. It is in full force in *every* encounter in any setting. It is most obvious between people, but it can be seen between a person and a thing or even a situation—my reactions to a seemingly willful computer, or to being lost while driving. However, the most serious destructive consequences flow from the paradox of defensive reactions against ourselves. This phenomenon is called Reactive Structure (Robert Fritz, 1984).

My experience with structured, appreciative environments in thousands of invention sessions, together with the experience of mental health professionals with "holding environments"—emotional safe zones created to encourage growth in both children and adults (Kegan, 1982)—tell us that alternate cultural structures are possible. This suggests concrete goals for reinventing the fields in the workplace to invite wholehearted, non-defensive involvement in the task at hand.

Validation and Effectiveness

In my observations of couples and groups I have also noticed that meetings are conducted on two levels. There is the polite, civilized level where everyone appears to be dealing rationally and constructively with each other on an assigned task—cooperating to help each other get the job done. Below this business (surface) level is a less visible, feeling level where the actions often seem to have little to do with the assigned task. It is rife with hidden agendas and competition. There are subtle attacks and counter-attacks, strategic maneuvers and areas of resistance that do not advance the agreed-upon purpose of the meeting. For example, I may use questions, not to get information, but to highlight someone else's wrong thinking, or to divert the group from the current topic to another where I may have more expertise or control.

Sometimes in an invention session one member will suggest a beginning idea—one that has not been developed enough to know where it might go. Another member says "The idea is fine, but it just will not meet our cost target."

> "Contemporary business life allows competitive relationships only, in which the major emotions are anxiety, tension, loneliness, rivalry, and fear."—Robert Bly

"Oh, yes, I guess you are right." says the proposer, in a reasonable way, and the idea is dropped.

But when we track the subsequent actions of that proposer, he gets even later in the session when his adversary is vulnerable or needs support. This is a gross example. Or he may produce more subtle actions of non-cooperation and sabotage, such as raised eyebrows, shrugs, inflections of voice, or cautionary comments that damn with faint praise: "Yes, that's a good idea, but…"

These and many other strategies are used apparently with no other purpose than to demonstrate power and control. They say, "I am meaningful, You had better treat me with the respect I deserve."

Cooperative or Competitive?

At a deeper level, my attempts to gain power and control are often ways for me to deal with rising anxiety about losing position. In every meeting and in every exchange with another, I have a secret priority (I may not even be aware of it) that is independent of the purpose of the meeting: to maintain my image of a competent, equal, worthwhile person—my appearance of validity. Studies of small group dynamics suggest that this hunger for validation—or the *appearance* of being valid—is the paramount force that governs whether I am cooperative or competitive.

Conventional vs. Validating

Over the forty-odd years of my research there have been many experiments to test the effectiveness of the procedures we were developing. Typically, two equal teams are formed, one is trained in Synectics processes, the other in

Brainstorming or some other meeting process. Each team is given the same problem and asked to invent a solution.

Almost without exception the Synectics-trained group wins. Comparative study of tapes reveals the secret. In the Synectics meetings people and ideas are systematically *appreciated,* that is, they are *unfailingly* listened to, supported, and protected from invalidating remarks or negative nonverbals by the appointed facilitator. Even evaluation is orchestrated to get the benefits of realism without the destructiveness of criticism and put-downs.

> "…the incredible power which verbal behavior seems to exercise in interpersonal situations."—Harry Stack Sullivan

If this sounds artificial and contrived, it certainly is. In order to maintain this constructive field, meetings need facilitators with the power to divert participants from their normal competitive, self-empowering behaviors that inevitably infect the field, and compel defensive maneuvers of one kind or another.

Validation Deficit Syndrome

When my validation needs are met, my mind is free for constructive use. To the degree that my validity seems threatened, however, I will apply myself to defensive, undermining, and adversarial behavior. The term we use for this phenomenon is Validation Deficit Syndrome (VDS). When I feel deprived of validation, I act *first* to compensate for that deficit by diminishing the validity of others, and/or enhancing my feelings of self-worth by whatever means available.

VDS is Catching

This syndrome can become contagious. When I observe someone in a group building himself up, or undermining my presentation or suggestions, it triggers in me the same need to affirm my self-worth. Therefore, the Validation Deficit Syndrome phenomenon has many of the characteristics of an infectious disease. Among many women, perhaps because of their long history of struggling against domination, VDS seems somewhat less virulent. Perhaps this is only apparent and not real. While many women seem to accept this discriminatory state of affairs, observations among couples suggest that they employ their own means of retaliation.

Validation Computer

I hypothesize that deep inside of me—at my very core—is a validation computer composed of part heart, part intellect. Originally it was dedicated to interpreting events in terms of their survival threat—to make a rapid, emergency decision to fight or fly. In either case, a large jolt of energy is instantly supplied. Unfortunately, our current computers have not been updated. They are primitive go or no-go machines ill-designed for the present delicate assignment: to determine not whether there is a life-or-death threat present, but whether or not I am in an emotionally safe zone.

> "...cultures with low synergy [are those] where the social structure provides for acts that are mutually opposed and counteract vs. [those] with high synergy, where the culture provides for acts that are mutually reinforcing."—Ruth Benedict, anthropologist

This simplistic device evaluates every situation in terms of its potential for evoking the painful and anxiety-fraught feeling of being rejected, humiliated, or held in contempt. The relative strength (or legitimacy) of this threat is not important; my computer is a simple, binary machine. No matter how complicated or subtle the information going into it, it spits out only one of two responses: *danger—mobilize!* or *relax—you are safe.* Alone or in a crowd, my computer asks, "How am I comparing with my standards for being seen as competent, equal to anyone here—worth anyone's emotional energy? *Am I being validated or invalidated?"* If it registers "invalidation", I still get that large jolt of energy, as though a primitive fight-or-flight response is necessary. That energy can spur me to overreact, to attack others or defend myself fiercely, even if I have only been caught in a slightly embarrassing situation, such as forgetting a fact or a date, or finding a coffee stain on my shirt. If it registers "validated" I am available for constructive connecting.

My validation deficit computer has a remarkable system of storage and continuing reminder called *shame.* Old humiliations remain there and are readily available for influencing and revisiting. They continue to revisit my consciousness, and heighten my sense of vulnerability and unworthiness for years to come. In some cases the humiliation is so painful I repress it and prevent it from coming into consciousness. It exerts a continuing toxic influence nevertheless. (Society even teaches us that it is healthy, when soaring on the wings of bliss, to stay in touch with shame to avoid overweening pride.)

In the other direction—circumstances that validate—I experience a strange, self-defeating phenomenon. As the degree of validation increases, like a standing ovation for an outstanding accomplishment, I reach a state of bliss for an instant and then my modesty circuit-breaker goes into overload. Feelings are shut off. I seem to have no preservation system for positive experience. Once felt and enjoyed in the limited amount permitted by my humility circuit-breaker, I may label it so it can be referred to, but the transient feelings of bliss, joy, and reassurance are difficult to recover, unlike the painful replays-in-living-color of humiliating downers.

The design of everyday life, particularly work life, is unfriendly to my hunger for validation. The rules of my culture, are focused on competition and dominance or

> "Normality of role is often set as society's highest goal. It is a matter of indifference to the social system if this is achieved with great expense to the self.—Sidney M. Jourard

power-over. Even with couples who are supposedly devoted to each other, when their relationship is troubled there is usually a power struggle going on as each attempts to get the validation he and she needs.

Self-Validation

Validation does not depend solely upon the feedback I get from others. There is a core of experience in me that is *self-validating*—activities or actions or accomplishments that feel good not because my mother or father, teachers or bosses, friends or lovers tell me it is good or correct or proper, but because deep down inside me it *feels right.* It is a satisfying demonstration of my competence or belongingness or courage that meets my standards for myself.

Although often overwhelmed by powerful people and imposing cultural forces outside myself that want me to meet *their* expectations, together with my own built-in reflexive urges that impel me to observe, imitate, and please others, there is also a stubborn voice that speaks directly from the deepest part of who I am.

The more validated I feel, and the less threatened, the easier it is to hear that voice, and be guided by it. Validation Deficit Syndrome and the compulsions of self defense, take me further and further away from my true needs; then I am struggling to maintain an image to satisfy others—to please parental and cultural icons that are not really me.

When my field is supportive and nourishing, I am able to relax my defenses enough to learn to hear that part of me that knows who I am, what I really want and need, and how I must act to be *right* with myself. My intense need for validation makes me acutely sensitive to *in*validation. When that happens, I am flooded with energy that cries out for *action.* The result is a phenomenon we call discount/revenge.

"Our survival and development depend on our capacity to recruit the invested attention of others to us."—Robert Kegan

Discount/Revenge

A discount is any action, body language or verbal behavior that I perceive as put-down, criticism, or denigration. Revenge is defensive, though it may appear as aggression. It is payback for a discount. It may involve openly discounting the person who injured me, subverting that person's goals or attempts at organization, being uncooperative, open rebellion or quietly going "on strike"—emotional withdrawal from a common enterprise, or any other form of retribution.

Discount/Revenge is an integral part of the Validation Deficit Syndrome. Whenever I am devalidated, the Discount/Revenge cycle is triggered. All my other agendas are put on hold, and I search for a strategy to recoup and put it into effect as soon as possible. If immediate action is not feasible, I wait for a better time to get revenge. *I do not forget.* I have had the experience of feeling discounted and resolving not to get revenge. At a later time when an opportunity for revenge occurs, I strike without conscious thought.

This compulsion to retaliate bears examination because it is a major destructive force in my life. I first observed the discount/revenge cycle as I was studying videotapes of invention sessions. The tapes make it possible to track back from a seemingly gratuitous hostile action and connect it to an earlier discount. Initially I considered retaliation childish. A mature person would not waste energy on such a useless activity. After seeing it happen several hundred times without once encountering a mature person, I revised my thinking. Invalidation begets revenge even in mature people. Discount/Revenge is a reliable behavioral law. It might be for behavior the equivalent of the law of gravity in the physical world and it has far-reaching implications for all acts that might be perceived as punishing.

The Impact of Discounting

Once aware of this phenomenon I began to use videotape review as well as direct observation to keep track of its various forms and their effect on the target person in invention groups.

> "An ocean of oblivion sweeps over a child when it is shamed..."—Robert Bly

True to Quantum field theory, it became clear that a discount aimed at a specific person had an impact not only on the target person, but on all who observed it. The higher the status of the discounter, the greater the increase in defensiveness in the group. Thousands of observations confirmed the concrete actions that affect the field and thus influence participants toward collaboration and building or toward competition and strife.

The simple social phenomenon of discount and revenge can, as you see, have far-reaching consequences. The effect on relationships is profound. From the growth and development of a child or an adult, to the nourishment of the connection-making capacity of group members, to the availability of participants in a group to work together constructively—all can be devastated. Discounting can create a hidden dynamic in any organization—one that impairs group efficiency and undermines the organization's goals because it fosters non-cooperation and worse.

If developmental behavior were a concrete substance, then the smallest component of developmental matter would be what we could call a behavioral sub-atomic particle. In the language of quantum physics, discounts and validations are two different kinds of invisible waves that create fields that bring out very different behaviors. The Discount field tends to evoke the disintegrating forces of agitation and entropy; Validation invites harmony and synergy.

When I present these actions in these black and white terms it oversimplifies. Many of the actions that trigger disorder have valuable contributions to make, for example, pointing out flaws, or insisting on precision, or raising questions. This is why these actions are so widely tolerated. They are like chemotherapy to a cancer patient—the side effects are devastating and he suffers them in the hope that the beneficial effects will outweigh the damage.

My task in Mind-Free is to re-examine my discounting actions with an open mind and invent transmissions to get the possible benefits without the toxic side effects.

Discounting in Childhood

I believe that discounting is qualitatively different from other forms of negative experience such as falling as I learn to walk. During infancy and childhood, discounting has side effects that can be lastingly destructive.

> "The half-life of a public criticism is about thirty years."—unknown

Abuse in the name of discipline is an example. When I realize that my parents' child-rearing practices, though well-intentioned, resulted in an adult me who is able to use only a fraction of my thinking potential, it seems obvious that those practices beg for reexamination. I now think of the process of parenting as helping a child develop an internal field that evokes behaviors that will assist him and her in fashioning rewarding relationships and developing the competence to achieve their life goals. Being newly aware of the discount/revenge cycle and the power of fields, I attempt to deal with my children, with myself, my partner, and with others quite differently. I attempt to model my actions to maintain a field of respect and synergy. I struggle to invent ways to minimize criticism. I believe *there is no such thing as constructive criticism.* This is a radical view and difficult to implement, and yet my traditional interaction models, which are discount/punishment based, have side effects that infect a relationship with reactivity and defensiveness.

"In the quantum world, relationships are not just interesting: to many physicists, they are *all* there is to reality." (Wheatley, 1994, Pg. 32). In my world, too, relationships are emerging as the richest, most influential, treasure-laden area of my life. Each one, beginning with my relationship with myself, begins as pure potential. Depending on how I manage my behavior, I can prejudice my life toward heaven or hell.

The Consequences of Discounting

The only counter to discounting is validation, but *even validation does not erase the consequences of discounting.* To the degree that validating experiences outweigh those of discounting, I dare to stay available to interact with others. My feelings of worth give me the courage to risk interchange. I have something of value to offer. But the two experiences are forever separate and immiscible, like oil and water. I retain the scars of discounting.

Validation is a way to nourish my intrinsic drive toward constructive growth. Validating actions are those that encourage responsibility, appreciate competence and risk-taking, demonstrate love and inclusion.

If I, as child, experience a great deal of validation and little or no discounting, validation begets validation; I will develop relating skills that recruit others into relationships with me. People will be drawn to me because the field we

> "Consider great teachers—inspiriting, inspirational, *empowering*, and the opposite: people like Frank [a negative, defensive boss] who is a dispiriting person. Think of the damage done to his subordinates."—Sidney M. Jourard

create together is nourishing and validating. On the other hand, if discounted (abused), I will tend to create a field that repels people. I not only fail to recruit others into relationship, I cannot be recruited. My internal field impels me to deal with others reactively—with discount and abuse. Our prisons and streets are filled with such people.(Kegan, 1982).

My tragedy, when I am a discounter, is that I become trapped in my field. My transmissions too often punish and stimulate reaction, defensiveness and reciprocal punishing. My first needs are for protection and nurturance so I can come out of hiding and become aware of my transmissions. Then I can invent ways to modify them to create a field that recruits rather than repels.

Transmissions With Unexpected Consequences

Below is a sample collection of everyday phrases that seem harmless, yet we have observed that when they are used, the person addressed reacts as though discounted.

That *seems* to make sense, but…
Better than that…
I've heard that before.
To be serious…
No, no. Absolutely not.

Let me challenge that.
I disagree with you.
Let me see if I can pin you down on that.
The trouble with that is…
Wrong.
Not where I come from.
I have a problem with that.
I question that. Let me play devil's advocate.
Not to contradict you, but…
I don't want to insult your intelligence, but…
I don't know about that.
What makes you think that is true?
I happen to know something about this.
That is against my principles.
That is ridiculous.
Get your facts straight.
Where did you get that idea?
Let me tell you how it is done.
What John means…
Let me ask you a question.

> "Perhaps the most effective way to avoid dealing with the proper friction of marriage [or any relationship] is through the establishment of a pattern of dominance and submission."—M. Scott Peck

Relationship

The fundamental assignment of my life is to grow so that I can be and feel meaningful. I do this by making connections to create an aware relationship with myself and with every person, activity, and thing in my life. To the degree my relationships are mutual, empathic, and realistic I will have the best chance for a full measure of effectiveness and satisfaction to more than balance my inevitable share of pain and frustration.

It may seem odd to extend the concept of relationship to include mutuality with an activity like eating, or with something like a house, and what I mean is that activities and things with which I interact provide feedback and the rewards of learning if I pay attention. Paying attention brings the field into awareness and the valence of that field—plus or minus—will influence how much I learn from the interaction.

Earlier we examined perception, connection-making and implication thinking. My courage and clarity in making connections to make meaning, govern the quality of my relationships and the most important relationship in my life is with myself. The underlying purpose of Mind-Free is to help me develop the most informed and creatively effective relationship with myself that is possible. Out of that positive internal field will flow good relationships with my world.

Relationship as an Entity

My relationships are on-going conglomerates of connections between me and another. According to the work of The Stone Center at Wellesley College, each relationship is an entity in the sense that it is coherent and different from the parties to it. The one exception is my relationship with myself. That *is* me and it is a major influence on all the other relationships in my life.

Janet Surrey in "Relationship and Empowerment" (1987, a working paper) and in workshops, emphasizes empathy in relationships. She defines relationship as: "Participating in connection with others…to be present with others in an empathic joining".

> "The growth of the human mind is still high adventure, in many ways the highest adventure on earth."—Norman Cousins

Each relationship persists over time, but loses energy when I do not attend it. When active, it is constantly changing according to changes in me and the other. Each of us influences these changes with the behaviors produced by our fields.

Transmissions are either validating or discounting. I believe there are no neutral actions. Intent may be neutral; perception never is. Actions vary in their impact on the relationship, but the valence is either positive or negative. Due to the preponderance of criticism and punishment over appreciation and approval in my upbringing, I am *hypersensitive* to negative actions—discounts—and they have a far greater impact on a relationship than a validating action. There is a saying, "The half-life of a critical remark is about thirty years." If you and I have had bitter words and actions, that will color my transmissions to you 'bitter', and vice versa.

"Women have gained the insight that events are important and satisfying only if they occur within the context of emotional relatedness."—Jean Baker Miller(1986, Pg.39).

Dissipative Structures

Ilya Prigogine, a Nobel laureate in chemistry, created the concept of dissipative structures. It refers to the ability of a complex system to extract energy out of entropy. Entropy is the law of nature that holds that everything is falling apart, moving toward disorder, dissipating, and running down. Unless there is a systematic force organizing them, their atoms become more and more dispersed and lost in random motion. For example, when a tree dies, it begins to rot and fall apart. When I do not use them, my muscles tend to lose strength.

Prigogine conceived of systems that harness energy that would otherwise be dispersed and lost in random motion as "dissipative structures". For example, the vegetable kingdom collects the random energy of sunlight and through photosynthesis organizes it into living entities.

Csikszentmihalyi (1990) believes that each reversal in my life is negative feedback that produces disorder (entropy) in my mind. Each threatens my self and impairs my functioning. My means for dealing with negativity and

> "All violent feelings produce in us a falseness in all our impressions of external things, which I would generally characterize as the "Pathetic Fallacy"."—John Ruskin

disorder are my dissipative structures: my courage, resilience, perseverance, and my transformational coping and problem-solving ability. To keep these capacities from being dispersed and lost to entropy, I need to use them continually, like muscles. I need to be available for connecting and learning, and I need to be informed about the effect of my transmissions—the words, vocals, and non-verbal actions I send into the field—do they serve entropy or synergy?

Relationships with people, ideas and things provide me with opportunities for connection. The meaning I make of these connections determines whether I grow and actualize my potential or deny and waste it. Relationships are the source of data that I can use either to validate me or plunge me into disorder and despair. This depends largely upon how I develop my relationship with myself to enable me to use *both* adversity *and* good fortune as material for growth.

Differentiation

As mentioned briefly before, this is a concept developed by Dr. Murray Bowen (1985) and it "...assumes the existence of an instinctually rooted life force—*differentiation,* or individuality—in every human being which propels the developing child to grow to be an emotionally separate person, with the ability to think, feel, and act for himself. Also assumed is the existence of an instinctually rooted life force—togetherness—that keeps...a family emotionally connected and operating in reaction to one another." (Kerr, Atlantic Monthly, September,1988, Pg. 37) To the degree I am differentiated I can take responsibility for myself and my development. My part of relationships are governed by where I am on Bowen's scale of differentiation. This scale specifies the characteristics of various levels of differentiation and fusion going from 100—complete differentiation to 0—complete fusion.

Bowen's Scale of Differentiation

0—10 Can't distinguish between feeling and thinking—has given up on relationships. No self. Incapable of being an individual in a group. Complete fusion/enmeshment—no separation from family. At this low level one is so highly sensitized to world around—has lost capacity to feel—is numb. Most energy into "loving" and being "loved". Difficulty maintaining long-term relationships. Much reaction to failing to get love. Hard core schizophrenic. High chronic anxiety—few situations are comfortable.

10—25 Functions almost totally governed by emotional reactions. Reactions range from automatic compliance to extreme oppositional behavior. Live in a feeling world. Skid row alcoholics, drug addicts.

May have been able to function in a favorable relationship, but when it collapsed through divorce or death, they did too.

25—35 Highly suggestible—ideological chameleons. Look outside for religion, culture, law, rule books, authoritarian figures to support their positions. Direct much life energy to being loved, loving. Little left for self-determined goals. Under stress—psychotic incidents, delinquency, intense symptoms. Lacking beliefs of their own, they adopt the prevailing ones. Low levels of *solid-self*...an important component of *basic differentiation.* Reasonable levels of *pseudo-self*, an important component of *functional* differentiation. Feelings soar with praise—dashed by criticism.

35—40 Better than the 0—25, but highly influenced by feelings. Sensitized to disharmony—to the opinion of others—to impression management—to tonals and non-verbals that may mean disapproval and therefore threat.

40—50 Poorly defined self, but a budding capacity to differentiate between feeling and thinking. Higher levels of *solid-self.* Many of the characteristics of those higher on the scale. When under stress develops neurotic symptoms—recovery after stress removed seems complete.

50—60 Well-defined opinions and beliefs on most essential issues. The intellectual system is sufficiently developed to make a few decisions of own. Hesitates to say what he/she believes. Knows there is a better way to live—still follows life course of those below 50.

60—75 The intellect recognizes that discipline is needed to overrule emotional system. Less emotionally reactive. Under sufficient stress, develops fairly severe physical, emotional symptoms, but they are episodic—recovers fast. Less chronic anxiety. Freedom to move back and forth between: a) seeking emotional closeness, b) pursuing independent goals, and derives pleasure from both.

75—85 Free to participate in highly emotional situations—confident can extricate self with logic and reason. When trouble comes, he/she can take over and deal with it to avoid life crisis. More *solid-self*. Individuality better developed.

85—95 Principle oriented and goal directed. Begins in infancy to grow away from parent. Sure of beliefs and convictions—not dogmatic or fixed in thinking. Capable of hearing and evaluating (entertaining) the views of others. Can discard old beliefs in favor of new. Can listen without reacting. Can communicate without antagonizing. Secure within self. Can respect the identity of another without becoming critical or emotionally involved in trying to modify that person's life course. Able to assume total responsibility for self. Sure of his/her responsibility to others, but not overly responsible. Realistically aware of dependence on fellow person—free to enjoy relationships. No 'need' for others that can impair functioning. Others do not feel used by him/her. Tolerant and respectful of differences. Not likely to engage in polarized debates. Realistic in self-assessment. Not status conscious. Expectations realistic. Tolerates intense feelings well—does not act automatically to alleviate. Chronic anxiety very low. Tolerates high anxiety well. Can adapt and/or self-soothe under most stress.

95—100 Person has fully resolved the emotional attachment to family. Emotional maturity. Can be an individual in the group. Responsible for self. Neither fosters nor participates in the irresponsibility of others. Differentiates clearly between feeling process and thinking process.

Relationship With Self

As I focus on my relationship with myself I have been impressed with how poorly I have devised my behavior for dealing with negativity in my environment. I have limited control over my external environment, but I *am* in charge of what goes on inside of me, even if I can't always control

> "Language nourishes or starves whatever grows between two people…if you can learn how to talk, you can be happy."—Miller, Wakman, et al.

all of my feelings. In that light, it makes little sense that I am my own most severe critic. All too often I am the target of my own negativity. In other words, I cooperate with the forces that damage me and I tend to downplay or ignore evidence of my own effectiveness. It is clearly important that I modify my strategies for dealing with myself. It also becomes important to be aware of the effects on me of destructive fields between me and others.

The *nourishment* of a relationship depends upon its mutuality. This, in turn, depends upon empathy. Empathy defines where the relationship will fall on the spectrum from controlling to mutual.

Relationship

Controlling **Mutual**

Dominance <——————————>Equality/mutuality
low <——Degree of empathy——> high

The characteristics of the two ends of this spectrum suggest the quality of relationship possible depending on where, along the spectrum, I locate myself and the other.

Dominance

- Power exerted over the minds or behavior of others
- Control
- In competition with
- Defensive
- High value on knowing
- Low tolerance of:
  —Unknown
  —Difference
  —Deviations from plan
  —Mistakes
  —Risk
- Faith in authority and structure
- Win/lose orientation
- Poor listener
- Alert for threat to position

Intimacy
Equality/Mutuality

- Collaboration/Cooperation
- Availability/Openness
- High value on learning
- Good listener
- High tolerance for:
  —Differences
  —Ambiguity/Uncertainty
  —Risk
- Connection-maker
- Improviser
- Lives trial and error/trial and success

- Win/win orientation
- Good listener

Mutuality and Relationship

"The capacity to engage in an open, mutually empathic relational process rests on [keeping defensiveness low] and openness to be responsive and moved by the thoughts, perceptions, and feelings of the other person. Each feels she/he has an impact on the other and on the flow of the interaction. Each feels heard and responded to—validated. Each experiences being through 'learning' [achieving increased awareness and understanding]" (Rogers, *Empathic: An Unappreciated Way of Being,* The Counseling Psychologist, 5, (No.2) pg 2-10)

Carl Rogers describes interacting as opposed to reacting and out of this capability comes relationships that are growth oriented. Janet Surrey in a seminar in 1991 also describes mutuality as communication between two people in which the transmissions of "A"contain something of "B" and "B's" answering transmission contains something of "A".

Participants in such an empathic relationship gain better connections with themselves and each other, as each risks self-disclosure and openness to be influenced.

The field of my early relationships with my parents and sister and brothers have a critical influence on my ability to relate in adulthood. Mother's generosity and appreciation can set me on a course that will enrich all future relationships. Emotional or physical abuse, even when

> "...bad is entropy—disorder, confusion, waste of energy, the inability to do work and achieve goals; good is negative entropy...harmony, predictability, purposeful activity that leads to satisfying one's desires."—Csikszentmihalyi

slight, can steer me toward defensiveness and an endless competition for the false safety of domination and control.

Relationship and Connection

Growth is about making connections to create relationships between me and people and concepts. It is how I make meaning and comprehend complexity. It is through this activity that I experience <u>be</u>ing—and if it works just right, I experience bliss—the rapture of <u>be</u>ing. The bliss of falling in love is a wonderful example of a relationship where nearly all the transmissions are strongly validating.

Connection-making is the source of validation and bliss, as well as discounts and misery. Every circumstance and action, usually a discount of some sort, that blocks connection-making leads away from <u>be</u>ing. I think of such acts as *anti-<u>be</u>ing, anti-bliss, anti-aliveness, anti-love.*

In fact, <u>*anything*</u> that inhibits or discourages connection-making is destructive to me. Mistaken connections (meaning) are inevitable and are not bad or punishable. They simply tend to obscure reality. The well-trained connection maker is constantly testing to see whether past connections (knowledge) are holding up. She is always prepared to modify or abandon them if necessary.

We saw in the section on Empathy that as a man, I am somewhat handicapped because of the early breaking away from mutually empathic relating to my mother. My focus shifts to independence, autonomy, and competition. The practice of competition leads toward concealing of any weakness and maintaining the appearance of invulnerability. It also leads to a certain unwillingness to admit mistakes and modify knowledge.

Relationship and Presentation of Self

Eighty percent or so of my energy can go into maintaining a facade. As Peck observes, "…what happens when we behave invulnerably, when we gird ourselves with psychological defenses and pretend that we are cool cats who have got it all together, rugged individuals who seem to be in complete control of our lives?

> "…the advance of civilization has consisted in creating small, protected areas of existence where competition and danger are minimized, where we can temporarily feel safe and relax our guard."—Csikszentmihalyi

"What happens is the other people gird themselves with *their* psychological defenses and pretend that they too are cool cats who have got it all together…"(Peck 1987, Pg. 217)

"As long as we look out at each other only through the masks of our composure, we are looking through hard eyes. But as masks drop and we see the suffering and courage and brokenness and deeper dignity underneath, we truly start to respect each other as fellow human beings." (Peck 1987, Pg. 69)

The goal in Mind-Free is to make each learning experience a rewarding relationship experience as well: people with both strengths and weaknesses struggling to help themselves and each other sample the behaviors that give surcease to loneliness and isolation. To do that I need to present my true self, undefended. Otherwise I attempt to make connections to my facade—a process with little satisfaction.

I also need to recognize and accept my personal limitations and failures openly before I can cope with them. For example, Kathleen and I were working with a group of men in their 50's and 60's who had all been laid off in the great downsizing of the 1990's. As each told his story, it seemed that each had been victim of being reorganized out of a job through no fault of his own. When asked to search for any personal responsibility, all declared themselves blameless. There is no doubt that most of these men *had* been caught up in events over which they had no control, yet these were men who had been in positions of considerable power. Until each could search his past and own responsibility for some part of what had happened, he was immobilized in a self-destructive place, incapable of first, forgiving himself, and then analyzing every aspect to see what he could learn from it. Denial is the great isolator.

When I have the courage to understand and cope with the anxiety of admitting failure (if I admit flaws I may be unlovable and may be rejected and abandoned) I have the basis for the most powerful forms of psychological learning. The act of avoidance (denying, blaming others) precludes my learning. Risk is the central issue in this self-disclosure and unless I summon up the courage to take that

> "The only criterion we have for what the…adult is learning or has learned is interaction. Can the person interact, or is his/her life one long chain of reactions to or acts of aggression against?"—J. C. Pearce

risk, I not only fail to learn, I undermine my self-respect by the act of the avoidance itself.

Relationship and the Tacit Self

In person to person communication I know there are three channels for transmitting: words, vocals (tones, emphasis, hesitations), and non-verbal actions(expressions, gestures, moves). Experiments tell us that words and vocals transmit about 50% of the meaning and non-verbals, 50% (Mehrabian, 1968) But in most human intercourse, there is a body of meaning transmitted which it is not possible to describe. It is information conveyed without speech, or clear reference. A shrug of the shoulders or raised eyebrows or eyes rolling are examples of the more obvious non-verbal element of this type of transmission. Another type that is even more difficult to indicate is information transmitted by body movements, muscle tension, and stance. These signals are so intimately connected to my inner beliefs, superstitions, and convictions that I cannot dissemble. These subtle signals are so revealing of character, aptitudes, attitudes, and inclinations that a comprehensive personality report can be derived from their study. (Lamb, 1975). Taken all together these transmissions make up a field.

In my early years, when I am totally dependent, I become skilled at understanding fields. As an infant of six months I can pick up anxiety as soon as I hear or see my anxious mother. (Sullivan, 1953, Pg. 9)

As I am socialized, I tend to suppress my direct awareness of these more subtle transmissions, yet I continue to be influenced by them. I believe I selectively ignore messages in order to reduce confusion because the tacit signals of my parents are often at odds with what is going on.

Relationship and Isolation

A narcissist is so focused on himself that he is in a state of spiritual isolation. To the degree I am unable or unwilling to make connections to others and to experience empathy and mutuality, I am estranged and alienated from the source of life's greatest satisfactions: relationship with community and my fellow human beings. To the extent my transmissions to another contain some empathy for the other and vice versa, there is mutuality and relationship.

> "The giant steps forward in the community building process are taken by those individuals of such courage that they are able to risk speaking at a level of vulnerability and authenticity at which no one in the group has spoken before."—M. Scott Peck

I have concluded from observations of thousands of interactions in groups we were studying, and from my own experience, that most of us approach new relationships fearing the worst. Even participating in a group discussion carries with it some apprehension that I will be rejected or made to feel inferior in some way. Knowing this, if I wish to develop mutual and empowering relationships with others, I will make kindness an habitual ingredient of every transmission.

Relationship and Chaos

Relationships like the weather, are influenced by a number of variables. In the weather, most of the variables are unstable, so that a small change in one *can* have a domino effect and create a large change over time—but then again, it *may* not.

Similarly, in the emerging science of chaos there is a phenomenon known as "the butterfly effect". As in: a butterfly stirring the air in Tokyo today may cause a thunderstorm in New York in a month. The butterfly effect has a scientific name: sensitive dependence on initial conditions. Wherever there is a sensitive dependence on initial conditions, a small change can create non-linear effects.

A relationship has a lot in common with the butterfly effect. It has a certain order and predictability, but *not necessarily.* Every relationship has a drift. When the total weight of the inputs is positive, the relationship drifts toward intimacy and satisfaction. The relationship is stable and can weather some reverses—some negative inputs.

When the total weight is negative; when the small daily inputs tend to be discounts, the relationship is unstable and one more small toxic input, when the initial condition is sensitive, can create a large change.

Relating, if we follow the quantum model, is not only my connection to the world and what is in it, the fields we generate together is what brings me into being. Thus my relating skills, particularly my relationship with myself, are a critical determinant of how well I will manage my life to be and feel meaningful.

> "For most people, the starting point is an orientation toward life that I call *reactive responsive.*"—Robert Fritz

Reactive Strategies

Why do I sometimes behave in ways that are destructive to myself—or fail to act to achieve some goal I am pursuing. For example,I am determined to lose some weight, yet I take a second helping of potatoes—or a first helping of chocolate sauce! I know I am going against internal policy, but I do it anyway and feel disgusted with myself. I may even bawl myself out; call myself names and punish myself.

Robert Fritz would say that my problem is that I have not been clear with myself about what I really want, and am not keeping myself aware of my impulsive reactions and their consequences. I believe these impulsive actions signal strategies—patterns of action I have devised to achieve something. The question is, what are these obviously counterproductive strategies attempting to achieve?

We have seen that my amygdala is sensitized by over-control. I rebel against accepting and conforming to these *directives* from an outside authority.

I know from my study of individuals in groups that criticism and comments that can be interpreted as critical are nearly *always* perceived by the target person as discounts. Authoritarian behavior—ordering, demanding, punishing—triggers anxiety about my meaningfulness. I react with fight, freeze or flight energy.

Reactive strategies are emotional decisions that often lead to patterns of resistance or rebellion to protect my *feelings* of autonomy and competence. These strategies are often subtle to avoid the certain punishment that comes with outright rebellion. Further, socialization is a complex activity. Some of it is done with open approval and praise, other parts are enforced by subtle non-verbal signals, and a very great deal of it is done by transmissions that are out of the awareness of both parent and child.

> "If your emotions become the dominant factor in your life, the power in your life becomes "how I happen to feel," not "what do I truly want."—Robert Fritz

Given the close-coupled nature of the parent child relationship, the way a child is tuned in to a parent, and the often conflicted feelings of the parent—exasperation, love, exhaustion, anger, and so on—it is natural that I absorb confused impressions—most of my reaction strategies are *felt out,* not clearly *thought* out.

Adding to the problem is the fact that a significant number of my reactive strategies operate out of my awareness. I am not aware that I am heaping chocolate sauce on my low calorie frozen yogurt because I am rebelling against the authoritarian voice in my head directing me, "You *should not* have any chocolate sauce, fatty!" and I am attending to the *feeling* "I feel like treating myself to some chocolate sauce" and responding to an unconscious urge, “I will show you, authoritarian voice, who is boss here”.

I have been taught that to be an effective person I need to develop will-power and the discipline to overcome those feelings of wanting chocolate sauce or acting in other self-destructive ways.

The trouble is that will power and self-discipline are intellectual, neocortical decisions. Reactive strategies are emotional, limbic decisions, and not very responsive to intellectual directives. The way to make them reliable is to make my reactive strategies visible in all their many manifestations. This will help me to discover the motives behind them and rethink and ‘*refeel*’ their usefulness to the adult me.

Split Screen Visioning

This is an operating practice that gives me a clear map of what is going on when I am attempting to achieve a result I want. The first step is to imagine a television or movie screen. On the screen I put a detailed image of what I want, and how I will feel when I achieve it. Continuing with the example of my weight problem, I image myself on the screen. I am lean. My tummy is flat, my chest and arms are muscular. I look the way I want to look. I imagine how I will feel then. That is my vision in living color, complete with accompanying feelings.

Now, I split the screen. On the blank part—for me it is on the right—I put an image of my present reality: an accurate picture of how I look right now. My tummy sticks out. I am not muscular and I have a layer of fat. I focus on how that feels. When I shift my attention back and forth between these images it becomes crystal clear what actions I need to take to make my current reality become identical to my vision—what I believe I want.

> "The shift of dominance from a life of *responding to what occurs* to a life of *creating what will be* invites us to focus on vision and new possibilities."—Robert Fritz

Having established my vision and my current reality I have activated a powerful motivator: imaging with feelings. I believe that all signals for action originate as images. Words and phrases are a modern rationalization and very handy for thinking, but when it comes to feelings, words are a foreign language to my limbic emotions. I need graphic images plus feelings to stir the needed emotional cooperation.

At dinner the bowl of frozen yogurt is passed to me. I help myself to three heaping spoonfuls. Reluctantly I light up my split screen. There I am in my vision, lean and excellent. It feels good. My current reality shows me fat with a tummy that sticks out, and I am helping myself to three spoonfuls of frozen yogurt. It feels bad.

I observe that my actions are inconsistent with both my intellectual *and* my emotional vision. I *do not scold or punish myself, I simply bring into my awareness this action that reveals a part of my reactive strategy. What I am doing gives me a bad feeling.*

When the chocolate sauce comes my way, I heap some on my frozen yogurt and again I light up my screen. No punishment, but that bad feeling is reinforced. According to Michael Pearlman, a psychiatrist who teaches split screen visioning as a means of personal change, each of us can profitably have thirteen split screens of things we want to accomplish. The critical step is to clearly establish the *feelings* that go with accomplishing, and those that go with failing to accomplish.

As I convert a current reality into a realization of a vision, I drop that and add another goal. These goals do not have to be earthshaking, they are simply things I want to accomplish to help me be and feel more meaningful.

As I systematically reinforce intellectual decisions with an emotional component, I greatly increase the probability of success.

As I become familiar with the myriad destructive maneuvers of my reactive strategies that work against my getting what I want, I become more and more able to act effectively in my own behalf.

It is of critical importance that I do not punish myself. If I punish, I will tend to stop lighting up my screen. Also my voice of punishment is an unconscious activator of my reactive strategies. It is as though that voice of punishment is an outside authority and awakens all the old inappropriate impulses to rebel, get even, and preserve my self.

> *"The clearer you are that as creator you simply make things up, the freer and more able you will be to make up results consistent with [your heart's desire]"* (Robert Fritz, 1984)

> "...intimacy may be nothing less than an avenue to an emotionally rich life."—Stephen B. Levine

Intimacy

Intimacy is the ingredient in a relationship that can take it from the level of a good and rewarding experience to an exhilarating, ever fresh, synergistic adventure. More than anything else, moving from the first level to the second requires that I get in touch with and nourish my *courage* to cope with the many faces of anxiety. It is no small matter to exercise the courage to connect. The visceral power of my fear that another will discover the true me, find it wanting and reject me, keeps me enslaved to putting up a front I believe will be acceptable.

Recently I spent five mornings in an experiential seminar on group therapy. At one point on the final day, there was a prolonged silence. The former inclinations to disclose seemed to have disappeared. As the silence continued, my anxiety increased. I became more and more panic-stricken. Part of me wanted to tell the group more about myself; part wanted to stay safely hidden. I was unsure which part would prevail, but as the silence lengthened I was moving toward self-disclosure. To my great relief, someone else broke the silence. Later, reflecting on my feelings, I realized that I was in the grip of the fear of being found out to be weak and unworthy, and at the same time wanting to reveal my true self in the hope that I would be acceptable. As I revisited those feelings, it seemed that they derive their enormous power from the struggle between fear of discovering that my low self-regard is accurate, and longing to be *known*—to stand revealed before another so I can better know the truth about myself.

The Path to Intimacy

Dr. Stephen Levine tells me that intimacy begins with my ability to share my inner experiences with another. This capacity depends on three separate skills: 1) my *knowing* what I am feeling and thinking (see Self-focus), 2) the ability to put my thoughts, feelings, and ideas into words, and 3) having the courage and willingness to say it to another.(1991, Pg. 259). Each of these skills is important to my emotional health, growth and development and one of the objectives of the Mind-Free program is to enlarge my capability in all three. I find it particularly useful to recognize courage as a skill.

> "We are dependent on interaction with other people to expand our knowledge of ourselves and the surrounding world..."—David Snarch

The Charmed Circle of Intimacy

As I move from infancy and enmeshment with my mother, toward differentiation and autonomy, my principal task is to make my *self.* I often hear the expression "I want to find myself" and "I am discovering myself". Kathleen has made it clear that a more accurate description is "I am making myself".

It has been helpful to me to think of this as a trial and error/trial and success process.. Unfortunately, in my early years the feedback I get from important others is as likely to be destructive to this process as it is to be helpful, not because of bad intentions of others, but rather because of their lack of appreciation of the importance of trial and error connection-making as the critical step in thinking-to-learn. As I trial and error in thinking, the reactions of parents and others to error convinces me that any error is unacceptable—which makes trial and erroring unacceptable. This cripples my effectiveness. Cripples may seem an extreme word to use, and yet when I consider that informed scientists believe that we use only a tiny fraction (between 2% and 10%) of our capacity, cripples seems accurate.

The normal mistakes of trial and error/trial and success or successive approximation, become frightening. This is reinforced by my confusion about my parents' standards. I believe they require perfection and any lapse on my part sends my anxiety soaring. These misunderstandings can lead to excessive caution in connection-making, or even avoidance when confused and uncertain.

Like so many of the lessons learned in infancy and childhood, the dangers of rejection and abandonment need to be revisited, clarified, and modified if I am to develop my full potential. For example, because rejection is so threatening in childhood, I have an unreasoning fear that it I will be rejected for *any* mistake, any failure.

Intimacy is the royal road to remaking myself. It is in intimate exchanges that I can observe me, and my old fears and decisions, from the perspective of another. I am free to modify. As I shape myself and become my unique self, I am also more and more able to be intimate. "Without the

> "...psychological intimacy's greatest potential is its capacity to enhance psychological functioning."—Stephen B. Levine

concept of self, there is not the possibility of intimacy since the ability to maintain the distinction of an "I" in the context of "you" is fundamental."(Schnarch, 1991, Pg. 111)

Sexuality, Secrets, and Practical IntimacyTM

In all cultures, intimacy has connotations of sexuality and secrets so intensely personal that they can be shared only with a lover. When I am seeking intimacy in a Mind-Free sense, I am aiming at a different level of self-disclosure that is not sexual, though it *is* personal. I call it *practical intimacy.*

Practical intimacy is defined earlier, in Empathy, as a state of mind and emotion in which it is possible for me to be unrehearsed and spontaneous—undefended and non-competitive. I am free to expose my weaknesses and failures, not without anxiety, but with assurance that I will be heard with empathy. It differs from conventional intimacy in that I do not disclose sensual experiences. My purpose in seeking practical intimacy is twofold: to give me opportunities to augment my courage in bearable steps; and to expose for examination, experiences that help me modify my dominant assumption that self-disclosure leads to rejection and ultimate abandonment.

As long as this old, childhood belief controls me, my habitual posture will be defensive. I will employ all my strategies to protect myself against the fatality of rejection and abandonment that I imagined long ago. Intimacy will be impossible.

Another of the drawbacks of our present culture of punishment and criticism is that it militates against intimacy between parents and children. As a child eager to measure up to my parents' expectations, I felt it necessary for me to spend more and more energy protecting myself. I avoided situations and even *thoughts* that might lead to disapproval and punishment. This pursuit of safety resulted in censorship and severely restricted my availability for connection-making. Modifying that belief opens connection-making opportunities.

Many parents make it a practice to criticize and punish their children as a way to teach them the proper way to act. In addition to making the child overcautious, as suggested above, this can lead to the belief that I am basically unacceptable. For many years I suffered the misconception

> "…events in the child's life that caused separation…and a mental environment which gave the child a feeling that normal love and affection was lacking, did far more to damage growth than did disease, and was more serious than all other factors combined…"—G. Binning

that if a person really got to know me, he would not like me. It seemed best to guard against being known. It took me a long time to realize that some people would like me and some would not. Keeping my guard up cut me off from those who would be my friends.

Intimacy and Trust

Trust is defined as a feeling of assured reliance on some person or thing—a confident dependence. Usually, my attention is focused on someone else who I am counting on to be trustworthy. This is always uncertain. I believe it is important to my capacity to be intimate that I develop my capacity to trust myself. Self-trust hinges on my *conviction* of being OK, even if rejected by others. This is not a simple matter of reason—of course I will survive rejection, says my adult self. However, deep inside me there is a left-over, unresolved *emotional* certainty that, if abandoned, I will die. The force of this underlying fear has an astonishing power to weaken my courage to risk. It not only cripples my ability to be intimate, it continually affects my openness to making connections of any kind. This is the well-spring of my anxiety. The urgency of that anxiety has resulted in its developing many faces to better control me in a variety of situations: shyness, boredom, anger, impatience, blanking out in the face of confusion—to name a few of the ways my anxiety attempts to curtail thinking and "protect" me from connecting.

This fear has an honest foundation. Every infant experiences abandonment through separations from his mother. My mother knows these separations are temporary, but I, as the infant, do not. I can get some understanding of the impact of these separation experiences by examining the effect of long separations on infants.

Bowlby demonstrated that when an infant is separated from its mother and is institutionalized, it loses the capacity for normal interactions and connections. "The dramatic and tragic changes in behavior and feeling which follow separation of the young child from his mother…are in fact available for all to see…" (1951, Pg. 22)

In spite of adequate food and care, the infant is severely retarded. He or she becomes vulnerable to infection and sickness and is listless and unresponsive. Studies of such

> "Differentiation is what permits an individual to participate in a system—without being captured by it."—David Schnarch

children in later life show permanent damage to their ability to interact.

As an infant I am totally dependent on others for survival and it is necessary for me to look to others for satisfaction and safety. But as I develop, I shift my dependence toward myself, and it is extremely difficult to learn that my feelings of life-threatening peril, aroused by rejection, can only be cured by learning to trust myself to my own ability to self-soothe and self-validate. Repeated experiences of risking, together with conscious focus on my being OK in spite of mistakes and rejection, help develop the critical ability to trust in myself. Once established, my self-trust frees me to be open to more opportunities to connect.

Intimacy and Self-Acceptance

Intimacy allows me to explore myself in relationship with others and to test my acceptability. It seems a fact of life that, as I get to know myself through intimate relationships, I am more and more able to deal with the formerly hidden, shameful elements and accept myself.

Intimacy then becomes the training and maintenance system for developing a satisfying self.

> "And it seems to be another fact that no man or woman can come to know him/her self except as the outcome of disclosing self to another person."—Sidney Jourard

Intimacy, Shame, and Self-Disclosure

One of the facilitating procedures of Mind-Free® is to create a relationship of Practical Intimacy to distinguish it from the sensual intimacy I think of as something that happens only between lovers. My goal in Mind-Free relationships is to establish *psychological intimacy* between me and other(s).."[This] is an elusive and transient state of grace that initially creates great private excitement…When this form of intimacy is maintained, a long term quieting of the inner self occurs."(Levine,1991, Pg. 259)

As discussed earlier, this state of grace "…begins with one person's ability to share her or his inner experiences with another. "(Ibid.) "…all participants in [this] relationship interact in ways that build connection and enhance everyone's personal power." (Surrey 1987) This non-hierarchical model of learning/teaching and growth contrasts with the traditional vertical or hierarchical power-over model and the outcome in terms of benefits to those involved is astonishingly different.

During the *uncivil* process of learning to be civilized, we absorb a punishing number of impressions of wrongness and shame from both adults and peers. As a result, "An unconscious feeling of unworthiness often crystallizes around some hectoring, negative view of one's self:.." Such shame-filled beliefs about the self have a peculiar relationship to the truth. They may be totally false…or they may have an element of truth in them…"(Karen, 1992, pg. 42) The problem comes when the feelings of shame are repressed.

> We have observed "the therapeutic effect of encouraging a person to *be.* To think and relive an experience without inviting disapproval or counter reaction."—Sidney Jourard

For many, the experience of self-disclosure like that offered by Mind-Free, can be critically useful because most of us, if not all, are suffering from shame about some aspect of ourselves.

This hidden shame "can stalk one's being, inflicting an unconscious self-loathing…Unacknowledged shame is a pathogen. It kills…it seems to block creative avenues. It *is* crippling, because it contains not just the derisive accusation that one is a wimp,…but the further implication that one is at core a defective being, fundamentally unlovable and unworthy of membership in the human community. It is the self regarding the self with the withering and unforgiving eye of contempt. And most people are unable to face it. It is too annihilating." (Karen 1992)

Mind-Free is ambitious in aiming to be a catalyst with such a grave and intimate problem, yet therapist participants suggest that this particular mix of creativity, self-disclosure, and wholehearted listening-to-connect creates a field that is surprisingly effective in dealing with shame. The rewards for success are great.

Part 5—Meaning and Learning

> "Autonomous self-acceptance develops from the courageous exploration of self-doubts."—David Schnarch

Meaning-Making

All of us are wired to make connections. Connecting to make meaning is one of my fundamental needs. According to psychologist William Perry, "What an organism does is organize; and what a human organism organizes is meaning. The activity of being a person is the activity of meaning making." (Kegan, 1982, Pg.11). For example, my granddaughter, Marjorie, is looking at the flash of a lighthouse in Gloucester harbor, "That is to warn ships that there is a dangerous rock there," I say.

"I know," she says comfortably, "like police car lights." She has created meaning for herself by connecting the new flashing light with something in her experience.

Meaning-making is creating/inventing sense out of confusion, inventing answers to questions, inventing solutions to problems. As Aldous Huxley notes, "Experience is not what happens to you. It's what you *do* with what happens to you." (Ibid. Pg. 11)

The essence of meaning-making is that effort I make to put the perceived stimulus (the flashing lighthouse) together with a known in my knowledge bank(flashing police car lights) to move me toward understanding. I believe that nature rewards the initial act of connecting with a tiny thrill of joy.

This seems clear and obvious and yet it somehow does not capture the overriding importance of meaning-making skills to my effectiveness and my well-being. I was lulled into complacency by my parents and other teachers. I slowly began to believe that the important skill to develop was that of *learning from them*; depending on them to make sense *for* me. My policy, when confronted with something that confused me, if I could not immediately make sense of it, was either to ask for help, or stop thinking about it. Not instantly knowing, being in a state of confusion raised my anxiety. It became undesirable, inferior, and to be avoided.

I believed that they, or *someone* could and would teach me the meaning of everything I needed to know, and while they did teach me a great deal, they never directly taught me connection-making and meaning-making. In fact, many of

> "You are talking about a search for the meaning of life?" asked Bill Moyers of Joseph Campbell. "No, no, no," he said. "For the *experience* of being alive."—*The Power of Myth.*

the thinking practices I learned ("if you don't know the right answer, don't…") prejudiced me against the very skills I need to be an expert meaning-maker. In other words, I became prejudiced against being a person.

Confronted with my observation of how, as I grew into youth, adolescence and adulthood, I lost much of my capacity for joy, I connect that to my training in *not making a connection unless I am certain it is precisely correct.* I am haunted by my anxiety, by my fear of making a mistake and being…what? Rejected? Ostracized? Abandoned?

In spite of this, like most other children I gradually developed an ability to "figure it out". Now, after many years of study of the invention process, I know there are effective procedures for inventing sense out of confusion. I could have learned these long ago and been far more effective in coping with the tasks of my life. And even now, I struggle with anxiety fueled by my fear of making a mistake.

If I could do it over, I would say to Marjorie, "What do you think about that tower with the flashing light?" and I would appreciate *whatever* connections she made, before sharing what *I* thought about that flashing light.

Meaning-Making and Validation

I am aware that Validation Deficit Syndrome has me testing every transaction to see whether it will validate or invalidate me and this creates a paradox. Making meaning out of confusion and uncertainty is a potent source of validation, yet my anxiety impels me to be cautious about leaping to a connection for fear it will be a mistake and will *invalidate* me. It might help me deal with this immobilizing phenomenon if I knew how it develops.

As an infant, I discover the fundamental nourishment of tenderness and love (appreciation of *me* transmitted by words, vocals, and non-verbal actions). It creates in me an awareness that I not only exist, I am meaningful. This is critical to my well-being. I also learn that love can be withheld, and I feel anxiety. To withhold appreciation (recognition, acknowledgment of worth—validation) is to deny that I have meaning. I experience the absence of appreciation (and unfortunately *attention* may equate, for

> "...greater than the inequalities of social class or achievement test scores is the unequal capacity of students to interest others in them—a phenomenon not reducible to social class or intelligence, and which seems to be the more powerful determinate of future thriving."—Robert Kegan

me, with appreciation) as a statement that I do not exist for Mother. It is literally annihilating and poses a terrifying threat to me as an infant. Life is not worth living if I am abandoned. When I am not lovingly appreciated, I will fail to thrive and may even die. We have discussed the catastrophic effects of abandonment (Bowlby, 1982).

Behavior to get validation and avoid abandonment become a high priority, second only to eating. As I trial and error to develop those strategies, anything that reduces appreciation and results in invalidation is an error—a mistake. It is easy to understand why errors and mistakes of any kind can seem so dangerous. My anxiety gradient is keyed to my foresight function to keep on guard. To complicate matters further, much of my training as I grow up, reinforces my fear of error and mistakes. If not reexamined and constantly taken into account, this terror of mistakes—terror of invalidation—will impair my perceptive and meaning-making abilities throughout my life.

Self-validation

At first, I am totally dependent on my parents for validation. I quickly learn that I get feelings of joy from my own accomplishments. Nearly every new physical and mental connection-to-increase-competence and create meaning is a tiny jolt of bliss. I discover the rewards of appreciating myself, of self-validation. The early physical developments, such as learning to walk, usually get validated by others as well. My parents feel no need to criticize or correct my mistakes as I collapse and fall, on my way to becoming a skilled walker. They can *see* that while the *goal* is walking, the *process* requires trial and error.

When I begin to talk, to reflect my thinking in speech, a whole new dynamic emerges. Because my parents cannot *see* my process—that I create meaning by trial connections—some of which will be mistaken, the error part of my process is less acceptable. Parents and teachers feel compelled to deny the value or otherwise punish errors because they cannot *see* the complete cycle of connecting-to-arrive-at-meaning. I use the word punish because, as we saw in Discount/Revenge, these criticizing actions are almost always experienced as discounts and are painful.

> "Bliss is the rapture of being."—Joseph Campbell

The Repression of *Be*ing

The inadvertent discouragement of my process for creating meaning has serious consequences. Not only do I lose much of the *intrinsic* bliss I felt in making connections and learning, I tend to repress my natural skills in trial and error discovery; I lose faith in myself and in my capacity to self-validate, and I subscribe to *immaculate knowing*—the myth that an intelligent person learns without going through the messy trial and error process. Further, I become more dependent on others for validation—for reassurance that I am meaningful.

In those early developmental years I struggle in this fateful battle between my drive to experience the joy of connecting-to-create-meaning, and my need for the love and approval of my parents, teachers and other important people. My *interpretation* of their correction of my errors is that I must not make errors in my thinking. I become inclined to deny error; to repress that part of my process that is messy and error-prone; that feels unacceptable to the outside world. In slow stages my real trial-and-erroring explorer and discoverer becomes hidden from others, and, sadly, hidden from me. Much energy goes into protecting myself from error and the appearance of error.

Two Paths to Regain Myself

The decision to go into hiding is itself made through trial and error. In early childhood it is a joy to share all my thoughts and feelings, and through the sharing, learn more about them. I gradually learn to be more self-contained to avoid the pain of disapproval. My self-protective secrecy is well-established by the time I am seven or eight. Harry Stack Sullivan, the great psychiatrist (1953), speaks of the importance of chumship, the close friendship with one of the same sex that occurs at about ten or eleven. I rediscovered self-disclosure as a learning practice. Then in adolescence I again retreat into self-concealment.

Falling in love and the intimate disclosures that are then possible, is another opportunity for learning about myself and another. Such intimacy is limited to that loving relationship, and all too often I find that I do not dare to continue full self-disclosure for fear of alienating my partner.

> "All people need help in development at all stages, but it is made to appear as if only children do."—Jean Baker Miller

In Mind-Free I have the opportunity to experiment again with self-disclosure. As I screw up my courage to disclose to others some of the shameful experiences of my past, I increase my courage and my tolerance. This has a direct effect on my ability to disclose *to myself* many limiting influences that I have repressed. When they are brought into my awareness I am in a position to deal with them. This is the first path to access more of my resources.

The second path lies in bringing into clear awareness, my perceiving and connection-making process, and whenever I engage it, to consciously applaud myself. Here is an example of how I wish to treat myself: my grandson, three-and-a-half year old Max, is visiting the Boston Aquarium with his mother. The display tank is four stories tall and spectators walk down a ramp to see the fish at different levels. Among the fish is something new to Max. It is a scuba diver swimming among the fish. Max is confused by a man under water with the fish. He notes the tank on the man's back and remembers a similar tank he had seen the summer before at my house. He had wanted to play with it and I had explained that it was used to squirt foam on fires to put them out. He made a trial connection. The man is a fireman!

Much depends upon how Max's discovery is treated. What he has done is a daring and admirable job of creating meaning out of confusion. His storehouse of possible connections for scuba divers is limited so his idea is quite approximate. It would be easy, and in fact, considered constructive for a knowing adult to laugh and say, "No, no, Max, that is not a fireman. What gave you that crazy idea? (but not pause for Max to answer) That is called a scuba diver, and…etc."

Max's ability to observe, feel confusion, search in his experience bank, retrieve a possibility and connect to make an idea that eliminates the uncomfortable lack of meaning, can do a lot for Max. It builds his feelings of competence, independence, and self-worth. It is a joyful validation. If he is appreciated for this, it will build his *speculative confidence*—strengthen his courage to continue to create meaning out of confusion. If he is punished, all these benefits are canceled out; he will feel devalidated and become more and more anxious cautious about future attempts to create meaning. He will lose his wonderful speculative confidence.

> "Any experimentalist looks for quantities that remain the same, or quantities that are zero. But that means disregarding bits of messiness that interfere with a neat picture." "...the disorderly behavior of simple systems acted as a creative process."—Thomas S. Khun

In the event, Max's mother asked him how he had figured out "fireman", genuinely appreciated his accomplishment, and went on to tell about firemen's breathing tanks for smoke-filled rooms, and the use of air tanks for scuba diving. This is how I would like to treat myself when I take risks to create new meaning.

The Meaning-Making Process

My ability to create meaning is the essential ingredient in my belief in my own competence; basic to my experience of *be*ing, it is critical for my own good that I understand and nurture this ability in myself. It is not ever easy because of my anxious prejudice about order and rightness. Meaning-making is not a smooth process. Here, again, is the step-by-step definition of meaning-making:

1) Perceived or sensed ignorance——> 2) Confusion or chaos——> 3) Semi-patterns——> 4) Search of knowledge bank for connection-making possibilities——> 5) Approximate trial connection (beginning idea, hypothesis/guess)——> 6) Testing against reality——> 7)

Modifications——> 8) Precise meaning (always subject to further testing and modification).

Optimism and Meaning-Making

I approach the world and meaning-making with one of two basic mind sets: optimism or pessimism. As an optimist, I operate out of an orientation of hope rather than despair. I believe that reality is not against me and I interpret actions and happenings hopefully. I create different, more hopeful meaning out of circumstances than does a pessimist.

As an optimist, I believe that the problems I encounter can be solved and this tends to create a self-fulfilling prophecy. I solve problems that pessimists do not—and I have a lot more fun in the process. Several years ago I interviewed some of the people who worked for Walt Disney. He emerged as a *determined* optimist. No matter

> "Habits of thinking need not be forever. One of the most significant findings in psychology in the last twenty years is that individuals can choose the way they think."—Martin E. P. Seligman

how difficult the goal, Walt believed he could attain it. "We will invent a way," he always insisted. Walt exuded confidence that the people who worked with him could rise to any challenge—he repeatedly made it clear that while *he* might not be able to do it, they *could*—and he would recognize it when they were there. He was a fanatic about being optimistic and he refused to suffer pessimists. I was told that whenever a person working with Walt said that something could not be done, he or she was not there the next day.

Even optimists get into circumstances where the realistic outlook is grim. In such a situation I focus on inventing my way out of it. I improvise. In 1964, when the Surgeon General announced that research demonstrated that cigarettes were poison, I struggled to stop smoking. As an aid, I used snuff and it helped me to shake the smoking habit.

My business was in serious trouble at that time, and if I had been a pessimist, I would have been looking for a job. As it was, I became excited about he possibility of making a "safe" cigarette using snuff as a cold source of nicotine. One of my partners and I made a crude model of a cigarette that, without being lighted, delivered a cool "smoke" made of fog and powdered snuff. We presented it to a client who became excited about it and supported a research project to develop the idea and it saved our company.

Another optimist who created hopeful meaning out of bad news is Norman Cousins, former editor of the *Saturday Review of Literature.* He was critically ill with a collagen deficiency; was in great pain, and his doctors told him he probably would not survive. He invented a surprising cure: he *made* himself *feel* better by continually watching movies that made him laugh, and he supplemented that with massive doses of vitamin C. He recovered and believes his invention did it.

The Destructiveness of Pessimism

At the other end of the spectrum is pessimism. As a pessimist, I always operate out of despair. I create, out of the data at hand, the least favorable meaning I can imagine. I project the worst possible outcome. While sometimes pessimism may seem to be prudent—it is safest to expect the worst, "Luck's a chance, but trouble's sure" (Houseman), it is a course of subtle destructiveness.

> "Each of us carries a word in his heart, a "no" or a "yes". You probably don't know intuitively which word lives there, but you can learn, with a fair degree of accuracy..."—Martin E.P. Seligman

Pessimism robs me of my sense of purposefulness; it numbs me to my surroundings, to others, to opportunity, to my relationship to my resources. In this state I am not able to search for useful connections to solve problems, learn, and grow. Pessimism about my competence to get what I want, when carried to the extreme, breeds helplessness—a state of powerlessness and hopelessness. If I feel helpless there is no point in making connections to create positive meaning for myself.

There is much data, in addition to my own experience, that show helplessness precipitating disease and even death. One study of 51 women given tests for cervical cancer (after routine tests revealed suspicious cells), demonstrated the effect of hopelessness. Eighteen of this group had experienced recent severe personal loss of some kind and were feeling hopeless. Eleven of the hopeless group(61%)

subsequently developed cancer. In the group not experiencing helplessness, only eight (24%) of the thirty-three developed cancer (Seligman, 1991).

Another study by Dr. Sidney Cobb focused on the helpless situation of losing a job. One hundred men laid off from a Detroit auto plant had their health monitored for a two-year period beginning six weeks before the layoff. The suicide rate among those one hundred men was thirty times the average rate. Twenty-nine of the group developed serious diseases, including ulcers, hypertension, depression, and arthritis (ibid.).

In a third study, a group of fifty-five women with an average age of eighty-two were interviewed prior to entering a nursing home. When they were asked about how much freedom of choice they had about entering the nursing home, thirty-eight (69%) indicated they had some, while seventeen (31%) said they had none. After ten weeks in the home, only one(2%) of the thirty-eight had died, while sixteen (94%) of those without choice were dead (ibid.).

Helplessness and the pessimistic attitude that goes with it, can be learned. For example, my daughter is a case in point. When visiting her and her family, I often joined my grandchildren for an early breakfast while my daughter and her husband slept. She encouraged her five and three year old children to make their own breakfasts—to help themselves to cereal and forage in the refrigerator for milk or anything else that looked good to eat. There were lots of

> "An aged man is but a paltry thing,
> A tattered coat upon a stick, unless
> Soul clap its hands and sing, and louder sing
> For every tatter in its mortal dress…"
>
> —W. B. Yeats

spills—bowls too full of cereal and too much milk added to that. I had to keep a tight rein on my impulses to take over the situation and create some order. Later, I brought up the matter with my daughter, carefully suggesting the need for more supervision. She responded that, "If I am always there to supervise them, they will get the idea that I have to be present, that they are not competent by themselves. I would rather clean up than have them get helpless."

Beginning List of Things that Increase Potential for Connection-Making and Meaning-Making

- Large vocabulary
- Willingness to be approximate
- Wholehearted listening
- Being awake and aware
- Willingness to make trial connections
- Tolerance for confusion and ambiguity
- Tolerance for anxiety—good self-soothing tactics
- Willingness to jump to conclusions/guess
- Willingness to image it (see it in my mind's eye)
- Willingness to postpone the safety of evaluating—evaluate only *after* I really understand both positive and negative implications

•Staying power in the face of confusion
•Interact vs. react
•Empathy vs. judgment and alienation
•Assume it can be done

> "Courage is not an *ability* one either possesses or lacks. Nor is courage synonymous with bravery, like falling on a grenade to save one's buddies from injuries or death. *Courage* refers to the *willingness* to engage in risk-taking behavior when one either does not know the consequences or when the consequences might be adverse. Anyone is *capable* of courageous behavior provided he/she is *willing.*"—Alfred Adler

Courage

In much the same way that I have been socialized into using a small fraction of my thinking horsepower—down to perhaps 10 from a possible 1000—I have developed an emotional *confusion* about my courage.

If I were given an owner's manual at the start of my life, and, at every developmental stage, I read and re-read the directions, I would know that in order to develop and maintain an effective self, I must deal with some of the pains and anxiety of becoming a wholly effective person. For example, when I make an error such as knocking my cup of milk on the floor, I need to own the responsibility for that. As it is, I grow up believing that I may be able to get away with denying responsibility when I do something that turns out to be a mistake. I am reminded of this when my grandson, Max, four, drops his cup of orange juice and instantly wails, "Mommie, look what you made me do!"

I am sure I did the same thing when I was four, and if I had my owner's manual (on audio tape because I could not read it) it would patiently tell me, "Georgie, it is not good for you to blame Mommie for your mistake. In fact, if you choose to eliminate blame of others altogether you can learn more. Think about how you happened to let the cup slip out of your hands. Then decide how you will hold it more securely next time. Mistakes are to learn from, not to punish for."

I am just a kid so I argue with this Voice of Wisdom. "It is easy for you to say "eliminate blame of others altogether". Try convincing my mom of that. My experience with mistakes and any kind of trouble I get into is that I can often avoid pain and sorrow if I deny it."

The Will to Persist

Courage is a mysterious, much admired *potential* that each of us possesses. Probably the first point to emphasize is that courage is not a gift that is bestowed ready-made.

"What a new face courage puts on everything!"—Emerson

The gift is the *capacity* for courage. The *ability to act courageously* must be developed. My Voice of Wisdom attempts to convince me that when I am involved in a mistake and am gripped with the urge to deny responsibility, I need to be aware I am making a choice. There are almost always two ways to go: one that appears to avoid or postpone pain; and another in which I own my full share of responsibility and risk anxiety, possible punishment, pain, and disapproval of others. Courage is the will or determination that *allows* me to choose the painful path—to persist in the shadow of threat without caving in, without compromising my respect for myself.

While my courage allows and recommends the difficult choice, it does not *force* that decision, nor make it easy. That decision is made by some kind of meeting between *my head and heart*, and if the field is right, I make the courageous decision. It is important to be aware that the decision to be courageous is made intellectually..It needs to be reinforced by emotional agreement. A process for obtaining that emotional support is to image the courageous act and *feel* what it will be like. Image failing to act courageously and *feel* what that will be like.

I do not always summon up my courage to cope rather than avoid. I am too afraid of the pain of punishment, and I retain a lingering belief that I *may* be able to escape the consequences later when they come due.

It has taken me a very long time to become convinced that I can *never* escape the consequences of avoiding the difficult path because the judge of whether or not I have compromised my respect for myself is my own, built-in Voice of Wisdom. I have learned a simple test (Bednar et al, 1989) that tells me the effect on my self-evaluation of any choice. First, I think of an experience in which I practiced avoidance. Then think of three words that capture how I *feel* about myself. Next I think of two words that capture what I *think* of myself for that decision.

For example, I remember a situation where my boss asked my opinion of something he intended to do. He was quite invested in it. I thought it was a foolish thing to do, but I knew if I told him that, he was going to be angry with me. I avoided telling him what I thought. Remembering, the three words that captured what I *felt* were: disgusted, sad, and impatient. I *thought* of myself as weak and cowardly.

In another situation a potential client asked me to give him an evaluation of the creativity of several of his subordinates we were training. I was afraid we would lose the business if I did not comply, but I summoned up my courage and explained that it was our policy not to give evaluations because it made people competitive and interfered with learning. I lost the business, but the words that captured how I felt were: calm, powerful, valuable. I

> "For when the One Great Scorer comes to write
> against your name,
> He marks—not that you won or lost—but how
> you played the game."
>
> —Grantland Rice

thought of myself as strong and courageous. Bednar points out that self-evaluation *does not depend upon the outcome* of such a decision.

Now, if I can run this test instantly *before* I chose whether to cope or avoid, I will stay in better touch with my courage. The magic question I have learned to ask myself: "Will what I plan to do help me be and feel meaningful—or make me less meaningful?"

The Temptation to Hide

I am conscious now of a continual inclination to take the easy way; to say to myself, "I have been on this developmental path a long time, I have made progress on most stages and I deserve a vacation from all this coping vs. avoiding. I will not really *avoid*, I will just relax a little and stand still."

This does not work for me. I am either coping or avoiding, and there is no in between. When Kathleen and I are working on a concept like this one on courage, I sit and stare at my computer and attempt to figure out a way to say something. Suddenly I connect with a clue to a way that might make the point clear. Along with the tiny blissful feeling that the connection brings, there is a tremor of anxiety. I am too thirsty to continue, and I go for a drink of water. There are some dishes in the sink, and I rinse them and notice that I have left a stack of papers in a mess on the porch…I know that I am moving away from effectiveness and meaningfulness, and I do it anyway. It is good for me, at such times, to call on what I might call "courage helpers". These are strategies to fight the temptation to hide, to avoid. One that I have found quite helpful in this particular avoidance pattern is to put on my Sony Walkman and play a recording of a mother's heartbeat. It usually helps me cope with my urges to get a drink of water and do other chores.

The Prudence of Policy

Whether it is the lack of an owner's manual or that I am a slow learner, I have not developed my courage enough for it to be completely dependable. I use all the help I can get to reinforce my will to chose the courageous course. Here are some of the policies or strategies I use to support my uncertain courage:

- Tell the truth whenever possible—even in small matters.
- Always accept the *possibility* that I am responsible for whatever is happening.

> "...it is in this whole process of meeting and solving problems that life has its meaning."—M. Scott Peck

- Avoid denial.
- Exercise courage in small matters to stay in touch with it.
- Use increasing self-disclosure to keep my image as close as possible to my reality.
- Remind myself frequently that choosing to cope vs. avoid is the *only* way I can move up the developmental ladder

Stay in Touch with My Stakes

A number of brilliant thinkers have devised developmental schemes to help people be more mindful of the path to self-realization. When I think of these as owner's manuals they become more meaningful. I use a combination of Erik Erikson's (1982) and Jean Baker Miller's (1982).

Below is Erikson's chart and it makes clear to me that in *every* developmental move, the key is courage. Others can help me, particularly in the early stages, yet each move—from mistrust to trust, inferiority to industry, isolation to intimacy, from despair to integrity—depends upon *my* head and *heart* deciding to risk the threat and take responsibility for coping rather than avoiding.

Miller's understanding of the pivotal role of relationship in each of these developmental moves illuminated the absolute necessity for me to learn to use my courage to disclose myself as I really am rather than a dreamed up image I design to impress others. This keeps me on the plus side of these psychological crises.

Forgiveness vs. Punishment

When my courage helper strategies do not work and I hide and avoid my developmental path, I observe myself drifting from my goals. Then I remind myself of the coping behavior I *wish* I were implementing, and then I forgive myself.

Punishment has no place in this lifelong effort to take full responsibility for myself. I believe that punishment, both self-punishment and punishment from others, is a perverse red herring dragged across the path of development. It creates a destructive diversion from learning. It focuses the punishee on his hurt and how to deal with that rather than on the opportunity to examine and

> "The search for safety, order, and lack of anxiety through prediction and mastery eventually arouses inward feelings of despair and feelings of loneliness."—Moustakas

learn from a mistake. Punishment is not only painful, it also distracts from the issue and will create hurtful dissonance within me. I need a healthy integrated self because none of the courageous victories on my journey assures a permanent state of effectiveness. I am able to be industrious at one moment, and slip into inferiority and incompetence in the next; feel secure in basic trust for a while and then descend into basic mistrust for another while.

Courage and Being

Avoidance behavior leads me to operate in ways that severely limit my effectiveness. Mistrust, shame, doubt, guilt, inferiority, identity confusion, isolation, stagnation, despair and disgust are states of mind that obstruct the processes of connecting and being. Being is a process and like, freedom, requires me to be constantly vigilant. To remain skillful at courage I need to partner with all the elements and facets that make me *me.* Courage itself is a process requiring continual practice.

> "If this is my vision, what courage is required of me at this moment?"—Anon

Chart 2

Psychosocial Crises

		1	2	3	4	5	6	7	8
Old Age	VIII								Integrity vs. Despair, disgust. WISDOM
Adulthood	VII							Generativity vs. Stagnation. CARE	
Young Adulthood	VI						Intimacy vs. Isolation. LOVE		
Adolescence	V					Identity vs. Identity Confusion. FIDELITY			
School Age	IV				Industry vs. Inferiority. COMPETENCE				
Play Age	III			Initiative vs. Guilt. PURPOSE					
Early Childhood	II		Autonomy vs. Shame, Doubt. WILL						
Infancy	I	Basic Trust vs. Basic Mistrust. HOPE							

"Perceptions of personal limitations are based on *untested* assumptions—perhaps arrived at when young and undeveloped."—Weik

Learning and Knowing

As a kid, I discover that I get an exhilarating feeling of joy from organizing random bits and pieces of observation and information into meaningful understanding. There is much trial and error/trial and success—guessing and testing. My feelings of competence and validity flourish on this do-it-myself kind of mental and physical connection making to arrive at knowing.

Lady Montegreens

As a child I am a master at making meaning/learning and I do it by jumping to conclusions. As data comes in, I quickly form a temporary explanation—what a scientist would call a working hypothesis. If the further data supports my temporary explanation or hypothesis, I solidify it. If the data does not support my hypothesis, I modify to suit the new information.

Some years ago there appeared in *Atlantic Magazine* an article entitled *Lady Montegreens.* It described a phenomenon of my childhood: my practice of hearing a statement and making my own temporary sense of it.

Lady Montegreen comes from the stories of knights and battles. Whenever a knight was sore wounded, they "laid him on the green". Here are some examples of Lady Montegreens:

- •In a warm house on the hay=In a one horse open sleigh
- •Maggie scuse=May I be excused (from the table)
- •East side giffs=These thy gifts (from Grace)
- •It's a marigold=It's a miracle
- •Drunk store=Drug store

As I grow to age four, I get the idea that school will be a feast of the kind of tolerant learning I am enjoying with my family. I *like* doing my own connection making. It is a major builder of self-esteem. It provides an exhilarating supply of endorphins. A part of me does not want anyone organizing meaning *for* me unless I ask for help. In fact, I defend myself against pre-organized meaning I have not requested; I am self-protective.

> There is "…no limit to the continual growth of meaning in human life."—John Dewey

With the imposition of schooling, I must shift my learning to more and more second hand connection making; integrating someone else's connections to arrive at knowing. I learn that the important thing is to *avoid being wrong.* To be wrong is to be invalidated, to feel meaningless. To protect myself against that, I rein in my urge to make my own connections. I ask questions or otherwise depend upon others for learning and knowing. This is less joyful for me. My source of satisfaction shifts from the wonder of making connections to the comfort of being right. I get my reassurance that I am OK from the teacher's approval rather than from experiencing my own competence.

As we have seen, the process of trial and error connection making—guessing and testing—triggers anxiety and is less and less tolerable. This leads me to some misconceptions about knowing.

1) Knowing is the most important goal of education.
2) Once acquired, knowledge is static, fixed, dependably unambiguous and always the same.
3) Knowing is superior, dominant; the learning posture is subordinate, inferior.
4) To know is to feel assured, confident, and competent; to be learning is to feel anxious, uncertain, and to *look* incompetent.

This creates a field that is anti-learning. When an event or observation is puzzling or confusing to me I feel anxious.. If there is no one to ask, I may ignore it. Instead of continually building my learning skills, I become less available to newness; more dependent on explanations from outside myself.

> "One characteristic of people in the creative orientation…how quickly [they] can alter the way they have been doing things."—Robert Fritz

Learning as Inventing

The process of inventing can tell me a lot about learning and the actions that facilitate it. The story of Alastair Pilkington and "float" glass is a slow-motion study of invention. In plate glass manufacturing, the constant problem was producing a smooth product. The process used mirror-smooth rollers to shape the molten glass. Even these rollers imparted enough imperfections so the glass had to be polished—an expensive operation.

For Alastair Pilkington, research chief at a glassworks in England, smoothness was the puzzle of his life. One evening as he was washing dishes, he observed a patch of grease on the water and paused. The grease was smooth on top. He connected with his knowledge that, because water seeks its own level, the bottom would be perfectly smooth too. He then connected grease with glass, and jumped to a new idea: float molten glass on water and it will be perfectly smooth without polishing! It was a thrilling connection.

Being a well informed thinker, Pilkington's instant reality test made the connection that the molten glass would explode on contact with water.

Because he understood the way invention, discovery and learning take place, he relished the "grease connection" for its elegance *even though it was in error*. He did not abandon it to avoid feelings of wrongness. He had learned tolerance of mistake anxiety and did not insist that a beginning connection pass or fail based on a reality test. He used it as an *armature*—a beginning around which he would build a new meaning by guessing and testing. Its great value lay in its suggestion of an entirely new direction of exploration: floating and using gravity vs. polishing.

He next began to trial-connect with *water-like* fluids that might be more practical. Over a two year period, he conducted experiments to find the right fluid and the right way to use it. From Pilkington's bold thinking—tested and informed by experiment—came a revolutionary new method of manufacturing plate glass: he poured molten glass onto molten tin. As the melt cools, the glass hardens to perfect smoothness—no polishing required.

From Pilkington's process I learn that each hypothesis is a trial connection—a conclusion "jumped to". It is then

> "One can think [creatively] only when one is willing to endure suspense and to undergo the trouble of searching."—John Dewey

tested to discover the truth about it. If it does not work, another conclusion is jumped to and tested.

Mindspring Theory

Mindspring theory, developed in the early seventies at Synectics®, holds that when I am available to speculate about what I observe, there is constant learning and creation of new understandings. These take place through the exercise of six thinking operations: wishing, retrieving, connecting, transforming, comparing, and storing. These may occur in any order.(Prince, 1975, 9,3)

In Pilkington's case, he was available to play with the implications of the grease floating on his dishwater. One implication of the floating grease that might have shut off further speculation, was that there was not enough soap in the water. The grease should not have formed, so he might have added more soap to get rid of it. But Pilkington was obsessed with **wishes** about smoothness, and here was an interesting smoothness. He **imaged** in his mind's eye the underside of the grease. He **connected** the implications of grease-on-water with his wish, and **transformed** the grease into molten glass. He **retrieved,** from his storehouse of information, relevant data on what might happen. He **compared** this result with his wish. When the result was promising, he pursued it. With the grease, it lead him to a further wish: he wished for a water-*like* fluid that could withstand a lot of heat. This promised a solution and he **stored** it for further work. Let's compare Pilkington's process with that of a child learning something new.

Physical Learning as Analogy for Meaning-making Thinking

When my daughter was learning to feed herself, I allowed myself to simply observe the process without attempting to teach. She went through a great many trials and errors to get small successes. She tolerated food all over her face and cheerfully continued her process of guessing and testing. Each successive approximation helped her get more effectively organized. Every increment of progress carried with it some satisfying awareness of increasing competence. It was easy to see that in these actions she was *be*ing. And with that comes joy—the rapture of being. Right beside love, it is one of the primary sources of bliss. Discovering their own growing competence is what makes

> "The purpose of education has been viewed primarily as learning about *other* people's connections and discoveries, not about making one's own."—Shilcock and Bergson

children's faces light up. It is what makes them dance because the feeling is too good for walking. Physical learning is easy for us to believe. We do not expect a child to *know* eating or walking or dressing. We can see that a child needs to trial and error—guess and test—and improve incrementally—in short, needs to go through the learning process. Coaches of sports know there is a physical organizing of meaning that requires practicing—trial and erroring as one works toward perfecting a backhand or serve. They are more tolerant of the learning process because they can see it.

Max invents meaning

The process of mental connecting is harder to tolerate. Recently I was telling my daughter about an acquaintance who had been sent to prison for drug dealing. Max, my 4 year old grandson, was playing nearby on the floor. A minute or two after I had used the word prison, Max said "George, do you remember that thing you showed me in your office?" I was at a loss. "It was glass, this long, and it made colors." said Max. I remembered the prism on my desk.

A year or so before, I had introduced Max to the prism. Max **wishes** to understand(organize meaning—learn) the concept "prison". He **retrieves** from his storehouse something that sounds like it, "prism". He **connects** this with an **image** of man-in-prism. He **compares** this connection to what he knows. It is puzzling, so he asks for clarification. As this new information comes in, he instantly, and without defensiveness, **transforms** his image to accommodate it. He **stores** this and begins a new file—under "prison". To invent is to learn, to learn is to invent

But most of the time, as a teacher and parent, the message I send is: "anything less than perfect is *wrong*-a *mistake.*" When a child exposes her early thinking-to-learn approximate connections, I react with punishment only. A typical exchange: son Winthrop, age three, sees his first horse. "Daddy! There is a *big* cat!" From me he gets laughter (ridicule) and the information, "No, Winky, that is a horse."("you are wrong in your connecting") Both my responses punish Winthrop for some very creditable connection-making.

> "There are some people who, if they don't already know, you can't tell them."—Yogi Berra

I see it as my duty to bring up my children to *know* instantly and precisely—an ambition that is a cruel illusion. A child suffers hundreds and hundreds of these well-meaning but destructive evaluations. It is at this time that my self-regard gets mortally wounded. My do-it-myself competence at making sense gets discredited. Confusion—one of the normal, healthy steps to figuring out—gets a bad name. Guessing—one of the more valuable thinking tools—gets abused and forbidden except for play. Approximate thinking—a process that enormously multiplies my chances of reaching understanding—gets sacrificed for the limiting belief in precision above all. Questions, that shift meaning-making away from me, are deified. No wonder much of the joy goes out of school (and thinking) by the third or fourth grade. The clearly established goal is rightness—knowing. We give lip service to learning, but only allow it with other peoples' ready-made connections.

Creating a climate friendly to learning

In the last thirty years I have studied videotapes of thousands of people—teachers, children, married couples—attempting to work together on a variety of invention tasks. As I learned to connect actions with consequences it became clear that most of us use our communication tools—words, vocals, and non-verbal actions—like blunt instruments. I have learned from thousands of observations that names, tones, even slight gestures can cause wounds. Such transmissions toxify the field and start cycles of rebellion, revenge and withdrawal that destroy cooperative impulses and contaminate even the closest relationships. My normal, careless transmissions almost insure high anxiety and defensiveness in others and low availability for thinking-to-learn.

A factor in understanding the field of a relationship, something discussed earlier, is an appreciation of relationship as an entity that persists—a sort of third party that mediates each transmission between the parties. The personality of the relationship is formed of all the words, vocals, and non-verbals that have passed between the individuals. For example, if the relationship between me and my boss has had few discounts or punishments in either direction, I would characterize our field as friendly to learning. I can afford to admit trial and error thinking with its attendant mistakes.

> "...there is comfort in sticking to what we have power over, and the use of punishment and rewards is nothing if not an exercise of power."—Alfie Kohn

But if the relationship has been *strict,* if the expectation is perfection, and any deviation disapproved, the field evokes defensiveness and I tend to avoid the risks of thinking-to-learn.

> "Every organism is a process: thus an organism is not other than its actions…it is what it does"—unknown

Limiting Learning

Anxiety is an enemy of learning. For example, I think of my mental model for meeting someone important for the first time. My mixed intention is to perceive and connect with this man or woman so I will remember her. I also wish to make a good impression so she will remember me. We are introduced and my internal field takes over. Anxiety rises and 95% of my perceiving is on myself—"How am I coming across?" 5% of my attention is on her. My inner field is not supporting me in operating in the way I wish. In this and in a great many other circumstances my field severely limits my effectiveness.

Anxiety and Change

Unless I become aware of the almost continual limitations my field enforces, and develop ways consciously to alter it, I am doomed to operate at a fraction of my potential. Anxiety is the key disintegrator of connection making and coherence.

Recent brain research has traced the effect of high anxiety. My amygdala identifies emotional threat in the situation. It triggers alarm and anxiety. It passes a strong signal to my hippocampus whose job it is to organize incoming information into a connected story. My hippocampus is overwhelmed by the strength of the alarm, and, to some extent, breaks down and fails to pull together relevant information for the rest of my brain to work on. I am fragmented and focus on holding myself together. I am not able to carry out my constructive intentions. I am out of my connecting and learning mode.

In the growing-up years everyone suffers a great many events that cause anxiety and fragmentation—operating in a defensive, "holding myself together" non-learning mode. Perceived threat triggers anxiety and I am impelled into defense. Because, as we saw earlier, my amygdala gets extra sensitized by repetitive early mistreatment, my field is not well defended against anxiety. Anxiety is so difficult to endure, I develop substitutes for it to make it manageable. Such behavior as impatience, blaming, procrastination, boredom, anger, suspicion, prejudice, antagonism, dominance, pessimism, and so on, are often anxiety in disguise. The characteristic that these field generators have in common is that they all interfere with perceiving/connecting. All can be ways to avoid *thinking* and *changing.*

Awareness is the first step in continued thinking. I use a simple strategy of absurdity that sometimes helps. For example, I was in a drug store buying a magazine. When I went to the cashier to pay for it, she ignored me as she talked with the cashier next to her. I felt a rush of anger and an impulse to reach over and whack her—an irrational and unacceptable behavior.

> "...the need for interpersonal security might be said to be the need to be rid of anxiety. But anxiety is not manageable."—Harry Stack Sullivan

I used a prepared ritual. I said to myself, "Are you really afraid that she will abandon you?"

This collapsed my anxiety and I was free to connect with the reality of the situation and use a sensible approach to get her attention. By absurdity and self-questioning I can often change my field to support better thinking. For example, when something is boring or irritating me it can change the field if I ask, "Why is this triggering anxiety in me?"

Anxiety is My Field saying, "Don't"

My foresight function is always looking ahead for possible threats to my meaningfulness and is ready to trigger an avoidance strategy. It is telling me not to risk this connection as it might hurt.

If I am to be all I can be, I need to be alert so that I can modify my avoidance impulses and engage my courage to think, learn and change. In reality, change is constant and what matters most is that my changes take me in directions of increasing effectiveness.

Goal-Oriented vs. Process-Oriented Learning

As we saw earlier, the general field punishes mistakes. The system operates on the basis of rewards and punishments. I get rewarded for reaching the goal of *knowing,* there is no reward for the activity of *learning,* and as a result, I may never really come to appreciate my process or continue to develop my perceiving and connecting skills. Alfie Kohn, in *Punished by Rewards,* says, "In a very limited sense…rewards and punishments do work. In the short term, we can get people to do any number of things by making it worth their while."(1993, Pg. 14).

> "…irrespective of who invents and owns our job, we can still be the creator and owner of our work."—Robert Kegan

The price I pay for this exclusively goal-oriented training is very high. In the work I do, my focus is nearly always on the end-point and how to get there with the fewest possible screw-ups and mistakes along the way; no experimenting or trial and erroring. This tends to make the process slightly unpleasant—something to be gotten through. The extrinsic reward is my driver. I do not attend to the minute particulars of how I am getting it done. I miss the perceiving and joys that accompany connecting to make new meaning. Since my reality is mainly process—a reward is a point at the end—to simply get through the process for the sake of the goal is to cheat myself of a great deal of being. As Carl Marden, one of my partners, used to say, "Work is a clumsy way of making a living."

Being Solely Goal-Driven has Problems

If I am solely focused on the goal I cut my chances of inventing a way to improve the process of getting there.

Another difficulty is that I am not used to dealing with the very *concept* of process. Almost always when a couple comes to therapy they are in trouble because one is attempting to *teach* the other how to act to improve their relationship. It is the therapist's task to help each one shift from that goal-oriented mode into a self-focused awareness of his or her own transmissions and *learn* their impact; to focus, each on his or her own *process* and self-teach how to manage that better. I am always impressed with how hard it is for them to shift from the goal of getting along better, to the process of how to get there.

> "The experience of cooperation will induce a benign spiral of increasing cooperation, while competition will induce a vicious spiral of intensifying competition."—Alfie Kohn

A further drawback of neglecting process-oriented learning is that I often experience goal-oriented teaching as a discount. I feel one-down in a power-over relationship. I may defend myself from being taken over and I have probably invented a number unconscious but effective reaction strategies to *resist being taught*—a built-in limiting factor in most teacher/learner relationships.

Field as the Medium for Teaching/Learning

There are two basic fields in people relationships: one that is grounded in equality/respect (as noted earlier, this equality does not depend upon equality of resources and experience, but on personhood), and the other—grounded in a superior/subordinate field.

As we have seen, the interpersonal field or relationship is very like a third party with a personality that is shaped by past interactions. It mediates the communications between me and another. When the field supports equality and respect, either one of us is free to negotiate with the input of the other. When the relationship has a history of respect and empathy for me and my needs, I can afford to be open to it. In contrast, the superior/subordinate relationship is based on power-over and is one-sided. Rather than a mutual situation it becomes a win/lose with the superior always winning. When I am in the inferior position, my self protective field will probably impel me toward defense.

> "The family is the civilian equivalent of Marine boot camp. Many simply are not fit for their members to live in."—Sidney Jourard

Defensive barriers protect me from being taken over by others, but they also limit my own access to my marvelous gifts for perception and connecting. Whenever the field signals power-over, I become less available. I am a self-limited learner.

> "At the quantum level we observe a world where change happens in jumps, beyond our powers of precise prediction."—Margaret Wheatley

This limiting field operates on me from infancy. Being a remarkable natural learner, I imitate that surrounding field inside me. I quickly reduce the importance of my own natural gifts for perceiving and connecting-to-make-meaning. I become skilled at taking directions from authorities. I ignore the joyful intrinsic rewards of my original perceiving/connecting process. My foresight function, anxiety gradient and selective inattention are dedicated to getting the extrinsic rewards dispensed by others and avoiding punishment. In brief, I dumb down. My internal field and strategies become consistent with the controlling field I must accommodate. My 1000 horsepower giant of a perceiver/connection-maker/meaning-inventor is controlled by a governor that keeps me idling at about 10 horsepower *except in special circumstances.*

Inventing A Field to Awaken the Giant in Me

In my experience the special circumstances that bring out the best thinking in people is a field that, by mutual agreement, outlaws discounting, exercise of power-over, and supports wholehearted listening. Destructive disorder is excluded by defining *roles* for each situation.(see Think Tank as Field Manager). The person with the most knowledge about it is temporary coach. The process systematically appreciates *all* perceiving and connecting and manages evaluation to make it *wholly constructive.* There is continuing focus on field so that each participant can learn to manage his and her actions to maintain the field.

I know of only three types of activity in our current culture that systematically embody most of these actions:

many sports, such as skiing, give much attention to the process of getting skillful. Good psychotherapy and well

> "What dominant groups usually cannot act on, or even see, is that the situation of inequality in fact deprives them..."—Jean Baker Miller

run invention sessions all provide the conditions for continuing growth.

Mind-Free is an attempt to examine the minute particulars that bring into being a field that nurtures process-oriented learning and behaving. As I examine and test the various ingredients of such a field, I can change my processes to create a field that awakens my 1000 horsepower giant of a mind more of the time in my everyday life.

"What's the matter with order? The problem is what people do to get order. They distort novel inputs to fit what they have known all along."—Weik

Addiction to Direction and Structure

For many years I have worked with a man who was repeatedly able to turn unfavorable—almost disastrous—situations into successes. He also seemed to have some talent for getting into these situations. Analyzing Bill Wilson's career, I began to realize that the qualities that made him so effective also made him unacceptable to his bosses. As a result, when he succeeded in one area, instead of being rewarded with promotion and bonus and appreciation, he was assigned to a backwater where he would cause no more trouble.

He would survey this new, seemingly unfavorable, situation, gather a new unconventional team, and proceed to turn the backwater into a golden opportunity. One example: after great success in developing not only new businesses, but new materials for his company, he had ruffled so many feathers that he was assigned the "safe" department of Energy and Environment. This was before the energy crunch of 1974. Although the company was an enormous user of energy, Energy and Environment was considered by Bill's friends to be a demotion—to be put in charge of a small police force to enforce government regulations.

Bill did not see it that way. Instead of enforcer, Bill saw himself and the staff he built as enablers. He developed roving invention teams that visited all the company installations to work with the local group to invent ways to increase productivity and reduce energy use, while complying with regulations. By the time he left a few years later, Energy and Environment had invented new ways of operating that saved the company more than $85,000,000.

Bill eventually gained some satisfying recognition—the company spent the two or three years before Bill's retirement attempting to figure out how to develop more Bill Wilsons—sincere flattery!

The characteristic that set Bill apart was that he *always* exceeded his authority. When given an assignment he did not begin to move toward a goal until he had a vision. Bill's

"No one is ever free to do something he can't think of."—Weik

visions grew out of a kind of confused and open-ended exploration of all the implications of a given situation. He did not let preconceptions of his authority or any limitations of the assignment blur the realities of feedback. He let the findings guide him and the team he assembled, to the discovery of the most promising possibilities. Then he and his team laid appropriate plans—always tentative and open to course correction as the realities continued to guide.

During the period of uncertainty—often many months—before there was any clarity that there was success at the end of the path, Bill's bosses had no continuing reassurance that no mistakes were being made. For a boss, this is the cruelest, most upsetting situation to be in. Bill was skillful in keeping his freedom of action, but in the end, no matter how wonderful the outcome, Bill's bosses seemed to act out of the discomfort they felt rather than in appreciation of Bill's real achievements.

Bosses, in this case, demonstrate the power of our addiction to the predictability that can come only through direction and structure. When Bill was given an assignment, the unspoken order was: "Do not surprise me. It is more important to avoid mistakes than to be successful."

This posture is epidemic and not only among bosses. We have a love/hate relationship with surprise. I love the feeling of a benign surprise. It is a pure sensation of aliveness. BUT I am usually gripped by fear that it will turn out to be a mistake. It feels out of my control—unpredictable and therefore likely to result in trouble for me. So I get powerfully conditioned toward hating surprises. Rather than experience the uncertainty of first hand contact with random reality, I seek instruction, "Is this what you had in mind?" "Am I getting into mistake country?"

The implications of this field of order and control are almost incalculable. Instead of being open to whatever pieces of information are coming to me, I insist that they be organized—that they be put into some logical order so as to make immediate sense. To avoid the anxiety of organizing meaning myself and possibly making mistakes, I learn to prefer that an authority tell me the meaning.

There is a kind of conspiracy to preserve the fiction of orderliness in the world. Many scientists dedicated to the truth, mislead us about how they make discoveries. As Beveridge in *The Art of Scientific Investigation* (1950)

> "Those studying chaotic dynamics discovered that the disorderly behavior of simple systems acted as a *creative* process. It generated complexity…"—James Gleick

points out, after a scientist trial and errors his way through confusion, painful uncertainty, and happy accidents to reach an unexpected new conclusion, he tends to reorganize and clean up the experience, after the fact, to present it to others as an orderly, logical procedure. There is even an accepted and orderly outline that one is supposed to follow. It is called The Scientific Method.

James Gleick in Chaos (1987) gives a stunningly different view of an emerging science that recognizes the overriding reality of randomness and disorganization in our world.

Some organization is useful in making sense of our world—and to simplify the passing of information back and forth from one person to another.

The difficulty seems to grow out of the kind of field generated by hierarchical structure. Information tends to flow one way—to control from the top down. "The hierarchical structure of a company [or a family] reinforces assertiveness and dominance by managers—and deference by the managees. Even General Motors and Conrail are realizing that the principles of organization that suit a baboon troop might not be the most efficient for running a complex corporation." (Csikszentmihalyi,1993, Pg. 49)

When a hierarchy governs my fate, as it does most of my life, I learn to lose my appetite for confusion, uncertainty and risk—the internal field created when I make meaning for myself. "Put a top monkey at the bottom of a new group, he "meekins" up and vice versa." (Ibid., Pg. 48). I meekin up and satisfy the hierarchy's demands for order. Sadly, I tend to stop thinking for myself.

Unless, that is, I behave like Bill Wilson and engage my courage. Then, I freely exercise my perception and connection-making-to-make-meaning gifts. I stay in touch with the confusion and disorder of reality and relish my ability continually to create something new out of it.

> "The initiative lies with the learner."—John Dewey

The Teacher Learner Field

A useful re-framing of the teacher/ student field is one of *managed mutuality*—a field of collaboration to bring out the most fruitful and satisfying connecting-to-learn for both parties. Framing the teacher as a learner can clarify his role. His objective then becomes how to learn to help each unique student develop his or her process of learning and relating. The student can wholeheartedly respect and join that effort and in doing so, give the teacher the satisfactions which led him to become a teacher.

Stability and Reality

The idea behind a classroom and a curriculum is to provide an orderly method to insure that each student gets a fully balanced education in the subjects required. If pressed, we might say the requirements are specified by the life the student is preparing for. There is a wish to be relevant. Most of us believe that the student is not far-sighted enough to decide what subjects are relevant.

The adult-designed learning system has long given the impression that educators know what they are doing. Almost the only dissenting voice has come from the students who make their opinions clear with their actions.

Their present drop-out rate, and failure to learn reading, writing, science and arithmetic send a message.

If we were in the education business the way Procter and Gamble is in the detergent business we would be paying close attention to attitudes and drop-out rates. We would be talking to the people who hire our graduates. We would know that our product is marginal. If we had any real competition we would be out of business.

Fortunately for the education business, virtually everyone is governed by tradition (except students and no one is listening to them…in any case, a little discipline is probably good for them). I was talking with one of my teachers at Exeter and I said I thought it would make more sense to learn conversational French rather than grammatical French. He said that what they taught was

> "…the ideas and images in men's and women's minds are the invisible powers that constantly govern them."—John Dewey

governed by what colleges want. "Parents send their sons to Exeter(it was not yet co-educational) to insure they will get into a good college, not to get a useful education."

So the educational system is solidly rooted in tradition which is enforced by the colleges which appear to be motivated primarily by the need to survive. A student, as a customer, choses a degree, the substance of which is governed by tradition.

Everything *seems* to have a reassuring stability. But the basis has little to do with the life problems of students.

Practical courses, like engineering and business appear to have a relevance to making a material living, while emotional development is left to chance. By the time I graduate from college, I can relax about education and begin the real learning and relating processes that will make my life worth-while.

A Startling Assumption

What if we assumed that as a child of 4 or 5 I am continually faced with a life situation that requires the same skills, knowledge, and attitudes right now that will be required all through my life.? Further, we might assume that I will be hungry to process all possible information that will help cope with the problems and confusions I am experiencing.

This would mean that we would need to discover a basic core that is needed (and wanted). Then we might add some courses that, in our adult judgment, will be useful.

This would allow us to look at areas that are not now on any curriculum—such as field and relationships. I will need to learn how to form and sustain healthy relationships with family and others. At present these skills are allowed to develop in whatever way learning happens. When I apply Margaret Wheatley's (1994) analogy of quantum physics to people, each of us projects an invisible field that structures behavior. I might call it vibes.

I know men and women who are anxious to find partners who unwittingly send transmissions that distance them from others. Some of us never develop the skills of relating and we pay a very high price for our ignorance. I am repeatedly impressed with the *carelessness* and *disrespect* that parents use communicating with their children. I experience the consequences in the destructive transmissions of well-

> "I am always ready to learn, but I do not always like being taught."—Winston Churchill

educated people in meetings. If we look to Csikszentmihalyi, who has made a study of the psychology of peak experience and flow, we find some definite skills that are valuable.

Some are:

1. Freeing and controlling consciousness
2. Knowing the dynamics of attention and memory (The shape and content of life depends on how we invest our attention)
3. Understanding the concept of self—the sort of actions that enhance and empower and those that diminish.
4. Understanding the impact of our transmissions on others.
5. Psychic entropy—the actions that disorganize the self and others and impair our effectiveness.
6. Growth and complexity—the actions that result in growth and those that inhibit.(1990)

These are samples. When we have thought through the possibilities and experimented with some of our student-consumers, we will have a better idea of curriculum. In addition, by creating in our students, a continuing posture of awareness of their own needs and anxieties as legitimate problems to be worked on, we will keep our teaching relevant.

What The Process Might Be

We focus on a concept, for example, denial, that influences how I manage my life. We self-disclose about the concept: I share with another person some of my experiences with denial. I listen to the experiences of others. Out of this I remake and enrich the meaning for me. I reflect on the implications for me of this new meaning. What problems or opportunities does this new meaning illuminate for me to entertain. I make a note in my work-book to spend the time to make some small or large decision about what action I will take as a result of making this meaning.

2/7/02The Tools

•Equality/Respect
•Self-disclosure
•Validation and Discount/Revenge
•Meaning making
•Self-focus

> "Our work then as men and women is not only to free ourselves from family cages and collective mind sets, but to release [our own] transcendent beings from imprisonment and trance."—Robert Bly

•Listening
•Implication thinking
•Collaboration
•Openness/availability/awareness/honesty
•Handling the three blocking beliefs
1. perfection
2. immaculate knowing
3. mistake prejudice
•Tolerance

Non-Defensive Availability

I am open to making meaning for myself out of what you are saying. I will resist my defensive impulse to say, "I don't get it" or "What has that got to do with what we are talking about?" I will be responsible for connecting, however approximately.

I will simultaneously empathize (sense what it is for you) and "try it on for size" to learn its significance for me. I will attempt to remain clear about the possible difference between its meaning for you and its meaning for me.

> "Advice is like castor oil, easy enough to give, but dreadful uneasy to take."—Josh Billings

Implication for Advice Giving

The usual advice is directive—"You should handle this situation this way…" It is quite likely to reflect *me and my point of view,* but I present it as though it is designed for you.

Since I cannot really be you, and since I am giving you advice from my own point of view, and you are responsible for deciding how to handle the situation, it seems most respectful for me to be absolutely clear about where I am coming from. *Instead* of telling you what to do, I help you use your own thinking power to invent something that works for you.

The Great Teachers

The characteristics shared by the great teachers I have known are:

- Interest and pleasure in and respect for the learning process going on in their students
- *No* discounting
- Creators of a field of mutual interest in and respect for the *process* of learning
- An uncanny ability to appreciate a direction of thought that leads toward a student's discovery of strengths
- Without the need for the defensive trappings of status and self-importance
- Accomplished and joyful learners themselves

"Everyone's perceptual grasp of her situation is partial. When one discloses his perspective he invites empathy. This can enlarge awareness and stimulate invention of a way to better the situation."—Sidney M. Jourard

Momentary Me

The idea of momentary me is borrowed from a manufacturing practice in the automotive industry called just-in-time inventory. Rather than maintaining a large inventory of parts stored in anticipation of use, it is much more efficient to have the needed part arrive just in time to be installed. I borrowed the term to describe the kind of learning that can happen in Mind-Free® relationships. Recently a student, I will call him Tom, was describing an experience with his fourteen year old with whom he had been having trouble communicating. It seemed that whenever they talked, his son was unavailable and would shrug off whatever Tom was attempting to say. As an experiment, he began a conversation by disclosing an experience when he had been dishonest, been caught and humiliated. To his surprise, his son empathized with him and they had a rewarding exchange. As I imaged along with Tom's experience, I connected to the impasse I was in with one of my children and I realized that I was keeping myself hidden from him. No wonder he was defended from me.

I think of this as an example of just-in-time information. I was needing to rethink my relations with my son, and Tom's experience came along to fill my need. I was available to make connections. I reflected on how much of the information I was taught in school was simply presented when I was ready-or-not. This led me to think of my experiences with psychotherapy clients, where I attempt to deal with whatever is uppermost on their minds. This is most effective when the client is relating an experience and disclosing his momentary me, self. Whenever he drifts into theorizing or describing something not in his own experience, the therapy loses force. I began to think of the effective moments as just-in-time self-presentation. Then it seemed clearer to call it momentary me to capture the way the disclosures revealed just what was going on right at the moment. Momentary me is in contrast to impression-management or rehearsed me.

I experience the momentary me disclosures of others as qualitatively different from the usual careful self-presentation. An example that illustrates this is some work I did with a brilliant man, I will call Sam, who was the CEO

"…disclosure is a reciprocal phenomenon."—Sidney M. Jourard

of a small, dynamic company. They were having growing pains as they moved from small to medium size and I was attempting to help them. The group surrounding him complained that Sam was like a dictator. I was surprised because I had attended several meetings at which Sam had *seemed* to be quite open to having his ideas modified or even changed. After the complaints, I listened to Sam's process more carefully. Whatever the issue, Sam presented a carefully thought out pro/con analysis which led to what seemed to be the only possible conclusion. I saw what his colleagues meant. Sam was such a quick thinker, he could look at all sides of the issue, summarize, and interpret in the direction he chose. He tended to control both the air time and the development of options. I videotaped Sam in action and as we reviewed the tape, I stopped as Sam made each point. I asked him to recall his thinking that came *before* he organized his presentation to make the point. If he could disclose that process as it happened, I thought, it would give his colleagues time to make their influence felt.

Sam was uncomfortable with his feelings of losing control, and he made a valiant effort to present his slightly disorganized, momentary me. The effect was dramatic. In later interviews they told me that instead of experiencing Sam as dictating (and slightly boring) he was stimulating and flexible. I found their meetings transformed. An issue would be raised. Sam would say something like, "Here is where I am on that at this moment," and then wait for someone else to give their thinking. Positions would change as the group thought it through together. It became a vital interactive process and perhaps the most heartening thing was that Sam, and everyone else, came to feel it was OK to change positions as new thoughts were shared. Before, positions were to be defended.

Momentary Me and a Field of Discovery

The practice of momentary me requires that I form my responses at the moment and it keeps me up to date with myself. Carefully thought out positions, carefully presented, are appropriate for debates, and for situations when I am feeling threatened, but as a communication policy they distance me from others and from making new connections. They have the further effect of keeping me stuck in my usual assumptions and conclusions and make it difficult for me to really listen to another.

Momentary me transmissions tend to be unstudied and undefended and have the beguiling ring of freshly minted thinking that conveys connectedness and availability. It

> "Translating a phenomenon into language alters the way it is represented and understood in our minds."—James W. Pennebaker

invites a momentary me response. This is the kind of interaction that nurtures discovery. As I disclose my instant connections and thinking and you respond with the thinking stirred by mine, we are present for the possibility of making unexpected new connections and building *new, mutual* meanings that transcend our going-in understandings.

In a recent Mind-Free meeting I was listening to Jerry (not his name) tell of the two kinds of self-disclosure he was experiencing. One kind, with its own characteristics, is the disclosing to others. The other kind is disclosing to himself. I was imaging Jerry with a cartoon strip balloon over his head. In the balloon was a disclosure to us. Inside him was another smaller balloon disclosing to himself. I suddenly connected with the thought that the two balloons are intimately connected. The better I am at disclosing to others, the better I get at disclosing to myself. Disclosing is the opposite of keeping hidden. As I shift my posture to disclosing, I move away from hiding and that applies to both outer and inner disclosing. I become more available to discoveries about myself.

Momentary Me and Relationships

Long ago I was told that the reason two people shake hands upon meeting grew out of a primitive custom of showing that one did not have a weapon in hand and had no destructive intentions. Momentary me is just such a demonstration. I am allowing you to see my thoughts as they form. They are not yet finished, perfected and protected. It is a way of inviting you to join in finishing and perfecting. Our conversation becomes a cooperative venture—the ideal of mutuality. Good relationships are built this way.

Momentary Me and Self-Acceptance

As I become more and more able to respond to what someone says with the thoughts that I process right then, without resorting to impression management and old ready-made stereotype thoughts, my true self becomes more available to me. I have increasing confidence in me; fewer self doubts. I am living in the present and using fresh thinking and creating fresh meanings. I find myself appreciating and accepting myself more.

> "…if narrative is truly fundamental to the way humans organize and give meaning to experience…an event only becomes an experience by being narrated."—Parry and Doan

Momentary Me and the Field

Even though I am committed to disclosing my thoughts as they form, I need to keep in mind the field I am creating. If my instant response is negative I need to reorganize it into an Itemized Response. I want to tell the truth as I see it, and I also want to keep the field positive. While this may seem paradoxical, it can work.

Part 6—Managing Fields

"Growth always involves a process of differentiation, of emergence from embeddedness."—E. Schachtel

Becoming a Recruiter

I remember certain boys and girls in school who always seemed to have friends around them. They attracted people. Robert Kegan, the Harvard psychologist and researcher, calls such people recruiters. He believes that as a result of fortunate loving and appreciative experiences when infants, these people have internal fields that are outwardly expressed in ways that help others feel meaningful.

Those who are attracted, he terms recruitable. Their upbringing was fortunate enough that they are open to receiving positive signals from the recruiters. There is a third group he calls the non-recruitables. These have suffered enough mistreatment in those early formative years so that they are too defended to be available to positive signals.

Of course these groupings are not black and white. There is a spectrum from Recruiter to non-recruitable with people located all along the way. So some non-recruitables are partly available while people at the extreme end are not. Representatives from all three groups can become successful in business or their life work, but recruiters and recruitables have much more satisfying relationships with others. Non-recruitables, not surprisingly, account for most of the prison population.

The field of a recruiter is greatly influenced by his or her inner conviction of his or her own meaningfulness and this leads to an empathic assumption that others are also meaningful and should be so treated. Countering this healthy and comforting inner field are the toxic forces described earlier that undermine my acceptance of myself. As a result, while I may still have the capacity to be a recruiter, my field conveys mixed signals.

If I am to realize my full potential for growth and positive relationships, I need to work on all three of the components of my inner field—empathy, self-awareness and integrity. The most fruitful place to focus is on my relationship with myself. If I can create an understanding, supportive, loving field within, it can serve as a model of how to treat others. As a recruiter, I am able to engage others in a collaborative approach to accomplishment.

> "This highly developed intimacy [of relationship] with another is not the principal business of life, but is, perhaps, the principal source of satisfactions in life..."—Harry Stack Sullivan

Think Tank as Field Generator

Think Tank is a design for relating to another person or group to achieve cooperation and stimulate connection-making—connecting both to my own resources and to those of others. I use the process to focus on problems or opportunities, and it is even more rewarding when I use it in everyday relationships. From childhood on, my models of relating tend to be distorted toward criticism, competitiveness and confrontation. The practices of kindness, listening, empathy, mutuality, building, equality, and the like are seldom explicitly taught. I grew up in what I thought of as a loving family, and yet, few of the transactions modeled careful intimacy; most were superior/subordinate. Even the transactions between peers were often confrontational. I recently watched a pick-up game of baseball in my neighborhood. Half or more of the event consisted in argument. I remember a ritual in college called a bull session. The process in a bull session was to argue. Whatever the point of view first voiced, my role was to take an opposite view and try to win converts. A *good* bull session developed heat and loud noises. It was thought to be a healthy learning process.

In Synectics when we began our study of meetings in 1957 we were interested in identifying the creative process and developing ways to evoke it. In the thirty odd years of studying videotapes of groups creating ideas it became clear to me that the most effective procedures for stimulating creative thinking resulted in an open, supportive and enjoyable field. In fact, as I became more interested in interactions, I realized that the field was probably the most important factor in producing the best creative work.

In Mind-Free® our focus is on the personal strategies that determine the quality of a relationship. When I know precisely the kind of transmissions that remove barriers to connection-making and those that *foster* making connections, I can become skillful in developing more rewarding relationships.

> "Be kind. Remember, everyone you meet is fighting a hard battle."—T. H. Thompson

Connection-Making and Endorphins

I have participated in hundreds and hundreds of creative sessions where the objective was to invent a new product or solve a problem. It was common for members of these groups to tell me of their feelings of well-being, even exhilaration, during and after these meetings. I explained it to myself as the feeling of pleasure that comes with discovering that I am a better thinker than I had believed; that I have surfaced resources that I had been unaware of.

This may be part of it, and since I have participated in Mind-Free meetings where the *objective* is to discover hidden resources, I have come to believe that a more important source of exhilaration is in the connection-making itself. When a Mind-Free meeting goes well there is a rising level of excitement. I am aware of internal sparks of connecting to another's experience and I sense others making connections. There is an air of breathlessness and joy. It is akin to the feeling that comes with jogging or distance swimming. A colleague suggested that perhaps connecting can produce endorphins—those hormones that produce good feelings—just as physical exertion can.

Connection-Making and Being

Whatever the chemistry of connection-making I have become aware that in the micro-second of connecting to form an idea or understanding there is a tiny spark of up-beatness or lightness usually too small to call joy, but a close relative to joy. Five quick connections might make a joy! Certainly there is a feeling of aliveness produced by connecting and there is often a chain reaction set off: A person tells me of a childhood experience when a grown-up unexpectedly expressed sympathy with her feelings of aloneness. I connect with a long-forgotten time when my mother came to comfort me after I was sent to bed for misbehaving. I reconstruct the event with new connections and understanding of the rebelliousness and rejection, and of the warm relief of Mother's comforting.

I believe that the defenses I develop to protect myself from the normal slings and arrows of our culture build *barriers to connection-making itself.* The implications for effectiveness in my life activities is mind-boggling. In order to make connection and be, I need to effort my way through my ever-present caution *against* making a connection for fear of making a mistake and being rejected.

"...I am satisfied that communication at every level, giving birth as it does, to the new body, the new idea, the new heart, is the most that life can be."—Sylvia Ashton-Warner

Life is a Series of Meetings

When I think of it carefully, my life is made up of meetings. Whether I am going over something with myself, discussing a ball game with a friend, talking with my boss, having an evening drink with my wife—I am engaged in relating, having a meeting. My behavior in the meetings of my life determines how satisfying my life is going to be. To be good at life, I will need to get good at meetings.

On pages 323 and 324 there are diagrams of concrete actions that take place in meetings. Some actions make for a harmonious, productive meeting, others lead to argument and dissention. This collection is based on many years of examining the minute particulars of what happens in meetings. It is the raw material that will allow you to design and practice your own meeting skills—your own life skills.

Meeting behavior is presented using group examples as that was how we did our research.. Most of these examples are relevant to any of the meetings you will be managing.

Think Tank—Practice in Being

Every part of the process of Think Tank is aimed at encouraging connection-making. We were designing to encourage creativity, the main ingredient of which is connection-making. I now believe that the reason creativity is such an important part of life is that it is the essence of being. To the degree that my creativity is stifled, I am deprived of originality and doomed to second hand thoughts and being taught rather than learning. Of course, everyone needs to be creative in order to operate. The issue is to continually enlarge my capacity for making connections to become ever *more* creatively alive.

Success in Think Tank thinking requires that I understand the difference between process and content. The easiest way for me to keep track of this is to know and understand the three roles played in Think Tank. If I am to make the most of my relationships with others I will need to internalize some form of these roles.

The Three Roles of Think Tank

In every meeting there are three basic roles played. First, there is the person who owns the problem. Then there is the person who is running the meeting. Finally, there is the participant. If we had a role-playing experiment and asked three people to play purely one role, the process person would ask the problem owner to state her problem. the problem owner would do so, and the process person would ask for ideas. The participant would then supply ideas. The problem owner would absorb these. The process person might then say, "Now it is time to evaluate the idea you liked best, problem owner."

Everyday meetings do not work this way. Role responsibilities are not explicitly assigned. Each of us feels free to assume any of the three roles. For instance, the chairperson might say, "It is time for ideas." I would feel free to interrupt with, "Before we go to ideas, I need a little more background."

Or, when evaluation time is at hand, even though I am simply a participant, I evaluate and give my opinion of the problem owner's decisions. This free-flowing model has the advantage of maximum involvement for all members and in fact, *when all members thoroughly understand the basic*

> "Creativity is the encounter of the intensively conscious human being with his or her world."—Rollo May

role responsibilities, it makes for an excellent meeting. When group members are at that point, they need only agree about how they are going to operate in this meeting. For example, at one meeting they may agree that everyone will be responsible for process. At another, in which they expect a lot of emotional involvement, they may agree that one of them will be facilitator and take charge of process.

Structure and Interactions

Every meeting is conducted on two levels. One level is the structure—The order of doing things, like statement of problem, analysis, ideas, etc.

It is needed and important, and if that is all that is taken into account, the meeting will be inefficient. The quality of interactions determines the quality of the *relationships* between people, and that largely governs the quality and quantity of connection-making and development of ideas and solutions. This is true in every situation where two or more people are working together. It is easier to see in a problem solving meeting. An example will clarify this critical point.

This group is working on the problem of automobile safety. The process facilitator has asked the team to develop a variety of ways of approaching the problem, a step in our structure called wishing.

Jim: I wish for a seat belt that fastens itself.

Joe: That doesn't really solve the problem. The basic problem is safety and that is only one aspect of it.

Joe has just discounted Jim and issued an invitation to a win-lose struggle. Jim, being a red-blooded he-man cannot refuse. If this is allowed to pursue its course, Jim and Joe would each spend some energy proving he is right. This would make *no* contribution to the problem-solving and would result in one or the other feeling as though he is one-down. The loser would then stop cooperating with the winner, and use more energy devising a way to get even.

The process facilitator intervenes.

Facilitator: Joe, it sounds as though you have a wish with a different objective than Jim's. Please frame it as a wish while I write up Joe's. Then I will get yours.

> "Men are brought to battle for any sign of undervalue, either direct in their persons, or by reflection in their kindred, their friends, their nation, their profession, or their name."—Hobbes

As the facilitator, I am not dealing with structure here; I am handling an interaction to minimize damage to the field. Because I *know* that discounts beget revenge and also hurt the general climate (every participant registers a discount and becomes a bit more defensive and cautious), it is important to prevent, as far as possible, *any* discounting. I believe it is possible to express virtually any difference without discounting. This also forces Joe to drop his adversarial behavior and focus on a wish that makes sense to him.

Joe: I wish everything about the car was designed with safety in mind.

Role of Client—the Problem Owner

I call the person who owns the problem our client. I want to make explicit the fact that the team is working for this person. We will really win only if we give the client what he or she needs.

My responsibility, as client, is to get from the team as much of what I need as possible. All of my actions are aimed at that. My relationship with team members is designed to increase their involvement. I keep focused on the idea of *relationship because that will determine how well the team works for me.* I will be more specific about this as we go along. Now, the responsibilities are the following(I describe these as though I remember to operate this way at all times. I wish I did!):

1. *I give the team enough information about the problem or opportunity so they can begin to work.* I have found that a brief period (about three minutes) to cover the answers to the following questions will usually do the trick: (a) What is the background? (b) Why is it a problem? (b) What is my ownership of the problem (do I have the power to implement a solution)? (c) What are some of the things I have thought of or tried? (d) What would be an ideal wishful solution for me?

2. *I contribute to the meeting as though a participant.* It can be particularly useful if I offer a far-out wish to demonstrate openness to such wishes.

3. *I am alert for opportunities to show appreciation for good thinking.* When a participant makes a pleasing contribution, I *connect* with it. I use words,

> "In the long history of humankind (and animal kind too), those who learned to collaborate and improvise effectively have prevailed."—Darwin

   vocals, and non-verbals to let him or her know about my pleasure. This is a positive addition to my relationship with that person and to the field of the session. It creates energy. I do not attempt to fake this.

4. *I resist the temptation to comment on the contributions when they do not please.* Negative comments and non-verbals are experienced as discounts and poison my relationship not only with that contributor, but with everyone. It builds a field of caution and defense. I have complete control over the direction in which the team will go. When making choices, I simply ignore those that do not aim where I want to go.

5. *I listen approximately.* Many of the suggestions made will not be precise fits to my problem. I exercise my skill in connecting. I listen for implications and triggers. When I make a good connection, I credit (see 6)

6. *I model the ways I wish participants to act.* For example, I credit: When someone says something that stimulates a connection in my mind, I let her or him know. "Sally, when you said that, it gave me the idea that…"

7. I *prove that I am there to find ideas that will work for me* For example, in the wish phase I will be given a mixture of ideas, wishes, beginning ideas, and directions. If an idea is offered that is new and looks feasible to me, I can say something like,

"Hey!, there is one I could experiment with next week." I may not choose to do so, but I have let my team know that I am alert for ideas that will be useful to me.

8. *I indicate the sort of direction that interests me* Here, again, I will not be reacting to every wish, but when one suggests a direction I particularly like, I let the team know.

9. *I am decisive.* When the facilitator asks me for directions, I give her what she needs. If I need time to consult, I take all I want, but when through, I am definite

10. *When I am not getting what I want, I let the facilitator know.* If the team is way off base, I ask for a break and discuss my thoughts and feelings privately with the facilitator. I am always careful not to discount what has gone on. I use wishes, "I wish I could get more thinking on how to increase distribution."

> "In this new world, you and I make it up as we go along, not because we lack expertise or planning skills, but because that is the nature of reality."—Margaret J. Wheatley

11. *When evaluating an idea I use Itemized Response.* This is a procedure that gives the members of the team a balanced evaluation that educates them about the kind of thing I am looking for and am concerned about. *Everything* I say affects the field.

> In any relationship, one negative comment outweighs five positives. With an IR I can be honest without negativity or discount. When evaluating, I *imagine* the idea is implemented and works. This helps me see all the implications. I tell the group three positives it will provide. Then I switch to my concerns. I Express them as *wishes or how to's*.

For example, in the car safety problem I am evaluating the idea of a padded mechanical bar that lowers to embrace the occupants of the front seat, much like the bar on a ski lift.

Me: I like the relative simplicity of that, and another plus is that it would be easier than a seat belt—the user just pulls it down. Another thing, it would be easier to automate than a seat belt. Another plus is that we could make it so that in the up position it would get in the way of driving. The user would almost *have* to put it on.

I have a couple of concerns: How can we make it comfortable, like a belt? Another is, how can we prevent sideways slip?

The underlying principle of Itemized Response is both to acknowledge the thinking of the idea giver and to help me stay open-minded and balanced. It is a wise and powerful process; a constructive way of relating to anything another person says or does. It allows me to validate another person without compromising myself.

The Role of Facilitator—the Process Manager

My responsibility as facilitator is to manage the process of the meeting to help the team do the best possible thinking to give the client what he or she needs. To this end, I guide the team, *mindful* of structure, but not bound by it. Everything I do is informed by my awareness of the critical importance of the field and that validation is the engine and fuel for accomplishment.

> "This simple truth—that the control of consciousness determines the quality of life—has been known for a long time."—Mihaly Csikszentmihalyi

My ideal image of the most effective possible group begins with everyone being in the state of Practical Intimacy. That is, I know enough of the others' background weaknesses and failures as well as successes to relax my impression management. I don't have any need to compete for status. I am knowledgeable about validation and discount revenge. My relationship to myself and to each of the others and to the group is so firm, relaxed and positive that I can listen wholeheartedly and speak without defensiveness—totally available to make connections with, and build on others' thoughts and wishes. Practical Intimacy may be capable, over time, of facilitating genius quality thinking because of the vast connection-making capacity that is freed up. To facilitate in a way to achieve something approaching this super-group I need to master the following:

1. *I need to be thoroughly familiar with the actions outlined in the table below—those that discourage connection-making, and those that encourage it.* I will be suggesting some ways of intervening or avoiding the discouraging actions, but the best way to facilitate is to know the basic principles and improvise in one's own style to create and protect relationships and thus the climate.

Actions that Discourage Connection-Making

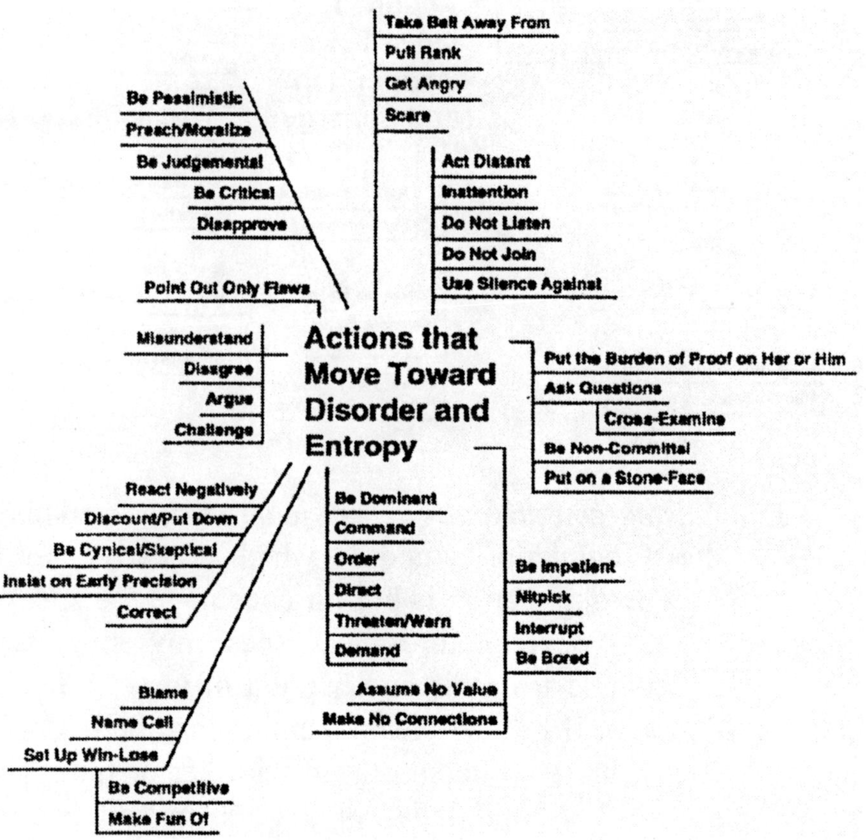

> "What play [wishing, excursion] does is unhook behavior from the limiting demands of real goals."—Weik

Actions that Encourage Connection-Making

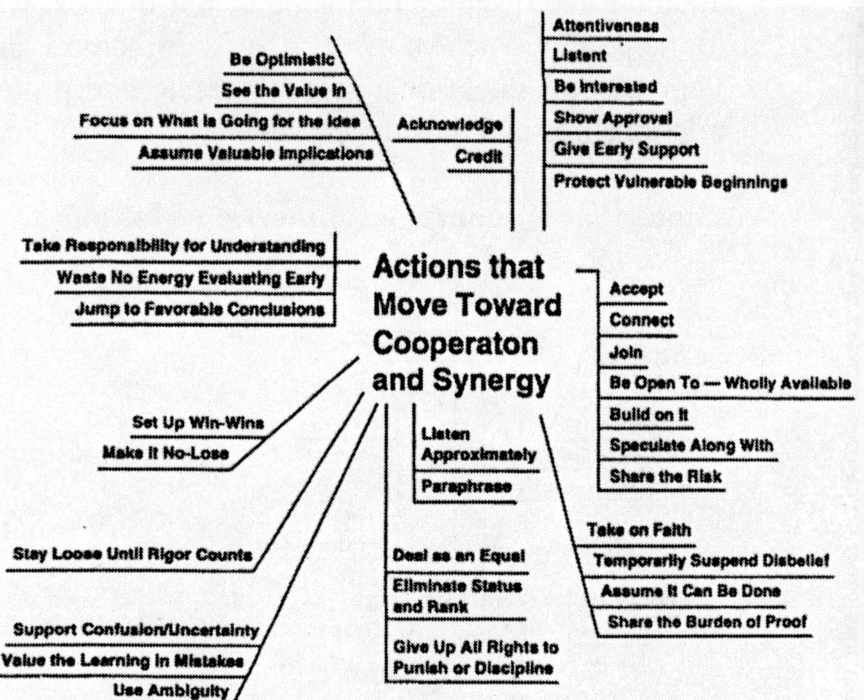

2. *I listen empathically to my team members.* This is the foundation upon which nearly *every* encouraging action is built. I encourage the speaker to paint any picture he wishes; my aim is to understand from his or her point of view. When in doubt, or if I think a team member may be in doubt, I paraphrase to be sure I am with her or him. This sounds easy, but it is not. I catch myself making judgments, tuning out, disagreeing, listening to my

own connections and otherwise getting in the way of really comprehending what the speaker is saying.

The importance of giving myself over to listening cannot be overemphasized. My good listening has a pervasive effect on the field. It brings out the team's productivity. It models the kind of listening I want them to do, and it shows each of them the way I will listen to them. It is the cement that holds a good relationship together.

I will occasionally have a member who takes too much air time. He or she is usually bright and valuable, but they can ruin a meeting. I need to manage him without ruining our relationship (he may be my boss!). Here are three ways I have used to deal with this—there are others and you can invent your own.

> "Problems call forth our courage and our wisdom; indeed they create our courage and our wisdom."—M. Scott Peck

- When I believe I understand his point, I interrupt to say, "Thank you, Sam, I've got it," and move quickly to someone else with, "anyone else have a wish?"
- I Avoid the compulsive talker's eyes when asking for a response.
- More drastically, when I ask for a response, I look away from Sam and hold up my hand in a casual stop sign.

3. *I work to keep the energy high.* This may seem an impossible assignment, but it is not if I stay aware of the need and improvise. There are a number of things that affect the energy in a group, including some beyond my control, like a member's hangover. But there is a lot I can do. Here are some suggestions:

    - My own interest, alertness, and intensity are contagious, so I give it my best.
    - I use excursions lavishly when the group is tired. It is often like an actual vacation from the problem and members return refreshed and with renewed connection-making material.
    - I keep the pace fast, but not hurried. I do not linger in any one step too long. When group members give signals of boredom, I do something different.
    - Humor can be invaluable. When amusing associations occur to me, I bring them out. When a member jokes, I show that I enjoy it too—if I really do.
    - I stay aware that the most energizing thing I can do is get the person to participate.

4. *I keep my eye on the client* When members are giving ideas, I watch my client with care. If he or she shows interest, I check to see if he or she would like to pursue that line of thought. When in doubt about what my client wants, I ask: "Client, we have 6 wishes. Would you like to select one to develop, or would you like some more wishes?"

5. *I arrange beforehand to take turns facilitating.* Like the Pony Express changing horses, it helps to change facilitators to keep up the pace.

> "It is the very nature of this play that nothing is taken for granted as being absolutely unalterable…its outcome and conclusion cannot be known beforehand. The creative person does not strictly know what he or she is looking for."—David Bohm and David Peat

It also signals that this power and control is temporary and others are welcome to share it with me.

6. *I do not pussyfoot.* Because relationships are so critically important, I may believe that being gentle and hesitant helps the participant feel safe and free to risk wild connections. There is nothing wrong with gentleness, but I can be crisp and definite in my directions and interventions. The intention behind my actions is always to honor and protect participants—the surest path to a productive field. It is my responsibility to be in charge of process and I have been given that authority by the group.

7. *I do <u>not</u> contribute ideas.* If I go into the idea-getting business I will neglect my process responsibilities. My attention inevitably shifts from my team to appreciating the beauty of my own thinking. I can't listen to them wholeheartedly. The exception to this LAW is when the group is small. If we number four or fewer, and I am disciplined to

give process my top priority, I can contribute to content.

8. *I value differences, but not disagreements.* Where differences enrich, disagreements create competition, win/lose and discounting. When I hear a budding disagreement, I intervene to get both points of view as wishes.

The Role of Participant—Connection-Making and Building

Participants are the heart of any meeting, All my facilitator skills and the constructive responses of the client are designed to help each participant *stretch* to make her or his unique contribution. To emphasize the true relationships in this kind of meeting, when I am facilitator, I think of myself as the servant of the group. When I am client, I am the problem's representative. When I am a participant, my job is to use my wits and wisdom to help the client get what she wants or needs. The best way to do this is to dig as deeply as I can into my personal potential. Here are some specifics I use to guide me:

1. *I pay intense attention to myself and my impulses.* I think at the rate of about 900 words a minute. People talk at the rate of 125 words per minute. I need only a small part of my energy to understand as a participant because I focus most of my energy

"Play…is the very essence of thought."—Bohm and Peat

in *imaging along with the speaker* and following the thoughts stimulated in me. I continually search for unexpected connections.

2. *I use my pad.* When I drop out of the meeting to listen only to myself, I take notes. When I connect and make an idea, I make a note. Then I can check back in without losing those 'out listening' connections and ideas.

3. *I don't censor something that feels important even if it does not make sense.* I share it with the group. They listen to it as a stimulus and may be able to make a connection where I was not.

4. *I practice open-minded listening and building.* It is probably impossible to listen without seeing the flaws in an idea. There are at least two constructive courses to take: (a) Focus on modifying the idea to overcome a flaw, and (b) repress my reaction to flaws and focus on the positive implications of the idea and look for other ways to accomplish the desired ends. For example,

Joe: The steering wheel is lethal in an accident. Let's eliminate it. We could use two levers like in a boat. Or one lever.

I image this and know that it will be hard to learn to use and will be resisted by consumers, but the

direction is promising. I credit Joe and propose a build:

Me: I like that direction, Joe. Another thought is, we could bring the steering wheel post straight up from the floor and have it hinged so it can move forward out of the way in an accident and to get in and out of the driver's seat.

Whenever I am unable to find positive implications in another's idea, I know that I am either adversarial to the idea proposer, or the idea makes me anxious and I need to reassure myself that this is only *thinking* and it is safe to think *anything.*

5. *I know the actions that discourage speculation and connection-making and I police myself so I do not slip into any of them.* I know the set of actions and I not only avoid the downers, I consciously use the uppers.

> "Playing may be defined as encounter in which anxiety is temporarily bracketed. But in mature creativity, anxiety must be confronted if the artist [and the rest of us…] is to experience the joy in creative work."—Rollo May

6. *I cooperate with my facilitator.* Even when I do not understand exactly what he or she is up to, I cooperate as well as I can. I guess and do it. In summary, as a participant, my responsibility is to bring my whole self and use as much of me as I possibly can.

The Scientific Method and Think Tank

The Scientific Method is widely thought of as the way scientists go about making discoveries and solving problems. In Synectics® research, as we studied groups attempting to invent, we could find some equivalent actions, but rather than follow the steps in the Scientific Method (Recognition or formulation of a problem, collection of data, formulate an hypothesis, and test it) we found it more useful to encourage the steps we observed people actually using when attempting to get ideas to solve a problem. (Formulating the problem, brief background, develop many wishful directions of thought, select one, stimulate connection-making to create options, select one and develop it). Where the Scientific Method is descriptive, the Synectics® Method is more operational.

Integrating My Facilitator, My Client, and My Participant

Both the Scientific Method and the Synectics® Method are attempts to introduce an orderliness into the thinking process to increase effectiveness.

I know, from a great many experiments, that a group organized to use the three roles of Think Tank will surface and use more of its potential than any other with which we experimented. I could observe the interactions and compare the effectiveness of such a group with that of a group using the conventional methods such as the Scientific Method, Brainstorming or Robert's Rules (Chairperson). There is no question that the three role method (originally developed by Synectics® Inc.) is best.

This suggested to me that if I could integrate these roles in myself, I would bring out my own most effective self for solving problems and capitalizing on opportunities. This requires a fundamental reorganization because I have spent most of my life "doin' what comes naturally". Upon examination, this has resulted in a rather chaotic use of my resources and an underlying poor field within myself. For example, it was a regular practice for me to punish myself harshly for the slightest failure to be perfect. Knowing what I do now about the effect of a discount on a relationship, it

> "Surely not to leave to fitful chance the things that *method* and system and science should order and adjust."—B. N. Cardozo

is clear that self punishment will set up defensive thinking and reduce wholehearted connection-making and building.

My Relationship Model of Organization

To take advantage of the learnings of Synectics® research, I deliberately revise my ways of relating to myself. My central, organizing concept is *relationship.* I want every internal action to reinforce my positive field within myself. When I feel critical of something I do, my facilitator self takes over and leads in an Itemized Response and the development of wishes for changing. I practice wholehearted listening and building with myself. Me, myself, and I form a team to help me be the most I can be.

Inside Me and Outside Me

In everyday life I constantly play all three roles, shifting from one to the other as the situation suggests. It will help me keep my transmissions constructive—clear of discounts and devalidations—and to build rewarding relationships, if I am aware of the probable effect of each of my transmissions, keeping in mind that I have both internal and external communications going on.

I use my outside behavior with others to reflect my inside behavior with myself, and I use my inside behavior with myself to model how I want to deal with others. This keeps my intentions in my awareness and can reinforce my determination to make the most of myself and of my relationships with others.

"In the kingdom of the blind, the one-eyed person can be king."—old saying

Managing Fields for Positive Interactions

As a Mind-Free person, I am aware of the field whenever I am in a meeting with one or more people. Most of my meetings are informal and there is seldom any explicit method or process, yet I know how to make the interchange more effective without formality. Below are some situations and ideas for managing fields without being intrusive about it.

Situation: I am a resource in a meeting and I want to have the support of other participants.

How to: How to win the support of others.

Analysis: An individual in a meeting is usually quite concerned with building and protecting his or her self-image. If I can assist him, he is likely to be supportive of my contributions.

Ideas: I select those whose support I wish to have. Whenever he or she speaks, I listen attentively. I give that person some acknowledgment that I have heard and appreciated what he or she has said. There are many ways to do this: nod, say, "That is a real point" or some other appropriate phrase, paraphrase, build, credit, etc.

It is unwise to be false or artificial. It is perfectly alright to have differences. The important thing is to hear and acknowledge the contributions of each of your allies.

+++

Situation: It is clear to me that one of the members of the meeting has clientship over the problem being discussed. The Chair or a senior person appears to be taking away the prerogatives of the client.

How to: Establish and protect the client without getting into trouble.

Analysis: It is common for a senior person to feel free to take over a client's role when the client is junior. It gets in the way of clarity and accomplishment.

> "Natural selection does not require competition; on the contrary, it discourages it."—Alfie Kohn

Ideas: Before any problems occur, I say something like, "Could I have some clarification? Who owns this problem…I mean, who will go out of this meeting and implement an idea we get?"

Or, if I know the answer to that, I can address the client, "Are you the problem owner?"

As the meting progresses and decisions are made by someone other than the client, I can say, "As problem owner, Jerry, how does that suit you?"

Prudence is necessary.

+++

Situation: There is no clear chairperson

How to: Make the meeting effective

Analysis: There will be continuing competition for control of the meeting and little will be accomplished.

Ideas: I offer to facilitate. If agreed by everyone, then I make some ground rules explicit.

If the there is competition for facilitator, I suggest rotating the chair. When it is my turn, I give some ground rules. Since my skills honor and validate, the chances are that I will be asked to continue.

+++

Situation: The manager who called the meeting has decided on a course of action. I believe it is premature.

How to: Avoid premature closure.

Analysis: When few options are developed, the manager may feel trapped into selecting a less-than-satisfactory one.

Ideas: I acknowledge the decision and say something like, "Jim, what possible troubles do you foresee that we might do some problem-solving on?"

> "Not only to say the right thing in the right place, but far more difficult, to leave unsaid the wrong thing at the tempting moment."—George Sala

Or, I acknowledge the decision and make a wish, e.g.., "I wish we could guess at the problems we might encounter—and solve them before they happen."

Or, I might suggest an IR

+++

Situation: I am in a meeting and a member is pointing out flaws in an idea.

How to: Make evaluations friendly.

Analysis: Untrained people naturally go for flaws, they do not know any better, and it feels safe to do so.

Ideas: I acknowledge the flaw, "I understand your concern, Jack, and before we work on that, I would like to look at some of the things going for this idea."

Or, "I hear you Jack, and I can also see some good plusses going for this idea."

+++

Situation: An idea has been offered and the group is evaluating it too early.

How to: Get developmental vs. judgmental thinking.

Analysis: Untrained people tend to go for immediate evaluation and discard an idea if it has flaws.

Ideas: I intervene and ask for help, "I hear us treating this like a fully developed idea…it sounds like a good beginning…maybe we can build on it."

+++

Situation: The meeting is cycling without going anywhere—from analysis and questions to ideas and back to more analysis.

How to: Make structure work for everyone.

> "Pioneers were not competitive people, they were cooperative. They wouldn't have survived otherwise."—William O. Johnson

Analysis: Often the chairperson does not have a structure *or* a process in mind and is not aware that wheels are spinning.

Ideas: I keep my Think Tank model in mind. When I believe that there is enough of one step, for example, analysis and questions, I suggest a next move and model it.

"Maybe we could move to ideas now…I have a beginning one."

+++

Situation: The meeting is bogged down in questions to the person who is seeking help—the client.

How to: Move the thinking from questions to ideas and speculation.

Analysis: The safest thing to do is to ask penetrating questions and it avoids the anxiety of developing an idea. If I ask enough questions perhaps an idea will come to me.

Ideas: "I am feeling as though we are beating on (client) with questions. Maybe we could shift to getting ideas for him."

Or (if groundwork is laid), "Maybe we could shift to How to's and Wishes."

Or, I introduce the idea of wishing and ask if they would like to try some.

+++

Situation: There is an adversarial person in the group—one who continually points out flaws and discourages connection-making.

How to: Counter an adversarial person

Analysis: One adversarial person can poison the field and ruin a meeting. Often an adversarial person believes his negativity will pass as constructive, but when you clarify what he is doing, he may resist.

Ideas: I acknowledge his point of view and then support what he is discounting, e.g.., "I hear your concern, Harry, but the idea seems interesting enough to develop a little more. Later maybe we can overcome your concern."

> "Intelligence is the ability to interact, and this ability can grow only by interacting with new phenomena…"—J. C. Pearce

+++

Situation: A person is dominating the air waves.

How to: Deal with a compulsive talker.

Analysis: Many meetings are ruined by a compulsive talker.

Ideas: I break into his or her monologue with "Let me see if I get your point, John." And I briefly paraphrase. I have picked someone who looks ready, and I say, "You were going to say something, Jack."

Here again, I use prudence.

+++

Situation: There is a bright member who is not offering anything and I know he or she has a lot to offer.

How to: Involve a quiet person.

Analysis: There are often quiet people in meetings whose good ideas are never heard because they will not 'fight' for air time.

Ideas: Whenever anyone expresses an opinion or offers an idea, I fix my eyes on the quiet one.

If this does not work, I try "What are you thinking Alice?"

Or, "How do you see this situation, Alice?"

+++

Situation: When I am a resource in a disorganized meeting I know I can improve the productivity by modeling building.

How to: Encourage connecting and building.

Analysis: Quite often other people are not acquainted with the idea of building on another person's idea. When they see how much credit I get for this, some will follow suit.

Ideas: Listen, image, and connect. See below:

"I am firm, thou art stubborn, he is obstinate."—unknown

Three Postures for Listening

To emphasize the ways I can listen, I have defined three different ways to focus my energy as I listen. In the first posture, I concentrate on the logical sense of what the speaker is saying. Let us say that he is describing an experience he had while skating. I listen in such a way that if he asked me to paraphrase, I could. This is *literal* listening.

In the second posture I am paying more attention to the person's tones, hesitations and his non-verbal expressions and gestures. I want to pick up what he is *feeling* about the experience he is describing. This is empathic listening.

In the third posture I focus on my own images, associations, and implications—I use what he is saying to stimulate connections of my own.
This is *metaphorical* listening.

Example: The problem is reducing alcohol related accidents. The person has just voiced a wish, "I wish drunks were required to ice skate to their cars," and he described a skating experience that would be impossible if he had been drunk. As he does, I listen for something that "catches my ear". I hear the scrunch a skate makes and I image the blade pressing against the ice. I remember being told that the reason a skate slides over ice is that the pressure of the blade raises the temperature of the ice and water forms. I focus on the formation of water under the blade. Then I connect back to the problem. I want to put some unusual pressure on the drunk. I image a navy decompression chamber where they put pressure on the diver and gradually decompress him to let the nitrogen (condensed in his blood by deep water pressure) escape so it won't expand in his blood and kill him. I connect this to some aircraft carrier pilots during World War II. They told me that when they came off shore leave and were hung over, they would sit in their planes and use the oxygen masks to sober up.

I say, "When you were telling the skating story, I connected with the skate blade pressing on the ice (crediting) and thought of another wish: "I wish every bar had a high-oxygen pressure chamber for quick sobering of drunks."

+++

"Repress that impulse...*pretend* that idea will work—Anon

Situation: I am a resource in someone else's meeting and I want to clarify the objective.

How to: Help the chairperson set a clear objective for the group.

Analysis: Many managers (and others) call a meeting without a clear notion of what they wish to get out of it.

Ideas: Before the meeting if possible, I ask what he or she wishes to get out of the meeting.

If that is not possible, I say something like, "It will help me to be useful if you would tell me what you wish to come away from the meeting with."

+++

Situation: The meeting is important to me, yet I have no assigned role except as a resource.

How to: Get a legitimate 'right' to intervene.

Analysis: Most meetings are rather disorganized. Since I have the knowledge of Think Tank, I can be both helpful and have an influence on the outcome of the meeting.

Idea: I volunteer to become secretary and keep notes. Then I can use my skills, "Jack, before we go on to your idea, I need to hear more about Sally's."

+++

Situation: It promises to be a long meeting and I would like to be a positive influence.

How to: Share the job of chairing.

Analysis: The meeting-caller may welcome some help in running the meeting if he or she is reassured that he can still retain some control.

Ideas: Before the meeting I volunteer, explaining my ground rules so she will be assured of getting what she wants.

> "Let the beginning idea stir up a build instead of a bust."—old Synectics® saying

At the meeting, I offer to rotate as chair with the meeting-caller retaining control of the content.

Situation: The group is working on a problem they have 'worked to death'. They are pessimistic about thinking of something new.

How to: Help the group think out of a rut.

Analysis: When a group is reworking a tough problem, minds slip into the same or closely related thoughts that have been explored before. If I can help generate one or two new ways of thinking about the problem, it demonstrates that new thinking is possible.

Ideas: After the group has experienced some frustration, I say something like, "You know, there is a thinking strategy that is supposed to help when we are going for newness…you want to try it?"

I always get permission. And if they agree, I explain wishing first and after playing with that I will take them on an excursion and demonstrate force fitting.

+++

Situation: There is time being spent arguing or differing about what the *real* problem is—the definition.

How to: Formulate the problem without wasting energy.

Analysis: Often when a problem is presented, each individual seems to have a need to interpret the problem for him or herself before going to work on it.

Ideas: My objective is to give each person who has the need, an opportunity to reformulate without argument. I say something like, "It often helps get ideas if I hear what others believe is the key issue in a problem—it gives me more points of view—and it helps if you express your thought as a wish."

+++

> "The environment remains uncreated until we interact with it; there is no describing it until we engage with it."—Margaret Wheatley

Think Tank Skills as Everyday skills

One purpose of the above situation analyses is to suggest that my skills in field management developed in Think Tank, put together with my Mind-Free understanding of relationships and creative effectiveness can be applied in almost every interpersonal situation.

Think Tank Steps

Roles: Facilitator, Client (problem owner), Participants

1. **Client states problem as "How to..."**

2. **Brief background**

3. **Several Wishes from participants and client**

4. **Client selects Wish to pursue and rewords it as a "How to..."**

5. **Excursion**
   "Give me an example of ____________
   from the world of________________

6. **Force Fit to get three or four ideas**

7. **Client selects an idea he/she want to implement**

8. **Open-minded evaluation (Itemized Response)**

9. **Problem solve on the "How to's"**

10. **Restate the modified solution**

11. **Next steps**

Worlds for Excursions

This list of worlds is meant only to suggest possibilities. Feel free to create your own worlds, for example, "the world of paint brushes" or "firewood".

(best with 'thing' problems)		(best with people problems)
Organic	**In-between**	**Inorganic**
Biology	Archeology	Physics
Tribal customs	Medicine	Mineralogy
Sports	Computers	Woodworking
Fashion	Models	Chemistry
Dancing	Noise	Electricity
War	Acoustics	Astronomy
History		Oceanography
Mythology		Rocks
Botony		

Part 7—Inner Field

"Bliss is the rapture of being."—Joseph Campbell

Bliss

In 1987, when I was sixty-nine, I was single having been recently divorced. I met Kathleen and, on the morning after our second date, I realized that I was thinking of nothing but her. As that day wore on, I could not seem to get my mind on anything else. I sat through a meeting of the executive committee and kept comparing the voice of one of my colleagues with that of Kathleen. The business of the meeting never really penetrated the fog of images of Kathleen. By dinner time I realized: this is *it!*

I was not a novice about love. I had fallen in love at eighteen and married the girl, and we had thirty-five loving years before she died of cancer. I subsequently tried marriage twice, to two nice people, but some essential ingredient was missing, and each marriage ended in divorce after a few years. I had finally accepted the fact that the kind of in-loveness that hit me at eighteen happened only once.

Kathleen exploded that despairing conclusion.

Falling in love at eighteen is marvelous and to remain in love through the slings and arrows that accompany graduating from college, getting a job, going to war, raising children, urging them out of the nest, starting a new kind of life without children under foot, had been immensely rewarding—a once per lifetime experience.

Falling in love at sixty-nine was very different from that earlier experience. There were none of the distractions and anxieties of youth, and I had a deep and sad knowledge of love lost and seemingly irrecoverable. I was blown away. After two weeks of intermittent dates with Kathleen (she was resisting me), I retired from Synectics to spend full time overcoming her resistance. Happily, I succeeded and it was not only the beginning of a blissful relationship, it was the beginning of the development of Mind-Free.

In-Loveness as a Model

The in-loveness feeling was so marvelous I began to think that those feelings of bliss should not be limited to my relationship with Kathleen. I wanted to have those same

> "Happiness is not a destination; it is a method of life."—Burton Hills

wonderful feelings about more of my life and so I began to analyze what was making my bliss so…*blissful!*

I assumed that since, in my work, I had discovered through research, how to increase the use of creative capacities, I would be able to increase my being-in-love capacity. Searching for the beginnings of in-loveness, I went back to infancy. My first want was for nourishment and this was easily satisfied by food and love. The hunger for food is easily understood. The hunger for love is more complex and strange.

The nourishment (and seduction) of love derives, I believe, from its power to evoke in me the conviction of being valid and meaningful. One of the earliest sensations is that of being *appreciated*, transmitted by words, tonals, and non-verbals (and perhaps by food), by the most important person in the world. Combine this with the more adult reward of self-discovery that comes when I respond to my love's and *my* longing to be *known*—to disclose to each other our most intimate thoughts and feelings and to be not only accepted, but *desired!* And to experience the joy of inventing ways of conveying to her all that she means to me. These form a template, a unique model of the ultimate way of relating, that stays with me all my life. The engrossing feeling of being *known to each other* and totally accepted and valid that is created by this field becomes the model of relationship I seek for the rest of my life.

At the Core is Field

As discussed earlier, Jean Baker Miller (1987) and the work at the Stone Center at Wellesley College have been redefining the process of development in women. Their findings have many implications for men, as well. We know that relationships grow out of the merging of two inner fields.They place these merging experiences, the fitting together of two different fields, at the very heart of becoming a person. They speak of this merging, this relationship, as though it is an entity—a third *being* between two people.

The skills I learn in fitting my field with that of others in the series of meetings that make up my life, will largely determine how fulfilling my life will be. Ideally, in relating, I participate in a mutually empathic joining. This is not always possible since the field of another may trigger anxiety and adversarial behavior in me. But if I am field aware, I can often modify my reactions and deliberately invite collaboration. The primary relationships are with my mother and father. The recent research of John Gottman establishes that my father plays a far more important role in my early development than had been thought.

The quality of those early experiences, the developing of my field and the fitting of it with those of my mother and father, establishes my capacity for joining in intimate relationships. If the bonding is ideal, rich in appreciation and mutuality (mutuality is defined as each having the power to move the relationship), I grow to be a recruiter, a person others are inclined to seek out because my field telegraphs that I am open to connect with and appreciate them.

> "…the incredible power which verbal behavior seems to exercise in interpersonal situations…"—Harry Stack Sullivan

If the bonding is mixed, too much early punishment along with appreciation, I grow to be *available* for recruitment, but not gifted in conveying appreciation and acceptance because the transmissions from my field carry punishing or critical elements. When bonding is poor, when there is much early punishment or even abuse, neglect and little appreciation, I am not recruitable for intimate, nourishing relationships. I have been denied that beginning validation I need and to preserve myself I do my best to shut down my vulnerability. My field is so defensive that I can't connect in intimate ways, and I may rely on power-over actions rather than mutuality to move others in my relationships.

Limerance-the Illusion the I *Can* Go Home Again

When early bonding is good, my model of love is wonderfully validating. I feel like the undisputed center of the world. Later, in adulthood, I use the ambiguity of the early stages of in-loveness to imagine that I have recreated that totally valid, center-of-the-world feeling. In the flush of imagined mutual approval, I have found the model of being loved that meets my dream specifications. Dorothy Tennov (1979) calls this intoxicating state of mind Limerance. For a limited time, I am able to delight in meeting my strict internal standards of perfection, proven by the total admiration and acceptance of me by my beloved.

One of the characteristics of Limerance is "a remarkable ability to emphasize what is truly admirable in my loved one and to avoid dwelling on the negative, even to respond with a compassion for the negative and render it, emotionally if not perceptually, into another positive attribute." (Ibid. Pg. 24).

As my love and I get to know each other better, our wholehearted approval of each other, gets tempered by the reality of our differences. How I deal with these facts of life will determine whether Limerance will develop into lasting in-loveness. I differentiate in-loveness from both limerance and loving, though they have common elements. Limerance attempts to be continuous explosion based on illusion and it cannot be sustained. Love is a steady, warm, solid underpinning to sustain affectionate regard through thick and thin. In-loveness consists of occasional glimpses of that everyday love through a kaleidoscope that flashes momentary patterns that incredibly fit a pattern of longing within me. These tiny explosions of bliss are ignited by a look, a gesture, a response, a thought expressed, that signal

> "Imagination…is the sensibility which transforms human love into something beyond…something magically and uniquely human."—Willard Gaylin

a special connection. They create a unique, paradoxical glow of excited comfort that reassures me that this *is* the embodiment of that model of bonding that I experienced long ago. In-loveness means that there is a continuing string of occasional tiny explosions of connecting that run through the steady background of a loving relationship.

The "Yes, But…" Response

Reflecting on my earlier life, I became aware that I dampened these sparks of bliss with judgmental thinking. My fear of being mistaken led to holding back. My love would do or say something that ignited the spark, and rather than give in and simply appreciate it, I had a "Yes, but..." response. My fear of losing my balance; of being wrong, being taken over, cautioned me to be evaluative. I cooled the thrilling with the irritating and created an uninspiring middle field of safety. With Kathleen there was a difference. As I slowly returned to sanity from limerance, I continued to delight in the sparks of bliss she ignited in me. Perhaps because of my age or because I had been so long deprived, I persisted in this wisdom. I dismissed the idea of balance and evaluation. Reservations were unimportant. This was reinforced by the Prathers (1988) whose *A Book of Couples,* appeared at this time. They counseled: focus on the sparks when they happen. Systematically diminish the importance of the imperfections.

I gradually realized that sparks of bliss are *not* decision points. They need no evaluation or balanced judgment. They are simply to accept with open heart as an unearned reward for being. This epiphany of understanding led me to reframe my everyday life. Sparks of bliss are scattered through my days, and I had been muting them with defensiveness by treating them evaluatively. My safekeeping self, to protect me from jumping to a mistaken conclusion, focused on balanced reality and mature sobriety.

The "Yes, Yes..." Response

My life with Kathleen has exposed me to a field of appreciation without criticism. Since infancy this has not happened to me, and the effect is quite remarkable. I became aware that a considerable amount of my every-day energy was used in being prepared to defend against criticism and other threats of rejection. My foresight function and anxiety gradient require energy. When the field is dependably without threat, I can relax and use that

> "Ideally, we should be able to express all our most intimate thoughts to someone."—James W. Pennebaker

freed up energy for more productive perceiving and connecting—for more of the rapture of <u>be</u>ing.

My life with Kathleen is not without differences, and the difference is in how she handles situations when my actions bother her. She signals a problem by saying, "I have an issue with you." and then, instead of attempting to *teach* me to behave differently, she self-focuses and tells me how it is with her. I have learned to respond non-defensively by self-focusing in turn. We negotiate a resolution. The blessings of this field of appreciation and no power-over or threat, are so many and so various they are difficult to count. It repeatedly brings into being for me an unconditional, welcoming "Yes, yes!" response to life.

Cultivating the Joy of Connecting

Much later, when we were running Mind-Free experiments, I asked people about their blissful experiences and we examined definitions and characteristics of bliss.

Some of their examples:

- •M. told of the birth of his baby. It went to sleep on his chest and he stayed quiet for four hours so as not to waken her.
- •G. told of writing his dissertation resisting including Hulian Drive until he watched his baby daughter wear herself out learning to walk.
- •T. told of going to visit his father and telling him that he loved him.
- •B. described going to Quebec as member of a Shriner championship football team and visiting burned children who embraced him for helping them.
- •H. told of going fishing in the middle of the ocean in a small boat and listening to the waves on the boat.
- •L. described her feelings when she finally got a new kitchen in her old house after being embarrassed about it for five years.
- • C. told of the feeling of singing in a choir together with three other choirs in Vienna.
- •A. spoke of his feeling at the birth of his third child.
- •L. described her fear of taking risks and how she was maneuvered into a white water rafting trip on her honeymoon and discovered her courage.

> "Learning is ever in the freshness of its youth, even for the old."—
> Aeschylus

- •J. told of her fear on a climb in the Alps. She is afraid of heights and found herself having to walk a

narrow ledge with an abyss—and she had to jump a gap.
- •C. described an encounter with a herd of Caribou while in the Arctic.
- •M. described the look in students' eyes when she teaches something and they really connect with it.
- •W. told about going out in a canoe to watch the sun come up and practicing his loon call and having a loon come up and respond to him.

Bliss happens when:

- •I make (or allow) a connection between my true self and a new piece of information.
- •I make a connection to a deeper level—I create a new meaning for me; comprehend a new implication.
- •It is a point in time for me, an instant, a few seconds…I am conscious of being a unique part of the universe…things *do* make sense.
- •I am aware of my uniqueness. I am the only one who can do the particular thing that I am "about"…that I am here for.
- •I am absolutely *alive!* Aware—all my senses are awake.
- •It is a reaffirmation of my self. Touches and engages an important part of me: my true self.
- •Instantly changes me. I am more alive and I will be more susceptible to bliss now.
- •Disconnects me from the everyday and connects me to the part of me that is most valid.
- •It validates me the way I am when I am the most I can be.

- •It is a moment of highest thought and feeling. It is me *transcendent!*
- •Total involvement—I am unaware of worries and frustrations.
- •Concern for myself disappears…yet a sense of myself emerges stronger afterwards.
- •Sense of time is altered.

> "Happiness, in fact, is a condition that must be prepared for, cultivated, and defended privately by each person.—Mihaly Csikszentmihalyi

Connections Generate Joy

Recently, I was player/coach in a Mind-Free® Group exploring Learning and Knowing. We were sharing experiences and the feeling of excitement gained momentum from a particularly vivid experience of a member. We were all making connections and eager to share them. I thought it was as though each connection gave off a spark of light and there were so many, the room was flashing like an electrical storm. All those shots of endorphin were lighting us up!

I don't know if endorphins work that way. I *do* know that since I have removed instant judgment, I am relishing connections even more, and finding more and more bits of bliss lighting up my days.

Who could ever have guessed that the years from 70 to 84 would be the most blissful of my life!

"Love is not the icing on the cake; it *is* the cake."—Willard Gaylin

Bibliography

Axelrod, Robert, *The Evolution of Cooperation,* Basic Books, New York, 1984

Bader, Ellyn, and Pearson, Peter T., *In Quest of the Mythical Mate, a developmental approach to diagnosis and treatment in couples t herapy,* Brunner/Mazel, New York, 1988

Bednar, Wells, and Peterson, *Self-Esteem, Paradox and Innovations in Clinical Theory and Practice,* American Psychological Society, Washington, D. C.1989

Belenky, Mary Field, et al, *Women's Ways of Knowing,* Basic Books, New York, 1986

Bergson, Peter A., and Shilcock, Susan D., *Open Connections: the Other Basics,* Open Connections Inc. 312 Bryn Mawr Ave., Bryn Mawr, PA, 1980

Bettelheim, Bruno, *The Uses of Enchantment,* Alfred A. Knopf, New York, 1976

Beveridge, W.I.B., *The Art of Scientific Investigation,* Vintage Books, New York, 1950

Bohm, David, and Peat, David F., *Science, Order, and Creativity,* Bantam Books, New York, 1987

Bohm, David, Edwards, Mark, *Changing Consciousness,* Harper San Francisco, 1991

Bowen, Murray, *Family Therapy in Clinical Practice,* Jason Aronson, Northvale, New Jersey, 1985

Bowlby, John, *Maternal Care and Mental Health,* World Health Organization, Geneva, 1951

Brown, Philip M., *The Death of Intimacy-Barriers to Meaningful I Interpersonal Relationships,* The Haworth Press, New York, 1995

Buzan, Tony, *Making the Most of Your Mind,* Simon and Schuster, New York, 1984

Campbell, Joseph, with Bill Moyers, *The Power of Myth,* Doubleday, New York, 1988

Csikszentmihalyi, Mihaly, *Beyond Boredom and Anxiety,* Josey-Bass, San Francisco, 1975

Csikszentmihalyi, Mihaly, *Flow,* Harper & Row, New York, 1990

Csikszentmihalyi, Mihaly, *The Evolving Self,* Harper Collins, New York, 1993

Dewey, John, *How We Think,* D. C. Heath, Boston, 1933

Edwards, Betty, *Drawing on the Right Side of the Brain,* Jeremy P. Tarcher, Los Angeles, 1989

Elbow, Peter, *Embracing Contraries, Explorations in Learning and Teaching,* Oxford University Press, New York, 1986

Erikson, Erik H., *The Life Cycle Revisited,* W. W. Norton, New York, 1982

Fritz, Robert, *The Path of Least Resistance,* DMA, Inc., Salem, MA, 1984

Friedman, Norman, *Bridging Science and Spirit,* Living Lake Books, St. Louis, MO, 1994

Gaylin, Willard, *Rediscovering Love,* Penguin Books, New York, 1986

Gazzaniga, Michael S., *The Social Brain,* Basic Books, New York, 1985

Gleick, James, *Chaos,* Penguin Books, New York, 1987

Goffman, Erving, *The Presentation of Self in Everyday Life,* Doubleday Anchor Books, New York, 1959

Goldberg, Herb, *The Inner Male,* New American Library, new York, 1987

Goleman, Daniel, *Emotional Intelligence-Why it Can Matter More than IQ,* Bantam Books, New York, 1995

Gordon, Thomas, *P. E. T. in Action,* Wyden Books, New York, 1976

Gordon, Thomas, *P. E. T. Parent Effectiveness Training,* Wyden Books, New York, 1970

Gottman, John, with Silver, Nan, *Why Marriages Succeed or Fail,* Simon and Schuster, New York, 1994

Gottman, John, with Joan DeClaire, *The Heart of Paarenting, How to Raise an Emotionally Intelligent Child,* Simon and Schuster, New York, 1997

Greven, Philip, *Spare the Child,* Alfred A. Knopf, New York, 1990

Harman, Willis W., *An Incomplete Guide to the Future,* W. W. Norton, New York, 1979

Havens, Leston, *Making Contact-Uses of Language in Psychotherapy,* Harvard University Press, Cambridge, 1986

Hirsch, E. D. Jr., *Cultural Literacy,* Houghton Mifflin, Boston, 1987

Jastrow, Robert, *The Enchanted Loom,* Simon and Schuster, New York, 1981

Jordan, Kaplan, Miller, Stiver and Surrey, *Women's Growth in Connection*, The Guilford Press, New York, 1991

Jourard, Sidney M., *The Transparent Self,* D. Van Nostrand Company, New York, 1971

Kagan, Jerome, *The Nature of the Child,* Basic Books, New York, 1984

Kayser, Karen, *When Love Dies,* The Guilford Press, New York, 1993

Karen, Robert, *Shame,* The Atlantic Monthly, February, 1992

Kegan, Robert, *The Evolving Self,* Harvard University Press, Cambridge, 1982

———*In Over Our Heads, The Mental Demands of Modern Life,* Harvard University Press, Cambridge, MA 1994

Kerr, Michael E., *Chronic Anxiety and Defining a Self,* The Atlantic Monthly, September 1988

Kohn, Alfie, *No Contest—The Case Against Competition,* Houghton Mifflin, Boston, 1986

Kohn, Alfie, *Punished by Rewards,* Houghton Mifflin, Boston, 1993

Laycock, Frank, *Gifted Children,* Scott, Foresman and Company, Glenview IL, 1979

Leonard, George B., *Education and Ecstasy,* DeLacorte Press, New York, 1968

Lewis, Thomas; Amini, Fari; Lannon, Richard, *A General Theory of Love,* Vintage Books, Random House, New York 2000

Lerner, Harriet Goldhor, *The Dance of Intimacy,* Harper & Row, New York, 1989

Levine, Stephen B., *Psychological Intimacy,* Journal of Sex and Marital Therapy, vol 17, No. 4, Winter 1991, Brunner/Mazel, Inc.

Malone, Thomas Patrick; Malone, Patrick Thomas, *The Art of Intimacy,* Prentice Hall, New York, 1987

May, Rollo, *The Courage to Create,* Bantam Books, New York, 1975

Mehrabian, Albert, "Communication Without Words", *Psychology Today,* Vol.2, No. 4, September 1968, p. 52

McEvoy, J.P. and Zarate, Oscar, *Introducing Quantum Theory,* Totem Books, New York, 1996

Melohn, Tom, *The New Partnership, Profit by Bringing Out the Best in Your People, Customers, and Yourself,* Oliver Wight Publications, Inc., Essex Junction, VT 05452, 1994

Miller, Alice, *For Your Own Good, Hidden Cruelty in Child-Rearing and the Roots of Violence,* The Noonday Press, Farrar, Straus, Giroux, New York, 1980

Miller, Jean Baker, *Toward a new Psychology of Women,* Beacon Press, Boston, 1986

Miller, Sherod; Wakman, Daniel; Nunnally, Elam; Saline, Carol, *Straight Talk, a New Way to Get Closer to Others by Saying What You Really Mean,* Rawson, Wade, Inc., New York 1981

Montagu, Ashley, ED. *Learning Non-Aggression,* Oxford University Press, 1978

Olsen, Shirley A.,Ed., *Group Planning and Problem-Solving Methods in Engineering Management,* John Wiley & Sons, Inc., 1982

Ornstein, Robert E., *The Psychology of Consciousness,* Penguin Books, New York, 1972

Parry, Alan; Doan, Robert E., *Story Re-Visions-Narrative Therapy In The Postmodern World,* Guilford Press, New York, 1994

Peck, M. Scott, *A World Waiting to Be Born,* Bantam Books, New York, 1993

Peck, M. Scott, *The Different Drum,* Simon & Shuster, New York, 1987

Peck, M. Scott, *The Road Less Traveled,* Simon and Schuster, New York, 1978

Pennebaker, James W., *Opening Up,* Avon Books, New York, 1990

Prather, Hugh and Gayle, *A Book for Couples,* Doubleday, New York, 1988

Prigogine, Ilya, *The End of Certainty,* The Free Press, New York, 1997

Prince, George M., *The Practice of Creativity,* Harper& Row, New York, 1970

——"The Mindspring Theory: A New Development from Synectics Research",*Journal of Creative Behavior,* 1975, 9(3)

——"Synectics®: Twenty-Five Years of Research Into Creativity and Group Process", *ASTD Journal,* 1982

——"Putting the Other Half of the Brain to Work", *Training,* Vol. 15, No. 11, November 1978, pp. 57-58, 60-61

——"Creative meetings through power sharing", *Harvard Business Review,* July-August, 1972, pp. 47-54

——"How to be a better meeting chairman", *Harvard Business Review,* January-February, 1969, pp. 98-108

Restak, Richard M., *The Brain,* Bantam Books, New York, 1984

Russell, Peter, *The Brain Book,* E. P. Dutton, New York, 1979

Sagan, Carl, *The Dragons of Eden,* Random House, New York, 1977

Schnarch, David M., *Constructing the Sexual Crucible,* W. W. Norton, New York, 1991

Seligman, Martin E. P., *Learned Optimism,* Alfred A. Knopf, New York, 1991

Semler, Ricardo, *Maverick,* Warner Books, New York, 1993

Senge, Peter M., *The Fifth Discipline, The art and Practice of the Learning Corporation,* Doubleday/Currency, New York, 1990

Siebert, Al, *The Survivor Personality,* Practical Psychology Press, Portland, OR, 1993

Sullivan, Hary Stack, *The Interpersonal Theory of Psychiatry,* W. W. Norton, New York, 1953

Taylor, Irving R., Getzels, J.W., Eds., *Perspectives in Creativity,* Aldine Publishing Co., Chicago, 1974

Tennov, Dorothy, *Love and Limerance,* Stein and Day, New York, 1979

van der Kolk, Bessel A., *Trauma, Memory and Self-Regulation Clinical Applications of Current Research,* Conference, Nantucket, MA September 18-21,1997

Wenger, Win, *Beyond Teaching and Learning,* Project Renaisance, Gaithersburg, Md, 1992

Weik, Karl, *The Social Psychology of Organization,* Random House, New York, 1979

Wheatley, Margaret J., *Leadership and the New Science,* Berrett-Koehler Publishers, Inc., San Francisco, 1992, 1994

Womack, James P., Jones,Daniel T., Roos, Daniel, *The Machine that Changed the World,* Harper Collins, New York, 1980

About the Author

George M. Prince

Is the retired co-founder of Synectics®, Inc., the company that initiated research into the creative process and then became the leading teacher of inventors for business and industry. As long time Chairman of Synectics, he and his partners originated the idea of videotaping invention groups to learn how the process of invention occurred. Based on their discoveries, they developed courses in creativity and innovation that have been taught all over the world. In 1970, Prince published one of the early books about the process: *The Practice of Creativity,* Harper and Roe, 1970. It became a best selling trade book.

Mr. Prince grew up in Rochester, New York and went to Exeter and Williams, where he graduated with honors. In World War II, he was an officer in the navy and served in a Destroyer Escort in company with an aircraft carrier on anti-submarine operations in the North Atlantic.

After the war he joined an advertising company in Rochester and rose to be Executive Vice President. He became fascinated with the process of getting ideas and when he heard of a creative experimenter in the Arthur D. Little Consulting Company in Cambridge, MA, he joined ADL as co-manager of their Invention Design Group. In 1960 he, together with three other members of the Invention Design Group, left ADL to start their own company, focusing on research into the creative process.

Mr. Prince lived in Winchester, MA with his first wife, the former Marjorie Morrison of Winnetka, IL, and their three children, Jonathan, Winthrop and Victoria. Mrs. Prince died in 1974.

In 1989 he married Kathleen Logan and they moved to Weston, MA where they live at present.

Kathleen Logan-Prince

Mrs. Logan-Prince grew up in Quincy, Massachusetts where her father was an attorney. She attended Thayer Academy, The College of New Rochelle and Boston College where she was awarded her MSW.

She has two children from her first marriage: Victoria, and Joshua. She is a Licensed Independent Clinical Social Worker, and is trained in marriage and family therapy. She is a diplomat in clinical social work and an associate faculty member at McLean Hospital, providing supervision to interns in the Human Sexuality Program of the Couples Institute. She is a member of the Board of Directors of the American Association of Sex Educators, Counselors and Therapist.

From 1987, in addition to her practice, she worked with Mr. Prince running experiments in the development of the Mind-Free® program in creativity. It is out of this work that she and Mr. Prince produced the present book.

Printed in the United States
6786